13.49

NJ 9/03
an.

FE and Lifelong Learning:
Realigning the Sector for the
Twenty-first Century

FE and Lifelong Learning: Realigning the Sector for the Twenty-first Century

Edited by
Andy Green and Norman Lucas
Lifelong Learning Group, Institute of Education,
University of London

Bedford Way Papers

**INSTITUTE OF
EDUCATION**
UNIVERSITY OF LONDON

First published in 1999 by the Institute of Education University of London,
20 Bedford Way, London WC1H 0AL

Tel: 020 7612 6000 Fax: 020 7612 6126
http:\\www.ioe.ac.uk
Reprinted 2000

Pursuing Excellence in Education

British Library Cataloguing in Publication Data
A catalogue record for this publication is available from the British Library

ISBN 0 85473 559 3

Design and typography by Joan Rose
Cover design by Tim McPhee
Page make-up by Cambridge Photosetting, Cambridge

Production services by
Book Production Consultants plc, Cambridge

Printed by Watkiss Studios Ltd, Biggleswade, Beds

Contents

List of Contributors

Patrick Ainley, School of Post Compulsory Education, University of Greenwich

Bill Bailey, School of Post Compulsory Education, University of Greenwich

Leslie Dee, Institute of Education, University of Cambridge

Andy Green, Lifelong Learning Group, Institute of Education, University of London

David Guile, Lifelong Learning Group, Institute of Education, University of London

Annette Hayton, Lifelong Learning Group, Institute of Education, University of London

Norman Lucas, Head of Lifelong Learning Group, Institute of Education, University of London

Anna Paczuska, South Bank University

Lorna Unwin, Centre for Labour Research, University of Leicester

Michael Young, Lifelong Learning Group, Institute of Education, University of London

Introduction and acknowledgements

For many years now colleagues in the Post-16 Education Centre [now the Lifelong Learning Group] and beyond have been talking of the need for a book that concerns itself with strategic and long-term concerns of the further education (FE) sector. The rationale for this book is to contribute to a much-needed strategic policy/practice analysis about FE. It is timely because, as the century draws to an end, FE has moved from its relative obscurity to centre stage. It is now seen as the key to many government initiatives around social inclusion – particularly, as the title implies, to lifelong learning.

Lifelong learning is a difficult concept to define and, as this book shows, is open to flexible interpretation. We use the term in the title of the book to mean post-16 education and training in all its forms, although informal lifelong learning falls outside this analysis. We focus on lifelong learning and the FE sector because it is uniquely placed between schools, universities and workplaces and has the potential to become the key player in providing education and training throughout a person's life-cycle. However, this requires realignment and some fundamental rethinking about curriculum and pedagogic issues.

This book examines the development of the FE sector from its roots in the nineteenth century to the phase of incorporation after 1993. As many of the chapters show, FE remains under-researched, although more interest has been shown in the last few years. The authors draw, where possible, on the most recent research, analysing the current situation, and plotting the progress, setbacks and contradictions of FE. However, the main focus is on the future, and the book looks beyond the Further Education Funding Council (FEFC) model of incorporation, arguing for a fundamental realignment of FE in relation to lifelong learning, schools and higher education (HE). The FE sector has changed dramatically since incorporation six years ago. It has undergone massive growth and has made significant efficiency gains and important improvements, however its strategic role has been lost and the incorporated model is in crisis. We argue that the crisis has four dimensions.

First, the strategic role of FE has become even more fragmented. The FEFC model of funding may have created a centralised national system of funding, but it has not led to the creation of a national sector. It is our contention that the distinctive role of FE colleges as institutions of lifelong learning and as engines raising levels of achievement towards national targets has been squeezed between the growth of sixth forms in schools, the role of Training and Enterprise Councils (TECs), and universities. In the scramble for units of funding, all notions of a distinctive national or regional role has been lost to cut-throat competition between providers.

Second, the massive quantitative expansion of FE has sometimes been achieved at the expense of quality. The national system of control via the FEFC's funding mechanism has pursued a process of efficiency savings and convergence of funding levels in order to drive down unit costs. Educational values and concerns with the quality of learning have been marginalised by funding and financial considerations. There are some very real worries about standards and quality as many of the recent efficiency savings have been achieved by drastically cutting course hours. We argue that performance could be regulated more by inspection and development than by pure unit funding and that a better balance between quantity of units and quality of learning needs to be found. As long as funding dominates the concerns of FE, fundamental lifelong learning questions concerning curriculum reform and new methods of teaching and learning cannot be given the consideration they deserve.

Third, we submit that the FEFC's model is over-centralised and is not responsive to regional planning or regional need. We believe that FE must move beyond the 'national contract model' of the FEFC to a more 'democratic' regional model with an integrated approach to delivering a post-16 education and training system linked to regional economic development and lifelong learning. Under a new system (as discussed in this book), the regional funding and planning bodies (the FEFC and the Regional Development Agencies (RDAs)) would encourage cooperation between all providers, including employers, TECs and local education authorities (LEAs), to produce regional plans with regional training and education targets. The wasteful aspects of cut-throat competition would cease with funding taking into account local socio-economic factors when setting the average level of funding or judging institutional effectiveness.

Fourth, we believe that the crisis facing FE is not just financial, but one of strategic drift. In the context of recent government initiatives on 14–19 curriculum reform and lifelong learning, FE is at a crossroads. On the one hand, sixth forms in schools are becoming broader and offering a range of 16–19 qualifications. On the other hand, HE is becoming more like FE, with a more flexible range of courses catering for returning adults and a more diverse range of students. There is a policy vacuum concerning FE's contribution to developments in the 14–19 curriculum, welfare to work, modern apprenticeships and lifelong learning. Although FE is potentially an important element of lifelong learning and has received important funds for that purpose, its strategic role is not clear. This book argues that FE needs to be redefined and realigned, with a move towards a distinct provision for 16–19 year olds, concentrating on preparatory education. FE colleges should become adult 18 plus institutions – more like community colleges in the United States – concentrating on becoming lifelong learning institutions.

This book addresses some of the major policy, professional, management, curricular and learning issues facing the sector as we move to the twenty-first century. Chapter One traces the emergence of FE sector from its nineteenth-century beginnings through to the present day and sets the context for the following chapters. It analyses the development of FE in five historic stages, arguing that incorporation is best understood by examining the points of continuity between past and present rather then seeing incorporation as a clean break with the past. It concludes that FE has not escaped from its fragmented and voluntarist past, and is not only in financial crisis, but also in a state of strategic drift.

Chapter Two builds upon the analysis of incorporation in Chapter One with a focus on the FEFC's funding mechanism. It traces the development of the funding mechanism in the context of the general 'marketisation' of education. Using recent research, it offers an assessment of the strengths and weaknesses of the funding regime. Although this regime has achieved some gains, it is seen to have forced colleges to focus on funding and meeting FEFC date demands rather then educational and strategic considerations. The chapter concludes with a critical analysis of recent developments, examining options for change that move beyond the present FEFC's funding model.

Chapter Three explores the provision of adult education in FE and raises a number of issues related to the lifelong learning agenda. It develops the view that FE has always had to cater for a diverse group of learners and be responsive to the needs of the community. It is argued that although FE is still responsive today, it is more to the FEFC and less to the community. This chapter describes the struggle to fit part-time adult education into the FEFC's bureaucratic framework, often for small amounts of money, leaving little time for innovation and change towards lifelong learning.

Chapter Four is concerned with the interface between FE and HE. It discusses the mergers, and the different partnership and funding arrangements that exist between the two sectors. It describes and analyses a complex interweaving of provision that crosses and blurs the HE/FE divide. It argues that some of 'new universities', although expanding student numbers and bringing about a curriculum convergence between HE and FE, are based upon a skills-based, not knowledge-based HE curriculum. Finally, the new landscape of post-compulsory education is discussed in relation to regional collaboration and planning.

The primary aim of Chapter Five is to examine how information and learning technology (ILT) can enhance teaching and learning. It is argued that this is not as straightforward as it seems, and that learning through

ILT is far more than an individual act of sitting a student down in front of a screen. The authors argue that like most learning, learning through ILT is a fundamentally social activity that needs to vary according to the situation and context. This means moving beyond current assumptions about learner-centredness to a position that allows the learner to collaborate and produce new knowledge within 'communities of practice'.

The thrust of Chapter Six is to examine inclusive learning and develop the approach adopted by the Tomlinson Report. The Report stresses the processes of learning and of creating an inclusive learning environment, which addresses the needs of all students, including those with learning difficulties and disabilities. The author takes the view that inclusive learning shifts the focus from seeing the 'problem' as lying with the individual student to considering the institutions capacity to respond to individual learning needs. This inclusive learning approach becomes the basis of widening participation, social inclusion and lifelong learning. The chapter explores factors that inhibit and promote this approach and suggests steps that could be taken.

Chapter Seven focuses on the student's experience of learning, relating it to current debates conducted under the banner of lifelong learning. It is based upon research undertaken in two FE colleges. It illustrates the diverse nature of the FE curriculum and the different learning experiences, intentions and progression routes undertaken by an ever-widening group of FE students. The chapter concludes with a call for increased funding for FE, a shift away from competition and efficiency savings and a greater focus on quality of curriculum and learning experience.

Chapter Eight discusses a more strategic approach to curriculum reform, suggesting that the government, although making some advances, remains trapped in an out-of-date view of qualifications. Furthermore, if lifelong learning is to become a reality, a radical reform of the qualifications system is required with a distinction made between the preparatory curriculum for 16–19 year olds and lifelong learning for adults. The author makes international comparisons and develops a conceptual framework, concluding with a way forward for curriculum reform into the twenty-first century.

Chapter Nine analyses the state of initial teacher education, staff development and professionalism in FE. It argues that professionalism has traditionally been weak and fragmented in FE and there has been very little discussion of pedagogy and professional practice. The authors analyse recent developments to raise standards in FE, including the establishment of the Further Education National Training Organisation (FENTO). They analyse the concept of the 'reflective practitioner' for FE teachers, suggesting that a broader concept of the 'learning professional' is more appropriate to teachers in FE. The chapter concludes by suggesting policy initiatives which would establish a new professionalism in FE, including a General Teaching Council.

Chapter Ten draws on all the other chapters and gives an overview of the position of the FE sector. The focus of the chapter is the strategic realignment of the FE sector in relation to schools, HE and the workplace. This final chapter reinforces the analyses running throughout the book. It shows the fragmented nature of the FE sector and how it has been squeezed by other providers, developing more by accident than design. It makes international comparisons with other tertiary systems, particularly community colleges in the United States. The chapter concludes with a view that strategic realignment should take place on a regional level in order to take account of different regional needs and existing provision. In general, the authors believe that separate provision for 16–19 year olds is needed along the lines of sixth form colleges or 16–19 tertiary colleges and that FE should develop a distinctive mission from HE. This would allow FE colleges to focus on becoming flexible adult institutions developing a new curriculum for lifelong leaning.

FE has become central to the government's aims to lift levels of skills and knowledge, to widen participation, to bring about greater social inclusion and to create a learning society. These are ambitious aims; the theme of this book is that a fundamental realignment, breaking with the old paradigm, is required to achieve this. We hope this book contributes to the debate.

Acknowledgements

We would like to thank all members of the Lifelong Learning Group for their help, particularly Michael Young for his constructive comments and encouragement. We would also like to thank Toni Griffiths, who saw the importance of this book and enabled its publication, and to Denis Gleeson for his helpful suggestions. Finally, a thank you to Caroline Steenman-Clark, who gave us her patient support when IT problems confounded both editors.

1 From Obscurity to Crisis: The Further Education Sector in Context

Andy Green and Norman Lucas

Introduction

This chapter argues that there has never been a national strategic role for further education (FE) and that many of the advances made towards local responsiveness in the post-1944 era have been weakened as the sector has become more fragmented, losing its links to local education authorities (LEAs) and employers. The Further Education Funding Council's (FEFC) model of funding may have created a centralised national system of funding; however it has not led to the creation of a national sector. Just as vocational and technical education and training was squeezed between schools and universities in the nineteenth and early twentieth centuries, FE under incorporation has been marginalised by the growth of sixth forms in schools, the expansion of the universities and the work of the Training and Enterprise Councils (TECs). In the scramble for units of funding, all notions of a distinctive national or regional role have been lost to cut-throat competition between providers.

The emergence of the further education sector

FE has a long, although relatively hidden, history, dating from the second stage of the Industrial Revolution. It was part of the formation of the modern state in the late nineteenth century, reflecting one of the many aspects of a voluntarist relationship between education, training and the state (Green, 1990). Adult or community education in its broadest sense can be traced back beyond the nineteenth century, for example to the

Sheffield Societies formed by mechanics in 1792 which were a mixture of self-education and radical political organisation (Thompson, 1963). For the purposes of this chapter, we will start at the nineteenth century and only mention community or adult education in as much as it illustrates and illuminates our analysis. Other studies may start earlier and definitions of further education could, legitimately, insist on the inclusion of community and adult education. Our analysis traces the development of FE from its early fragmented and voluntaristic start to the present. We characterise the emergence of FE through five historical stages of development.

Stage 1: The nineteenth century (the Mechanics Institutes and the voluntary principle)

Nineteenth-century technical education and training in England had a number of strands. These included the work-based apprenticeship, the various schools and self-improvement associations of the labour and cooperative movement, and the Mechanics Institutes and other adult education institutions which received philanthropic and state funding.

The dominant form of training in England during the first half of the nineteenth century was the apprenticeship, which was organised by independent employers and craftsmen with no public funds and little public regulation. This usually involved on-the-job training with little or no theoretical or academic study, and was generally marginalised from mainstream educational provision and low in status. As a voluntary provision made by employers without state regulation, it well suited the dominant liberal philosophy of 'voluntarism' in education and training, and in many ways set the parameters for all further developments in post-school technical education and training (Green, 1990).

The other main tradition of adult education in the early nineteenth century was that of working class 'self-education', often organised through small associations and clubs and, on a larger scale, through the institutions of the labour and cooperative movements. In this political tradition, adult education took many different forms – from the common reading circles of working men and women to the Owenite Halls of Science and the 'schools' organised by the Chartists, Christian Socialists and others.

An example of the latter was the London Working Men's College formed in 1854 by the Christian Socialists to provide education for working men (Harrison, 1954). Although 'useful knowledge' was highly valued in this tradition, the emphasis tended to be on developing working-class literacy, general culture and, above all, political awareness.

The principal precursors of the late-nineteenth-century technical colleges, however, were the Mechanics Institutes, the first of which was founded in Edinburgh in 1821. These were initially organised on a subscription basis, with substantial additional philanthropic funding, and aimed to provide useful and self-improving education for adult workers. Their evening classes proved to be quite popular, particularly amongst artisans and the lower middle class, and by the mid-nineteenth century there were 610 Institutes with a total membership of more than half a million. However, the Mechanics Institutes did not gain credibility as genuinely mass adult education providers. Their increasingly middle-class ethos alienated potential working-class recruits, whose initial education was, in any case, often too limited to allow them to benefit from what the Institutes had to offer. In fact, the Institutes established the dubious tradition of separating general, scientific and technical education from practical craft instruction (Evans, 1975). The working-class self-education movement was often critical of the Mechanics Institutes, seeing them as middle-class organisations dedicated to counteracting the supposedly radicalising effects of working-class self-education (an argument that re-emerges in the twentieth century between community educators and technical colleges) (Simon, 1969).

What was common to these three strands of adult education and training was their predominantly voluntary and part-time character. The state played a relatively minor role in apprentice training and formal technical schooling, at least until later in the century, as it was generally opposed to the tradition of radical working-class self-education. Michael Sadler later summarised the strengths and weaknesses of the part-time, voluntary tradition of evening classes in the nineteenth century:

> Thus alike in their excellence and their effects, the evening classes have borne the characteristic features of the English educational organisation.

Free in their development, vigorous in some of their achievements and
often well-adapted to the requirements of the persevering and strong,
they were unsystematic in their arrangement, weakened by deficits in
the early training of their pupils, and from the national point of view
insufficiently adjusted to the needs of the rank and file. (Roderick and
Stephens, 1978: 21)

By the mid-nineteenth century there was increasing criticism of this
voluntary tradition. Great concern was expressed about the state of technical education following the Great Exhibition of 1851 and a Department
of Science and Art was established under the Board of Trade in 1853 to
stimulate and coordinate efforts in technical education. This had some
success in the establishment of schools of art and design, but had little
impact until the next decade in establishing science classes. A mere £898
was spent on science classes in the first six years, underlining the initial
intention that the Department of Science and Art would only exist to
provide support to an existing system which would continue to be local,
voluntary and, in the main, self-supporting (Bishop, 1971).

It was not until the late 1880s that a more dynamic and systematic
approach was adopted to the development of public technical education,
in part as a response to the criticisms of the existing system made by the
Samuelson Royal Commission on Technical Instruction in 1884. Examination boards had been established with the foundation of the Royal
Society of Arts (1856) and the City and Guilds of London Institute (1879);
the latter created by the City of London Livery Companies to give accreditation to the growing number of vocational students. The City and Guilds
played a part in the foundation in 1883 of the Finsbury Technical College
which offered daytime and evening courses, including mathematics, science
and vocational subjects such as engineering and building. They also col-
laborated with the new Regent Street Polytechnic, opened by Quinton
Hogg, which offered instruction in bricklaying, plumbing, electrical work,
watch-making, printing, photography and tailoring. With the passing of
the 1889 Technical Instruction Act and the 1890 Local Taxation ('Whiskey
Money') Act, more public funding became available for technical education. This allowed a range of technical colleges and polytechnics to be

set up in the 1890s, which provided the foundation of the twentieth-century technical college system. This was a late outbreak of good sense, but in many ways it came too late to alter the patterns which had already been established.

The overall picture of nineteenth-century technical education is one of a fragmented, *ad hoc* and marginalised provision. Initially, the state did not play a direct role in fostering industrialisation either by directing capital into industry or by training in new skills. Companies were left to invest in training as they saw fit and many did not see it as a high priority (Barnett, 1986). The liberal, voluntarist creed, which generally preferred voluntary initiative to state intervention in education and training, applied particularly in the area of technical education, which was seen as a low priority for government and whose public promotion raised fears about increased taxation, loss of trade secrets, restrictions on child labour and the undermining of employer initiative. The developmental role played by the state was, therefore, limited until the latter part of the century.

The pattern of technical education that developed in the nineteenth century was not only institutionally marginalised from mainstream education; it was also intellectually adrift. Whereas in most of the more advanced northern mainland European countries, such as France and Germany, technical education was closely allied to general education, in Britain a sharp divide grew up between the two, separating skills and knowledge.

The main institutions for technical education in France – the trade schools, the *écoles des arts et métiers* and, at the higher level, the *écoles centrales des arts et manufactures* and the *École Polytechnique* – all combined theory and practice in their teaching. Their full-time students typically spent half their day in classrooms learning general subjects and the theoretical background to their vocation, and the other half in workshops learning practical skills. The acquisition of general culture (*culture générale*) was seen as a right and a responsibility for future citizens of the Republic in the post-Revolutionary era. Equally, the combination of theory and practice was regarded as essential for the cultivation of applied science (*la science industrielle*) and the latter was the intellectual legitimisation and bedrock of the engineering professions which the French state and its public works helped to raise to such high esteem (Day, 1987; Green, 1997; Weiss; 1982).

The system had undeniable strengths in the preparation of those who, in time, would come to occupy higher level positions as technicians and engineers. Comparing the products of the English apprentice system and the French trade schools, Flemming Jenkins (Professor of Engineering at University College) argued that although the English system cultivated practical skills as well as the French system, the latter had the advantage in the long term:

> When in after life the two men came to fill the higher stations, the English engineer would begin to feel the want of elementary training very severely, and would be at a disadvantage compared with the man abroad in judging the new problems which came under his eye. (Select Committee, 1867–68: 130)

By comparison with the French system, English technical training was a very minimalist affair. Its prototypical form was the employer-controlled apprenticeship, whose archetypal product was the useful 'practical man' and whose main standard of quality was time served. Sylvanus Thompson (the first Principal of Finsbury Technical College) referred to the apprenticeship as six years of dull, repetitive drudgery that failed 'to make anything but a bad, unintelligent machine' (Thompson, 1879). This was no doubt a bit harsh, as, although with a neglectful employer the apprentice might learn very little, with a conscientious one he (rarely she) might at least get a good grounding in the basics of his trade. However, what he did not acquire, at least not through his apprenticeship, was any broader culture or much theoretical knowledge. The technical colleges later made up for the latter, but not the former.

Despite advances towards the end of the century, nineteenth-century technical education in England left a distinctly impoverished legacy. Usually, part-time, intellectually narrow and institutionally marooned between school and work, it never acquired a status comparable with that achieved in certain other continental states. Its form became characterised by an historical absence – the lack of any legitimised notion of general culture and general education with which to frame technical skills. FE colleges would find it hard to break out of this mould and to rectify this absence.

Stage 2: 1900 to 1944 (indecision, marginalisation and drift)
Public funding for technical education became available following the 1889 Technical Instruction Act. The 1902 Education Act laid the basis for the expansion of post-primary and secondary education. This, together with the economic growth of the late nineteenth century, should have provided the basis of growth in technical and further education. Yet it was only partially the case. Technical education did expand, particularly in the commercial fields whose popularity grew in line with the growing army of clerks servicing Britain's imperial expansion in the period before the First World War. However, the school sector, and especially the growth of state grammar schools, continued to receive higher priority than the technical colleges, and all areas of education were squeezed through the expenditure cuts in the inter-war era.

With the end of the First World War and the rhetoric about creating a 'land fit for heroes', came the 1918 Fisher Act which required all LEAs to provide free and obligatory day continuation schooling for those leaving school at the age of 14. However, economic depression and public expenditure cuts after 1926 ensured that few authorities met the requirements (Frankel and Reeves, 1996). Junior technical schools providing post-elementary vocational education did continue to expand with enrolments reaching around 30,000 students in 1937, but they did not develop into a comprehensive national system, and no more achieved parity of status with academic secondary schooling than did the secondary technical schools which followed the 1944 Butler Act (Bailey, 1990; McCullough, 1989). During this period, there also was some development of adult non-vocational education. Henry Morris pioneered community education in Cambridgeshire in the 1920s and 1930s and the Women's Institutes were founded in 1924, some years after the inauguration of the Workers Education Association in 1903. All of this added to the diverse landscape of post-school education, but fell far short of creating a national FE system.

By 1937–1938 only one in five children leaving elementary school at the age of 14 went on to any kind of full-time FE and the rest went straight into the job market. Of the 3.3 million 14–18 year olds in England and Wales who were receiving no full-time education, one in 25 were on part-time courses and one in 123 in voluntary day continuation schools. Of the 80,000 pupils in 1937 who began secondary school one in 12 ended up with the Higher School Certificate, one in six went to some form of further education and one in 20 went to university. Most people went into the job market with no training (Barnett, 1986).

Stage 3: The 1940s to the mid 1970s (expansion, technical colleges, apprenticeships and the relationship to employment)

The war years saw a large increase in training programmes in colleges and universities. There were 6,000 state bursaries for two-year university technical degree courses; more than 4,000 students in technical colleges following six-month courses for Higher National Certificates in both industry and the armed forces; and nearly 4,000 engineering cadetships. There was further rapid growth after the Second World War as troops returned home requiring training for civilian life. Alongside the technical colleges, adult education institutes started to cater for part-time academic, vocational and leisure activities. Regional Advisory Councils led to a National Advisory Council on Education and Industry and some national colleges were set up, reflecting the growing interest amongst employers. Consequently, day-release expanded to over 350,000 by 1955, building on breakthroughs achieved during the war years (Evans, 1975).

The 1944 Education Act sought to achieve for FE what the 1918 Fisher Act had failed to achieve with its largely unimplemented policy of day continuation schools. The new Act was the first to make it a legal duty for the LEAs to provide FE. Although no specific timetable was set, the LEAs were required to establish and maintain county colleges which were to provide school leavers with vocational, physical and practical training. In the first year after the Act nothing extra was spent on colleges and in the next six years the total spent was half of that spent on school medical care and nursery schools (Barnett, 1986). However, gradually, progress was made. Employers were asked by the government to associate and cooperate with the new colleges. This approach led to the growing occupational training role of 'technical colleges', which gradually became institutions for 'day-release' vocational education of the employed or those serving apprenticeships.

Table 1: Growth of student numbers in further education (in thousands)

Course type	Year							
	1951	1953	1955	1957	1959	1961	1963	1965
Full-time and sandwich	55	61	67	89	119	132	176	202
Part-time and others	1,956	1,831	1,985	1,960	2,063	2,398	2,584	2,856
Total	2,011	1,892	2,052	2,049	2,182	2,550	2,760	3,058
Day-release (incl. block release)					440	526	586	653

Note: From 1961 colleges of advanced technology are excluded. These figures include those at Polytechnics (Bratchell, 1968: 19).

In 1956 a new urgency was manifest with the publication of a White Paper on Technical Education, which announced legislation for FE and HE. The White Paper's rationale made a direct link between these sectors and growth of the economy and called for increased work in higher technological and advanced technical education. It proposed a new Diploma in Technology leading to postgraduate studies. It set targets to double day-release students in five years from the 335,000 in 1954. These targets were not met. Even 10 years later, those on day-release had only risen to about 650,000 (Bratchell, 1968). In 1959 the Crowther Report identified FE as a crucial sector for generating economic growth, but criticised it for its confusion and proliferation of courses, its high part-time attendance and low retention rates, calling for more day-release and sandwich courses.

The 1961 White Paper, *Better Opportunities in Technical Education*, put a greater emphasis on lower levels of study, concentrating on technicians, craftsman and operatives. By 1960 the numbers in these categories had risen to 283,000 on part-time or block-release courses, 152,000 on evening-only courses, and 14,000 on full-time courses. Between 1959 and 1965/66 there was a significant shift towards full-time, sandwich and day-releases courses (Bratchell, 1968). Throughout this period, colleges were seen as responding to government initiatives, reaching a high point of work-relatedness in the late 1960s/early 1970s.

Throughout this period, the apprenticeship remained the main vehicle of vocational training and was usually completed without any parallel off-the-job general or technical education. For all its strengths as a means for imparting job-specific vocational skills, the apprenticeship system was never an adequate vehicle for meeting the skills needs of the economy. The craft unions tended to see the apprentice system as a means by which they could protect their skill status and differentials through restricting entry into tightly demarcated trades. Employers often valued the system as a way of gaining cheap labour without statutory obligations to provide expensive investment in training to given standards (Rainbird, 1990). Both sides of industry agreed on limiting the numbers of apprentices so there were repeated skills shortage crises not only before the First World War to the end of the Second World War, but also increasingly during the expansionary post-1945 period.

Not only did the apprentice system provide an inadequate supply of skilled workers, it was deficient in many other ways as the 1958 Carr Report made clear (Perry, 1976). It involved unduly lengthy periods of time-serving, failed to train to any specified standards, was overly narrow in the skills it imparted and was impoverished in terms of general education and theory. Most damagingly, it ignored the training needs of semi-skilled workers and severely limited access to many groups, notably women (Sheldrake and Vickerstaff, 1987). According to some (Gleeson and Mardle, 1980) the role of technical colleges during this period was to prepare apprentices to fit in with the existing occupational structures and cultures. Any questioning of the dominant assumptions were not tolerated either by the technical teachers or the college administrators.

Numerous reports (including the government's own 1956 White Paper on Technical Education) pointed to the relative deficiencies of British training and the 1945 Ince Report called for the creation of a national training scheme (Ainley and Corney, 1990). However, no government action was forthcoming. In 1952 the Ministry of Labour and National Service was still upholding the traditional government line that 'employers bear the major responsibility for the training of their own employees' (Sheldrake and Vickerstaff, 1987: 27). Thus, the *laissez-faire* era in British training policy continued until the beginning of the 1960s, when renewed skills shortages, the challenge of Soviet technology and the growing youth cohort finally convinced the government that policies on vocational training had to change.

The 1964 Industrial Training Act inaugurated the tripartite Industrial Training Boards (ITBs) to promote and coordinate training in the different sectors, and it empowered them to redistribute the costs of training between employers by means of the levy-grant system. Being organised by industrial sectors, but without achieving full coverage, this was never quite a national apprenticeship system, still less a national training system for all grades of employees. However, it was as near as Britain had come to such a thing in its history. In the brief period of ten years during which the system was in operation the volume of training did increase marginally (up by 15 per cent in those areas of manufacturing covered by the ITBs between 1964 and 1969) and notable advances were made in improving the quality of training (Sheldrake and Vickerstaff, 1987). Day-release became common in many apprentice schemes; group training schemes proliferated, helping smaller firms to participate in formal training programmes; and the engineering ITBs' modular training systems paved the way for greater flexibility and breadth in apprentice training (Perry, 1976). However, the system was not achieving its objectives.

The quantitative gains in training provision were limited to certain skilled areas and were, in any case, soon wiped out by the secular decline in apprentice places, which followed the onset of the recession in 1973. The ITBs failed to open up access to apprenticeships for previously excluded groups and did little to change the old practices of time-serving and age entry restrictions. Most seriously, little headway was made in the setting and monitoring of standards in training.

These shortcomings were not attributable to the principle of social partnership in training and did not undermine the argument for government intervention. What they did show was that a national training system could not be created on the basis of devolved sectoral organisation and that the social partners in the different sectors could not be induced to act in a coordinated way to create a national system of training to standards without a strong central body to coordinate them. Unlike in Germany, Britain's national federations and 'peak bodies' for employers and unions (including the Confederation of British Industry and the Trades Union Congress (TUC)) lacked binding powers over their members and the local Chambers of Commerce never attained great influence. The Central Training Council, as the TUC frequently complained, never had adequate powers to compensate for this and to ensure that the system fulfilled its objectives in meeting those long-term skills needed by the national economy which individual employers were always prone to ignore (Perry, 1976; Ainley and Corney, 1990).

Stage 4: 1970s and 1980s (further education colleges, local diversification and responsiveness)

Despite the advances of the post-war years what had emerged was a highly uneven provision that varied substantially from one locality to another. Legislation had been permissive, allowing LEAs wide scope for interpretation. Vocational education and training remained low in status and apprenticeships were dominated by the engineering and construction industries which, by the 1970s, were in decline along with other traditional industries, such as shipbuilding and heavy engineering (Gorringe, 1996). By the late 1960s technical colleges had begun to transform themselves into colleges of FE, providing a wider range of academic, vocational and pre-vocational courses, acquiring a multi-purpose educational function (Tipton, 1973). Their diversification was however, accompanied by the decline of their economic and work-based role from the mid 1970s due to de-industrialisation, particularly in areas such as engineering.

Throughout the late 1970s and 1980s, full-time participation in FE was rising steadily and colleges were required to respond to the needs of new types of learners, including, notably, adults and school leavers who previously would have entered directly into the labour market. Colleges increasingly saw themselves as 'responsive' institutions, catering for a diverse student population and with a mission of offering a second chance to learn and achieve. During this period there was a shift from the typical technical college focus on vocational day-release and evening study to the far more complex offer of the new style FE college with its increased load of full-time students following a variety of vocational and academic courses. Two trends had particularly important influences.

First, there was the growth of academic courses for both adults and young people who wished to have a second chance at 'O' and 'A' Levels. This growth was stimulated by the expansion of HE, which was now becoming accessible to those who would previously have been excluded, and the fact that many schools found it increasingly difficult to maintain viable sixth forms. Many LEAs attempted to establish cooperation between schools and sixth-form consortia or sixth-form centres in order to offer a reasonable range of academic courses and to maintain reasonable class sizes. Other LEAs removed sixth forms from schools and merged them into sixth form colleges or combined sixth forms with FE colleges to form tertiary colleges that provided both academic and vocational courses. Some tertiary colleges included adult education, whereas other LEAs maintained separate adult provision.

The second important and related factor was the decline in youth employment from the mid 1970s. The government, in reaction to the crisis, took important initiatives in vocational qualifications for the unemployed school leaver (Avis, 1983), such as the Youth Opportunities Scheme (YOPs) and, later, the Youth Training Schemes (YTS) and the Certificate of Pre-vocational Education (CPVE). For adult returners there was the Training Opportunities Scheme (TOPs) and, later, Employment Training (ET). These government-sponsored initiatives did have a limited effect on the levels of youth registered as unemployed and led to some young people finding employment, although the extent of this varied from region to region depending upon the local employment opportunities. During the mid-1980s the growing realisation that youth unemployment was not a temporary phenomenon was combined with reports that stressed the importance of increasing the knowledge and skills of the workforce for changing economic production (Gleeson, 1996). Comparisons with other countries' participation rates and education levels were made and a systematic look at the post-16 curriculum took place, leading to proposals for a national qualifications framework.

However, despite all these new initiatives, the institutional structures of post-16 education and training were not rationalised and England and Wales continued to have a uniquely mixed system of provision. Although FE colleges were increasingly becoming the main providers of full-time 16–18 education, they failed to become the normative upper secondary institution. The common 6-3-3 pattern of primary, lower secondary and upper secondary schools, typical of the majority of advanced countries, could not evolve in England and Wales because of the prestige attached to the 11–18 secondary school, which was still the preferred option of many parents. Where tertiary colleges developed, and in the rare cases where they became sole 16–19 provider in an area, a new institutional model could be seen to exist in embryo, but even here the mission of the institutions was made more complex by the fact that they continued to serve adults. Further education and tertiary colleges continued to be an awkward mixture of what in the US context would be a comprehensive high school combined with a post-high school community college. These mixed purpose institutions continued to form part of a complex institutional patchwork which included sixth forms, sixth form colleges and training providers, all of which came under different statutory regulations and state bodies. The last chance to reform this system and produce an institutional structure that would be more simple, coherent and transparent then disappeared amidst the vagaries of electoral politics. The MacFarlane Report, recommending what amounted to a new national structure of 16–19 tertiary colleges, was published just as a new Conservative Government was installed in 1979 with a quite different agenda.

As organisations, colleges were often rather loose conglomerations of departments with little overall cohesion. Colleges reflected social divisions between 'graduate and non-graduate, industrially experienced and non-experienced, craftsmen, white-collar workers, managers scientists, social scientists' (Tipton, 1973: ix). This meant that colleges were identifiable not as single organisations, but as competing departments to which staff had allegiance. However, by the end of the 1980s, the issue of corporate identity and strategic planning was beginning to be discussed. Colleges were extremely diverse in character and had different levels of resourcing, reflecting the priorities of their respective LEAs, the different communities and the labour markets they served. They also reflected the diversity of policies of the different government departments and agencies to which they were accountable. The effects of the growth of FE in the 1980s was to produce a sector which had experienced 'expansion without strategic leadership' (Green, 1995). Government-commissioned reports from the mid 1980s, such as *Managing Colleges Efficiently* (DES, 1985), noted the inefficient use of resources in many colleges, with poorly utilised space and enviably small class sizes, and argued persuasively for greater consistency in resourcing and efficiency in the use of resources. It was hard at this time to argue that FE formed a sector in any real national sense.

During this period of expansion and change, FE failed to achieve anything comparable to the statutory status of schools or the prestigious autonomy of universities; nor did it have the benefit of a formalised contractual relationship with employment. The 'technical phase' of FE, related to the expansion of the economy and the development of apprenticeships, was relatively short-lived, being confined the period of the 1950s and 1960s. Vocational education and training in England was not institutionalised in the same way as in other systems in mainland Europe, where specialised vocational institutions were closely tied to vocational qualifications and the labour market. The English approach to vocational education, even at the height of its close relationship with the economy, always reflected its minority status. In the late 1960s only a small proportion of 16–19 year olds were involved full- or part-time and the majority of young people in work did not receive any form of further education and training. The process of detachment of colleges from the local economy, particularly in inner city areas, was brought on by de-industrialisation and was further compounded by government policy.

During the 1970s and 1980s a 'new vocationalism' developed which emphasised preparation for work. As Bloomer (1997) illustrates, this development fuelled a debate that is still ongoing about the purpose and content of such courses. Bloomer argues that recently there has been recognition that vocational education is complex and far more than training for job specific skills:

> Many of the reforms to have taken place in post-16 education since the early 1980s, despite the problematic nature of their underlying evidence and logic, reflect a clear and visible attempt to shift from narrowly focused 'preparation for work' towards some notion of preparation 'for life', for 'citizenship', 'for multi-skilled work' and for 'collaborative work relationships'. While the effects of such shifts are most evident in full-time vocational courses, and to some extent in 'A' Level programmes, they receive little or no recognition in National Vocational Qualification (NVQ) levels 1, 2 and 3. Consequently, the once clear purpose of vocational education has become bifurcated into 'vocational education' based in some broader concepts of vocation and preparation and 'occupational training', whose primary concern is to equip learners with skills for jobs. (Bloomer, 1997: 14)

Since the mid 1980s and the development of NVQs, the emphasis has been on an employment-led approach to qualifications for those in the workplace rather than an 'alternance model' which would formally involve colleges as training partners.

By the end of the 1980s FE colleges had acquired a much more diverse mission than had previously been the case. In addition to their traditional – and still primary – focus on vocational education and training, they were now also responsible for some 40 per cent of 'A' Level teaching. However, unlike school sixth forms and sixth form and tertiary colleges, they tended to have a disproportionate share of more disadvantaged students and those seeking a 'second chance' after unsatisfactory previous experiences of learning. Colleges were both locally and nationally funded with approximately 20 per cent of their budgets consisting of targeted funding from central government departments and national Quangos. Funding levels in FE colleges were very uneven, reflecting local political decisions. However, pressure for cuts in public expenditure and the introduction of Local Management of Colleges following the 1988 Education Act were creating very real tensions between colleges and their LEAs. The division and rivalry of the Department of Employment and Department of Education perpetuated FE's ambivalent position in local and national priorities as well as its traditional marginalisation between schools, HE and TECs.

Stage 5: The early 1990s (incorporated colleges and the Further Education Funding Council's 'national sector' and mixed system)

As outlined above, incorporation was in many respects a continuation of existing trends rather than a clean break with the past. The ground for incorporation had already been laid with the growth of targeted funding and the introduction of the Local Management of Colleges in the 1988 Education Act. Incorporation came about in a political climate of a government in its third term of office determined to give education greater autonomy from LEAs and to introduce competition between providers. The example of the polytechnic sector under the Polytechnics and Colleges Funding Council (PCFC) had demonstrated that efficiency gains could be achieved by incorporated institutions competing for funds.

However, the particular context of incorporation reflected political pragmatics. By 1990 the government was keen to remove financial responsibility for certain services from local government so as to reduce the burden of the unpopular Poll Tax which it had miscalculated. Removing FE colleges from LEA control was an easy solution to bringing the Poll Tax levels down to their predicted targets – particularly as a similar thing had been done to the polytechnic sector. To everyone's surprise, sixth form colleges, traditionally identified with the school sector were, for good measure, included into the incorporated FE sector.

Beyond the political context, two particularly important documents influenced the form that incorporation, and perhaps more importantly the funding mechanism, took. The first of these was the White Paper, *Education and Training for the Twenty-first Century* (DES/ED, 1991). The second was *Unfinished Business* (Audit Commission/OFSTED, 1993). The former placed FE at the centre of a national strategy for raising levels of skills and qualifications, whereas the latter pointed to inefficiency, waste and poor completion rates for younger full-time students. Indeed the central concept of the FEFC's model of funding was to raise levels of participation, with a particular emphasis on 16–19 year olds; improve retention rates; and create a national sector of funding which would be more efficient and effective. The wide range of funding levels was to be tackled by a process of convergence towards an Average Level of Funding (ALF), achieved by setting growth targets for high ALF colleges, where the additional units were funded at rates below that of other units. Units replaced the traditional student full-time equivalent (FTE) and were linked directly to funding levels. Unit funding was based on the stage process of 'entry', 'on programme' and 'achievement', with other units available for additional learning support, fee remission and child care. This was designed both to reflect real costs and to provide incentives for improving attainment.

Although FE has undergone massive change in recent years, we would argue that incorporation is best understood by examining the points of continuity between past and present rather than seeing incorporation as a clean break with the past. (A more comprehensive discussion on the funding mechanism takes place in Chapter Two.) Recent research into the effect of the funding mechanism on colleges (Leney, Lucas and Taubman, 1998) confirms that it is having quite contradictory effects on different colleges and different parts of the curriculum, for example between low and high ALF colleges, and full-time courses and part-time courses. The research, which was based on 12 different colleges, showed that although class size had increased and course hours had been cut, these were trends already taking place before incorporation (FEFC, 1993).

Research on colleges seems to suggest that the early optimism towards the FEFC has shifted to a more critical attitude within a sector that is divided and suffering from excessive internal competition. If the FE sector could be characterised as fragmented and diverse in its pre-incorporation phase, the post-incorporation phase is characterised by competition and division often based on high and low ALF factors. Some colleges in inner cities claim that the methodology is fundamentally flawed and that an institutional weighting factor should be introduced (Chambers, 1995) to compensate for extra costs associated with catering for different socio-economic deprivation. This idea, initially rejected by the FEFC, has been given fresh impetus following the recommendations of the Kennedy Report (1997) for extra funding for persons from certain postcode areas to encourage widening participation in FE. The FEFC has decided to add a widening participation factor to its funding methodology based on postcodes. In its first year of operation in 1998–1999 'widening participation' funding will only apply to 15 per cent of the most deprived wards and includes an allocated sum of £10 million. According to the FEFC, only 32 colleges in the country have 60 per cent or more of students coming from the relevant deprived areas. Thirteen are in London with Tower Hamlets College attracting additional funding for 98 per cent of its students (Education and Employment Committee, 1998). How much money is allocated to 'Kennedy students' in the future remains to be seen, as does its potential effect on colleges enrolling students from the 'right' postcodes at the expense of others.

The FEFC's centralised system of funding requires very rigorous audit. Some anecdotal evidence suggests that petty scams are taking place around registers at the census points, with some students being kept on courses when they would previously have been asked to leave, and funding units being created by 'unit farming' and franchising in ways that were certainly not intended by the FEFC. Systems to maximise units are being learnt very quickly by colleges. It would certainly seem that the existing system is easy to 'manipulate', particularly because units are not the same as funded students. Maximising funding may benefit individual colleges, but it does nothing for the sector as a whole. The Hodge Report (Education and Employment Committee, 1998) suggested that such practices waste precious resources and that the FEFC should ensure that such 'perverse incentives' be dealt with through a process of simplifying the funding mechanism.

Most commentators agree that FE is in some sort of crisis. The main complaint about the funding methodology is the bureaucratic complexity of the data demands of the FEFC creating excessive paperwork, particularly at middle management level, which absorbs valuable college resources. However, it is important in reflecting upon the incorporated model, to distinguish between incorporation, the funding methodology and the overall amount allocated to the sector by national government. Although in the past many failed to distinguish between what are essentially methodological, political and organisational dimensions of incorporation, there now seems a far greater willingness to do so by separating the arguments for increasing the quantum from government with reforming the FEFC's model of incorporation. There is a growing consensus that after five years of FEFC funding, a change of government and recent reports such as Tomlinson (1996) (see Chapter Six), Dearing (1996), Kennedy (1997) and the recent Green Paper, *The Learning Age* (DfEE, 1998), changes to the funding methodology are due. However, if the recommendations of the House of Commons Education and Employment Committee (1998) are adhered to, the changes will not be fundamental, as the Committee's analysis concurred with that of the FEFC that the crisis of FE is primarily one of quantum not funding methodology. No serious commentators suggest that colleges will return to LEA control. It seems incorporation will remain, albeit on a regional rather then national model, although the FEFC's methodology seems likely to be made more flexible with the emphasis changing from cut-throat competition to one of regional planning and co-operation between providers. If, as expected, regional planning takes place, and certain types of students begin to carry more units than others do, the whole edifice of the FEFC's funding methodology – with its emphasis on national formulae funding and national convergence – becomes more difficult to sustain. If this scenario does come about, the national bureaucratic model of incorporation will need to be redefined as FE enters yet another stage of development. Chapter Two analyses the funding of FE in more detail.

Further education and the government's education and training policy

The role of the incorporated FE sector can be seen in the context of over-all government policy for post-16 education and training since 1991. This has five basic dimensions. First, there are the National Education and Training Targets linked to raised levels of participation for the 16–21 age group. Second, there is the expansion of a broad vocational track through the development of GNVQs and, more recently, the development of modern apprenticeships. Third, there is the encouragement of institutional competition and market logic as a means of stimulating quality and driving down costs. Fourth, there is the use of national and local quangos as a means of coordinating delivery. Fifth, there is the attempt to raise the profile of FE linked to the notion of lifelong learning and the government's 'New Deal'.

In the 1990s it is possible to see FE symbolising the movement from a 'low-participation mixed system' to a 'medium-participation education-led system' in which the majority of the age group stay on at 16 (Spours, 1995). Following rapid rises in full-time participation in 1987–1993, the role of colleges has grown so that in 1993–1994 they held a larger share of 16-plus full-time participation than schools and catered for about 35 per cent of the age group. Now the sector offers more 'A' Levels than schools, as well as catering for many more 16–19 year olds and adults than the school or HE sectors, on both a full-time and part-time basis.

Yet, despite this expansion, the relationship between FE and the education and training system could be seen as one in which FE is being standardised to play a increased 'quantitative role' related to 'second chance populations' to complement other organisations which have more elite participants. Aspects of the recent initiatives on the New Deal would be an example of this. This approach could be characterised as attempting to reform the FE sector without reforming the ET system a whole. Indeed, as Unwin (1997) argues, vocational education and training have not only been the victim of political ideology in the attempt to tackle the problem of mass youth unemployment, but have also been shunted from one government department to another until the creation of the DfEE. The English system of ET has no tradition of strategic reform and because of its scale and diversity consensus has proved difficult to achieve (Hodgson and Spours, 1998), particularly within the context of English voluntarism and competing awarding and funding systems. Indeed, in recent years, efforts have been made to create a market that sets schools, colleges, TECs and other training providers against each other. The consequence of this has been the further fragmentation of provision, the strategic drift of FE, and although there has been some success with modern apprenticeships, a general failure to create a credible high-status work-based route (Unwin, 1997). Despite many recent reports and initiatives from the New Labour Government it seems that the piecemeal approach of reforming education and training continues. The New Deal, lifelong learning, modern apprenticeships and the curriculum reform advocated in *Qualifying for Success* (DfEE, 1997) are on the whole being considered in isolation with no unified or strategic view of encompassing the tertiary sector of education and training as a whole.

Despite the growing role of FE, the ET system has continued to exhibit features of a mixed system. The role of colleges is best understood by an historical analysis of its changing role and the relationship between the development of the education and training system as a whole. In the mid 1980s, the ET system in England and Wales was described as a 'mixed system' in which there was an absence of any dominant form of delivery (OECD, 1985; Raffe, 1992). In France, the dominant form has been school-based, linked to the development of the *baccalauréat*. In Germany the Dual System has been predominantly work-based. The English situation could be described as a fragmented delivery system. Throughout the 1980s, the participation of 16–19 year olds was finely divided between school sixth forms, sixth form colleges, the private sector, FE colleges, YT schemes, work with training and work without training and with a large residue not involved in any type of education and training. Colleges by the end of the 1980s had come to symbolise both the strengths and weaknesses of the ET system as a whole – diversity and innovation, but accompanied by fragmentation and incoherence (Green, 1995).

Although predominantly education-based, the ET system in the 1990s saw the focus of fragmentation move from between education and training to division within full-time education itself. This is symbolised for FE by the complexity of its boundaries (Hall, 1994; Hughes, 1994) and the problematical interface with schools, employers and HE (see Chapter Four). Most serious is the problem of school sixth forms competing over 16 and 17 year olds, which has been actively encouraged by the government. Colleges also have an uneasy division of labour with TECs, which have responsibility for the organisation of employers and work-based youth training, and modern apprenticeships. The problem of the relationship between colleges and TECs was aggravated by the unwillingness of the then Tory Government to support an 'alternance model' of vocational education and training which would provide a more explicit role for FE in relation to employers. There has also been a rapid decline since the late 1980s in the numbers of part-time students enrolling in FE (Spours, 1995) and there is increasing competition with HE over HNDs and other sub-degrees courses. In this context of being bounded by more prestigious or high profile organisations, it is not surprising that FE colleges continue to be dogged by low status.

In the late 1980s, the concept of the low-skills equilibrium (LSE) became influential in the analysis of the ET system. The LSE was described as a mutually reinforcing syndrome in which low-quality production demanded low levels of skill from industry staffed by managers with inadequate training and reinforced by a divided education and training system (Finegold and Soskise, 1988). There have been several important changes since this analysis was first published in 1988, the most significant being the rise in full-time participation which begs the question as to whether elements of the ET system have released themselves from the LSE. At one level, colleges appear to be breaking out of the LSE by recruiting more students and by focusing on keeping them on course. The language of quality and high skill is certainly looking beyond the LSE. On the other hand, colleges may be being driven back into the LSE by the focus on quantitative growth. There are accusations that colleges are becoming like 'factories' for processing students where real skill gain or value-added is in many cases questionable.

In a later article, Finegold (1991) focused on the institution (in this case, the private firm) rather than the whole ET system, to analyse movements from a LSE towards a high skill equilibrium. The main features of this type of development are represented by a strategy of long-term skill investment, clear rewards for training, decisions being taken in operative units or cost centres, employment security and promotion structures linked to a structure of qualifications and an emphasis on cooperation. The experience of the FEFC's model over the past five years would suggest that colleges conform to only a minority of the symptoms of a high skill equilibrium organisation. Many colleges are now better managed than they were in the past, but the relationship between colleges as incorporated entities, the FEFC's model and overall government policy of the education and training labour market has driven these organisations back into the low skill equilibrium. There is still a focus on the short-term, driven by the need to maximise revenue, too little collaboration both internally and between providers and not sufficient investment in the future. Any efficiency gains provided by the FEFC's model have at the same time had the tendency to reduce college effectiveness by stretching the organisations to the limit.

Staffing issues under incorporation

Significant changes for FE staff have taken place since incorporation (see Chapter Nine), yet here too these changes had started earlier. By 1993, class size, numbers of hours taught, student-staff ratios and the proportion of part-time staff had all been tightened to reduce unit costs. At present it is impossible to generalise about the contractual position and average number of teaching hours because, in practice, the number of local variations approximate to the number of colleges. Although the exact picture is difficult to ascertain, there is little doubt that the number of teaching hours for FE staff has increased. Even more significant has been the extra pressures outside of 'formal' teaching hours, regarding curriculum development, tutoring, and responding to the massive increases in information required by the FEFC's funding regime such as Individual Student

Records. As colleges have driven down their unit costs, class sizes have shown some increase, but more importantly course hours have been cut to the minimum with teachers teaching more groups and consequently a greater number of students.

While full-time posts have been lost, the growth areas have been taken up by greater employment of part-timers. On average, colleges are spending around 30 per cent of their staffing budgets on part-time staff. This statistic hides a huge variation in local practice – one (large) college devotes just 5 per cent of its budget to employing part-timers, whereas another (small) college is spending 64 per cent (Lucas and Betts, 1996); the majority of colleges fall in the 20–40 per cent category, but a significant minority lie on either side of the middle range. The trend to employ more part-time and less qualified staff is occurring right across the FE sector with assessors or instructors, who have no training other than the Training and Development Lead Body (TDLB) D32/33 assessor awards being used as teachers. The implications of this are quite complex. FE has always had a 'core' and 'periphery', although since incorporation the 'contractual fringe' or 'flexible labour force' has grown. *Quality and Standards in Further Education in England* (FEFC, 1996: 6) also confirms this trend, reporting that funding and financial considerations, not educational ones, are dominating the debate in FE. It also maintains that fears of redundancy are sapping staff morale as the shift from full-time to agency part-time staff raises concerns about quality which 'are not always in the best interest of student'.

The FEFC makes no recommendation regarding expenditure on staff development. Today the average for each college is still about 1 per cent of total budget, yet the variations around this mean are quite wide, within an overall range from approximately 0.33 per cent up to 2 per cent. Research (Young *et al.*, 1995) suggests that most of the money spent on staff development by colleges is not part of a long-term strategic plan, but is spent on immediate needs, such as staff achieving D32/33 assessor awards and management receiving training on Management Information Systems, Individual Student Records and other immediate aspects of administration arising from the demands for data from the FEFC.

The future of initial training, staff development and the professionalism of FE staff is at a crossroads. At present, neither the Teacher Training Agency (TTA), the FEFC nor the DfEE takes responsibility for FE staff training and professional development. Each college operates on its own, increasingly influenced by financial considerations and the entrepreneurial activities of examination boards, universities and national agencies such as the former NCVQ. Much will depend on initiatives from national government and how the new Further Education National Training Organisation (FENTO) operates. Standards and quality of FE teaching staff are being taken more seriously and there is some hope of combining ITE with a coherent set of standards in a framework of professional development for all staff, including part-timers. (A fuller analysis of ITE and CPD takes place in Chapter Nine.) The FEFC's funding mechanism could be changed so that colleges are rewarded for taking a strategic approach to human resource development (HRD). HRD could also become stronger criteria in the FEFC's inspections. These developments, which are discussed in more detail in Chapter Eight, hold out the possibility that the sector could in the future take a more long-term and strategic approach to professional development and that, for the first time, a professional body for FE might be established. There is growing recognition that quality learning relies on highly skilled staff and that both staff and management must change the present culture of neglect. Initial training in this scenario would be a stage of professional development rather than the professional qualification. Placing initial teacher education (ITE) within a new qualification framework would allow colleges and universities to discuss their respective contributions in a new and more constructive way and to develop their human resource strategies accordingly.

Has the Further Education Funding Council created a national sector?

Part of the problem in creating a national strategy for the FE sector is that although FE caters for many more 16–19 year olds than schools, it also caters for older students (see Chapter Three), with 76 per cent of all

FEFC-funded students now over 24 years of age (AFC, 1996). Whereas full-time 16–19 year olds need well-defined structures, provision and support, adult students have many different needs from younger students – they are more likely to need more flexible modes of study, locally available provision, recurrent patterns of participation, accreditation of prior learning, child-care support and relatively inexpensive provision (Derrick, 1997). In responding to adults in the mid 1990s, colleges have had to become more customer-oriented. In a market environment driven by the funding methodology, colleges are tempted to try to broaden the basis of their courses and to create a learning process which is so generic that it can be conceivably applied to all types of learning. This may be the meaning of the movement towards the 'counselling and guidance college'. This could be appropriate for some types of students, but not others. Colleges appear to be meant to cater for everyone, 16–19 year olds, both academic and vocational, adult returners, access students, HE students, those with special needs (see Chapter Six), the socially excluded and those not involved anywhere else. As part of the growing ethic of lifelong learning, if you are not in a school sixth form, at work or at university, then you should be involved with the local college. Within this catchall vision of colleges there is great diversity and excellence, but alongside the virtues there are potential pitfalls. The virtue is increased commitment to access and achievement for all, but the possible pitfalls are that FE lacks a clear strategic role, either nationally or locally, and is rather marginal to high prestige areas. There is a danger that in concentrating on basic skills and access FE will fail to attract its fair share of faster, more capable students.

Few supporters of incorporation realised that the move away from LEA control would mean so much regulation from the FEFC in order to create a national sector of FE out of a fragmented and diverse local provision. Incorporation has been by characterised as a 'national bureaucratic model', contrasting this with a 'local administrative model' when under LEA control (Spours and Lucas, 1996). It is an application of a national framework of funding, inspection and auditing within which colleges (and schools and TECs) compete in what was seen by the government of the time as an education and training market (Gleeson, 1996) or a 'quasi market'. The funding mechanism over the last few years has tended to focus the attention of colleges on the FEFC's short-term financial considerations with more long-term strategic plans being pushed to one side. In the efforts to drive down unit costs, to increase efficiency and to bring about convergence, the FEFC stands accused of concentrating on quantity and compromising quality. Funding considerations, not educational concerns, dominate the college management agenda, as course hours are drastically cut and more part-time lecturers are employed in order to achieve 'efficiency' (FEFC, 1996; Leney, Lucas and Taubman, 1998).

We would argue that although the changes are still impacting on the sector, the FEFC's model of incorporation has failed to create a national post-16 sector. The Hodge Report recognised the lack of leadership and strategic direction given to FE and called on the government not only to increase the quantum but also to explain its priorities to the FEFC. Several issues appear to stand in the way of national coherence. First, the institutions now contained within the FEFC sector are still very varied, ranging from small sixth form colleges, tertiary colleges and specialist institutions (such as agricultural colleges) to very large FE colleges. Each contains within them different cultures and traditions. Some are predominately 16–19 academic institutions, some offer HE courses, others vocational courses, and yet others offer nothing above level two qualifications catering for more part-time and full-time adult returners. College incorporation and the creation of the FEFC have done nothing to rationalise the overall structure of post-16 education and training. In fact, in many ways, they have made such rationalisation impossible, as there is now an even greater diversity of controlling agencies in the sector, including not only the FEFC for colleges, but also the LEAs for schools, the Funding Agency for Schools for Grant-maintained schools and the TECs for youth and adult training. Such a proliferation of overlapping control has already made the extension of tertiary system an impossibility as no one agency has sufficient authority to plan across a whole area. Without more consolidated regional control for the sector, any other forms of comprehensive institutional reform will face the same obstacles.

Second, the recruitment of 16–19 year olds is divided between schools and colleges which compete under different funding systems, therefore reinforcing features of fragmented delivery. Third, the move towards local FE pay bargaining may accentuate different conditions of service. The different emphasis given by individual colleges to staff development and initial teacher training, plus the tendency to replace full-time lecturers with part-timers and instructors, may undermine a common concept of professionalism. Fourth, the doubtful division of adult education between recreational (funded by the LEA) and vocational (funded by the FEFC) further increases fragmentation. Fifth, TECs, which are responsible for government-funded training schemes, have a funding methodology and set of performance criteria that differ yet again from those operating under the FEFC. The introduction of the welfare to work schemes will add yet another piece to the mosaic.

Conclusion

Since incorporation, the FE sector has undergone massive change and made significant efficiency gains. However, local links with employers have been weakened and the sector is still very fragmented despite the centralised national system of funding – all in all it is still a long way away from the promised national sector. The one-time possibility of a distinctive role for FE as an engine for raising levels of achievement towards national targets has been lost somewhat, not least as it has been squeezed between the role of TECs and the growth of school sixth forms and HE. In the effort to maximise funding, compete with other providers and survive the first five years of 'efficiency savings', FE has lost any notion of having a distinctive national or regional role. The sector is not only facing a financial crisis, but is also in a state of strategic drift. The recent Education and Employment Committee Report (1998), and the announcement of an 8.2 per cent increase in FE spending over the next three years (Crequer, 1998), both suggest some acknowledgement of the strategic and financial problems. We are of the view that there needs to be a fundamental review of FE leading towards its renewal and realignment for the new century. This will be explored further in Chapter Ten.

References

AFC (Association for Colleges) (1996), *FE Now*, *24*, February. London: Association for Colleges.

Ainley, P. and Corney, M. (1990), *Training for the Future: The Rise and Fall of the Manpower Services Commission*. London: Cassell.

Audit Commission/OFSTED (1993), *Unfinished Business: Full-time Educational Courses for 16–19 Year Olds*. London: HMSO.

Avis, J. (1983), *Curriculum Innovation in FE: A Case Study*. Occasional Paper. Centre for Contemporary Cultural Studies. Birmingham: University of Birmingham.

Bailey, B. (1990), 'Technical Education and Secondary Schooling, 1905–1945'. In P. Summerfield and E. Evans (eds), *Technical Education and the State since 1950*. Manchester: Manchester University Press.

Barnett, C. (1986), *The Audit of War: The Illusion and Reality of Britain as a Great Nation*. London: Macmillan.

Bishop, A.S. (1971), *The Rise of a Central Authority in English Education*. Cambridge: Cambridge University Press.

Bloomer, M. (1997), *Curriculum Making in Post-16 Education*. London: Routledge.

Bratchell, D.F. (1968), *The Aims and Organisation of Further Education*. Bath: Pergamon.

Cantor, L., Roberts, I. and Prately, B. (1995), *A Guide to Further Education in England and Wales*. London: Cassells.

Chambers, R. (1995), 'Lewisham not Lewis! Profligate Colleges or penalised students'. *Praxis Papers 1*, London: Lewisham College.

Crequer, N. (1998), 'Colleges Hit the Jackpot', FE Focus, *Times Educational Supplement*, 17 July.

Day, C.R. (1987), *Education and the Industrial World: The École d'Arts et Métiers and the Rise of French Industrial Engineering*. Cambridge, Mass.: MIT Press.

Dearing, R. (1996), *Review of Qualifications for 16–19 Year Olds*. London: SCAA.

Derrick, J. (1997), *Adult Part-time Learners in Colleges and the FEFC*, Post-16 Education Centre Working Paper No. 21, University of London Institute of Education.

DES (1985), *Managing Colleges Efficiently*. London: HMSO.

DES/ED (1991), *Education and Training for the 21st Century*, Vols 1 and 2, Department of Education and Science/Employment Department. London: HMSO.

DfEE (1997), *Qualifying for Success*. London: The Stationery Office.

DfEE (1998), *The Learning Age: A Renaissance for a New Britain*. London: The Stationery Office.

Education and Employment Committee (1998), *Sixth Report of the House of Commons Education and Employment Committee*, Vol. 1, 19 May. London: The Stationery Office.

Evans, K. (1975), *The Development and Structure of the English Education System*. Sevenoaks, Kent: Hodder and Stoughton.

FEFC (1993), *Funding Learning*. London: FEFC.

FEFC (1996), *Quality and Standards in Further Education in England*. Coventry: Further Education Funding Council.

Finegold, D. and Soskise, D. (1988), 'The Failure of Training in Britain: Analysis and Prescription'. In Glesson, D. (ed.), *Training and Its Alternatives*. Milton Keynes: Open University Press.

Finegold, D. (1991), 'Institutional Incentives and Skill Creation: Preconditions for a High Skills Equilibrium'. In P. Ryan (ed.), *International Comparisons of Vocational Education and Training for Intermediate Skills*. London: Falmer Press.

Frankel, A. and Reeves, F. (1996), *The Further Education Curriculum in England: An Introduction*. Bilston: Bilson College Publications.

Gleeson, D. (1996), 'Post-compulsory Education in a Post-industrial and Post-modern Age'. In J. Avis, M. Bloomer, G. Esland and P. Hodkinson (eds), *Knowledge and Nationhood*. London: Cassells.

Gleeson, D. and Mardle, G. (1980), *Further Education or Training?* London: Routledge and Kegan Paul.

Gorringe, R. (1996), *Changing the Culture of a College*, Coombe Lodge Report, *24(3)*. Bristol: The Staff College.

Green, A. (1990), *Education and State Formation*. London: Macmillan.

Green, A. (1995), 'Exam Sitting Targets', *Times Higher Educational Supplement*, 17 March.

Green, A. (1997), *Education, Globalisation and the Nation State*. London: Macmillan.

Hall, V. (1994), *Further Education in the United Kingdom* (2nd edition). Bristol: Collins Educational and Coombe Lodge.

Harrison, J. (1954), *History of the Working Men's College. 1854–1954*. London: Routledge and Kegan Paul.

Hodgson, A. and Spours, K. (1998), *Dearing and Beyond: 14–19 Qualifications, Frameworks and Systems*. London: Kogan Page.

Hughes, C. (1994), 'FE-All Dressed UP – But Does It Know Where to Go'. In M. Austin and C. Flint (eds), *Going Further*. London: Association of Colleges.

Kennedy, H. (1997), *Learning Works: Widening Participation in Further Education Colleges*. Coventry: FEFC.

Leney, T. Lucas, N. and Taubman, D. (1998), *Learning Funding: The Impact of FEFC Funding: Evidence from Twelve FE Colleges*. NATFHE/University of London Institute of Education.

Lucas, N. and Betts, D. (1996), 'The Incorporated College: Human Resource Development and Human Resource Management – Contradictions and Options', *Research In Post-compulsory Education, 1(3)*, 329–345.

McCullough, G. (1989), *The Secondary Technical School: A Usable Past?* London: Falmer.

OECD (1985), *Education and Training Beyond Basic Schooling*. Paris: OECD.

Perry, P.J.C. (1976), *The Evolution of British Manpower Policy*. London: BACIE.

Raffe, D. (1992), 'Beyond the Mixed Model: Social Research and the Case for Reform of 16–18s Education in Britain'. In C. Couch and A. Heath (eds), *Social Research and Social Reform: Essays in Honour of A.H. Halsey*. Oxford: Oxford University Press.

Rainbird, H. (1990), *Training Matters: Perspectives on Industrial Restructuring and Training*. Oxford: Blackwell.

Roderick, G. and Stephens, M. (1978), *Education and Industry in the Nineteenth Century*. London: Longmans.

Select Committee (1867/68), *Report on Provision for Giving Instruction in Theoretical and Applied Science to the Industrial Class*. London: HM Government.

Sheldrake, J. and Vickerstaff, S. (1987), *The History of Industrial Training in Britain*. Aldershot: Avebury.

Simon, B. (1969), *The Two Nations and the Education System, 1780–1870*. London: Lawrence and Wishart.

Spours, K. (1995), *Participation, Attainment and Progression*, Post-16 Education Centre Working Paper No. 17. London: University of London Institute of Education.

Spours, K. and Lucas, N. (1996), *The Formation of a National Sector of Incorporated Colleges: Developments and Contradictions*, Post-16 Education Centre Working Paper No. 19. London: University of London Institute of Education.

Thompson, E.P. (1963), *The Making of the English Working Class*. Harmondsworth: Pelican Books.

Thompson, S. (1879), *Apprentice Schools in France*. London.

Tipton, B. (1973), Conflict and Change in A Technical College. London: Hutchinson Educational.

Tomlinson, J. (1996), *Inclusive Learning*. Coventry: Further Education Funding Council.

Unwin, L. (1997) 'Reforming the Work-based Route: Problems and Potential for Change'. In A. Hodgson, and K. Spours (eds), *Dearing and Beyond: 14–19 Qualifications, Frameworks and Systems*. London: Kogan Page.

Weiss, J.H. (1982), *The Making of Technological Man: The Social Origins of French Engineering Education*. Cambridge, Mass.: MIT Press.

Young, M. Lucas, N. Sharp, G. and Cunningham, B. (1995), *Teacher Education for the Further Education Sector: Training the Lecturer of the Future*, Post-16 Centre Report for Association of Colleges. London: University of London Institute of Education.

2 Incorporated Colleges: Beyond the Further Education Funding Council's Model

Norman Lucas

Introduction

This chapter will build on the analysis of incorporation developed in Chapter One, but will focus on the effects of the Further Education Funding Council's (FEFC) funding mechanism which gave incorporation its particular shape. It analyses the major influences that informed the development of the funding mechanism, including the ideology of the 'marketisation' of education and the creation of a 'quasi-market' in which providers compete. The difficulty of objectively analysing the FEFC's model of incorporation is discussed, and, building on previous research (Spours and Lucas, 1996; Leney, Lucas and Taubman, 1998), the chapter arrives at an assessment of strengths and weaknesses of the FEFC's funding regime. Recent emphasis given to cooperation to counter the worst aspects of the marketisation and 'efficiency savings' of the past few years are welcomed. However, the chapter takes a critical stance towards the present funding methodology of the FEFC, arguing that it has reduced colleges to scrambling for units and focusing on meeting the FEFC's data demands rather than addressing educational and strategic considerations. Despite the new emphasis given to further education (FE) the government still seems wedded to the FEFC's model of incorporation, which my analysis suggests is unable to respond adequately to the new demands being made on the FE sector, such as those of widening participation and of lifelong learning. The chapter concludes by examining options for change, arguing that strategic planning and funding should take place at a regional level, involving all post-16 providers, which means moving beyond the present funding model of the FEFC.

Further education under local education authority control

During the 1980s FE was funded by a mixture of local and national taxation. No national funding formulae existed, although college allocations were all retrospectively calculated on the previous year's full-time equivalents (FTEs). Central government used advisory formulae as part of its assessment of need in arriving at the Standard Spending Assessments which underpinned the Revenue Support Grant, but these were indicative not prescriptive. The detail and level of funding varied from one local authority to another, with different models and calculations reflecting the complicated funding formulae used by local government. In many areas local education authorities (LEAs) were able to influence colleges to ensure that minority groups had a place in the college plan and that the college had links with local industry and was responsive to community needs.

Minimal quality control took place; perhaps the LEA following a poor inspection report would express concern, but this would be retrospective and rarely have any funding implications. LEAs had long-term influence on priorities, but change was evolutionary. Although this provided security and continuity, the model was not conducive to change, rapid expansion of student numbers or curriculum development. Even within the context of public expenditure savings forced on local government by successive Tory Governments in the 1980s, which included the growth of targeted funding, there was little change in the culture and values of FE. By the late 1980s college funding was a mix of contradictory trends, with LEA funding provision alongside a growing, more targeted funding system. At the time of incorporation, this developed to about 20 per cent of the budget, with developments such as Technical and Vocational Education Initiative (TVEI). Change was marginal rather than fundamental until the 1988 Education Reform Act (ERA), when cuts in public expenditure and Local Management of Colleges (LMC) did begin to have profound effects on FE colleges just prior to incorporation.

Many qualitative changes associated with incorporation, such as targeted funding from central government (i.e. Youth Training Scheme or TVEI), took place in the 1970s and early 1980s whilst under LEA control. It was in this period that FE colleges began to change in two major ways. First, there was the shift from their predominately part-time, day-release role to becoming more diverse institutions responding to de-industrialisation and the consequent rising levels of unemployment amongst youths and adults. Second, colleges started offering a variety of academic courses responding to the expansion of higher education (HE) and the increasing difficulties schools were having in maintaining viable sixth forms. Thus, the technical colleges of the post-war years dominated by employed part-time vocational students were transformed into more diverse FE colleges. The 'new FE' offered more full-time courses for 16–19 year olds whilst developing part-time courses for adults (see Chapter Three), many of whom were unemployed. Throughout this period colleges began to feature in government thinking, partly because of the growing numbers of full-time 16–19 year olds, partly as institutions for coping with mass unemployment and dealing with the 'skills deficit'. One difficulty in defining FE as a national sector prior to incorporation was that it remained obscured by political localism.

Incorporation: the Further Education Funding Council's model

As Chapter One outlines, incorporation came about within a particular political context. The political thrust from central government of the time was based on undermining the power and influence of LEAs and the belief that introducing markets and competition would improve provision. Removing education from LEA control had been successfully achieved in the polytechnic sector and it suited the ideology of the time to apply it to FE colleges. It was also a timely and pragmatic solution to reduce the burden of the Poll Tax, which the government had miscalculated so badly. The inclusion of sixth form colleges in the incorporated sector was either a mistake, caused by the rush in which incorporation came about, or was needed to make up the Poll Tax miscalculation (Ainley and Bailey, 1997). Either way, sixth form colleges found to their surprise that they were incorporated into the FE sector, making that sector even more diverse then before.

The foundations for incorporation had already been laid with the local management of colleges (in the 1988 Education Act) which changed college governance and gave delegated budgets, although at this point colleges were still under the auspices of the LEAs. The move away from LEA control to incorporation came in the 1992 Higher and Further Education Act. The driving concept behind the FEFC's model of incorporation was an expanding sector linked to improved 16–19 participation, improved retention rates and the promotion of more adult learning. The aim was to create a sector with a higher national profile, being more standardised so that it could be judged by national criteria for efficiency and effectiveness and operate at reduced unit costs.

Alongside the political agenda of the government, the form incorporation took was particularly influenced by two documents. The first important strategic document, which signalled the direction for FE in the 1990s, was the White Paper *Education and Training for the Twenty-first Century* (DES/ED, 1991). It placed FE, for the first time, at the centre of the strategy for achieving higher levels of skills and qualifications (Green, 1995). The main objectives of the White Paper were to raise levels of participation and achievement, to create a more integrated FE sector and to force colleges to be more dynamic and efficient by placing them in a competitive market situation.

The second important influence was the seminal report *Unfinished Business* (Audit Commission/OFSTED, 1993). This was concerned with 16–19 year olds across the school and college sectors. Its major findings were those of poor retention, poor success rates on 'A' Level and vocational courses, and a wide variation in costs per student between institutions. It reported that on average 12 per cent of 'A' Level students left early and 20 per cent failed the examination. Vocational courses did worse, with 18 per cent leaving early. The report also noted that annual revenue costs of courses involving three 'A' Levels, BTECs or Diplomas all varied from just over £1,000 to almost £7,000 per student following the same course in different colleges. No link was found between the cost of courses and the subsequent examination results achieved. The report concluded that typically 30–40 per cent of 16–19 year olds who started a course did not succeed 'at a cost of £500 million – as well as substantial amounts of a student's time' (Audit Commission/OFSTED, 1993: 2).

The legacy of historical funding which the report highlighted was to be resolved by the process of 'convergence', in which the average level of funding (ALF) of each college was designed to converge by 1996–1997 to plus/minus 10 per cent of the median. For a minority of colleges this meant coming down from high ALF levels. For most it meant a decrease in the level of funding per unit, because the movement towards convergence, greater efficiency and a generally more level playing field, would be brought about by rapid expansion of student numbers, generating extra units, at a lower rate. If colleges had problems with meeting their targets, then there were two options: either they could revise down the targets and extend the time-scale of convergence, or they could start to close or merge. To date no colleges have closed, although many are in financial difficulty, seeking amalgamation and merger as a means of survival. Some are calling for the strategy of national convergence to be reconsidered (Leney, Lucas and Taubman, 1998), with the suggestion that national convergence should be replaced by regional convergence based upon a regional strategic plan.

Atkinson (1995) argued that although the funding methodology introduced several new concepts, two are of key importance. First, the currency of the system is the 'unit of activity' or simply the 'unit' which replaces the student FTE, thus in theory, the funding actually follows student learning. College targets are set in units and units are linked directly to funding. The second key principle is the concept of unit funding being based upon a three-stage process – 'Entry', 'On-programme' and 'Achievement'. The bulk of units are earned by the 'On-programme' element with relatively small amounts for 'Entry' and 'Achievement'. Other units can be earned from fee remission, child-care and additional learning support. Different quantities of units are awarded according to the type of course students follow, with 'load banding' reflecting 'cost weighting factors' according to the different resource needs of programmes. The basic purpose of the funding mechanism is to focus colleges on recruitment, growth and course retention. The vast majority of FE funding (90 per cent) is viewed as 'core', with 10 per cent being 'margin' and unit based. However, with the value of the unit dropping, colleges have had to increase their total number of units in order to maintain their budgets. This has led to the other function of the funding methodology, that is to bring about expansion at lower unit costs. Amidst all of this, the actual amount of funding attached to student output or achievement is small. Of the unit-based element only 8 per cent is output related in the pure sense.

The 'marketisation' of education and training

The incorporation phase of FE was an attempt at modernisation through the application of a national framework of funding, inspection and auditing. Within this framework, colleges, schools and other providers compete in what is seen by government as an education and training market (Gleeson, 1996). Although colleges have governors, the real line of accountability is to the FEFC and within the framework of local competition there is a strong strand of national regulation. In a sense, FE colleges could be seen as 'marketised bureaucracies', which are no longer locally accountable but are in an education and training market in which they compete, adopting a managerialism more associated with private companies in which students become customers.

The idea of markets is clear, but it is hard to see how colleges can operate in a market in any classic economic sense, because the relationship between colleges and the vast majority of students is not determined by price. College incorporation is perhaps better described as the creation of a 'quasi-market' with incorporated colleges, schools, TECs and private sector trainers competing. A quasi-market is one where on the supply side there is competition between providers, but on the demand side purchasing power is not expressed in monetary terms but by a centralised purchasing agency influencing policy decisions (Le Grand and Bartlett, 1993). The idea of a quasi-market in FE goes something like this: on the supply-side FE is being forced to compete by the FEFC's methodology, while on the demand-side the FEFC's funding mechanism is highly regulated, exerting enormous power over dependent colleges. There is some market responsiveness in the incorporated model due to local institutional competition and unit-based funding; although in some areas colleges have a virtual monopoly. The combined effect of this is the creation of 'bureaucratic-markets', in which a centralised authority exercises control by making funding conditional on obeying rules and regulations it lays down.

It is argued that a 'quasi-market' does not just apply to FE but is an increasing feature of the 'contract-state' (Ainley, 1993). Ainley argues that the contract or 'contracting-state' is characterised as meeting short-term quantitative performance targets. He contrasts this with the old 'corporate-state' which met the needs of the social partners in the former mixed economy. The contract-state represents a centralisation of power, which operates by franchise, contract and consumer charters untrammelled by social obligations, or even of representative democracy. Developing the concept of the contract state, Spours and Lucas (1996) suggest that another way of understanding incorporation is by analysing it as a 'national bureaucratic model', contrasting this with a 'local administrative model' when under LEA control.

There is still some way to go before the boundaries of the 'marketisation of education' (Ball, 1993) are fully explored or exhausted. Perhaps the FE experiment represents a market hybrid in which strong local competition is combined with strong central control and regulation. More research needs to be done in this area, particularly in relation to the resources used in marketing and the cost of responding to the ever-greater information demands of the FEFC. It would also be interesting to research how far the FEFC's funding has reduced overall costs by taking into account former LEA administrative costs, cost per FTE student, the FEFC's current administrative costs and current college debt. However, comparisons between the old LEA funding costs and the FEFC's costs would be difficult, if not impossible on a national level, as units are counted not FTEs, and as outlined below, units of activity and numbers of students do not necessarily correspond. Recent research into 12 different FE colleges (Leney, Lucas and Taubman, 1998: 24) reported FE staff complaining that the auditing demands of the FEFC were out of control, taking 'a whole new industry to support it', with colleges directing resources at the FEFC's data requirements, diverting resources from teaching, learning and curriculum development. One college was offering Argos shopping discount points to attract students. Other methods of attracting students include offering free uniforms and knives to catering students, free materials and carrying cases for those following Art and Design, and driving lessons to keep students in school sixth forms (Carlton and Nash, 1998). In addition to these sorts of practices, Perry (1997) suggests that the complexity of the funding methodology, the demands of the Individual Student Record (ISR) and management information systems (MIS) has led colleges to invest large amounts in new computers and software, including the personnel and consultants to go with it, costing the average large college approximately £500,000.

Although the 'quasi-market' seems to represent a 'grey area' to economists, the belief in the efficiency of the marketisation of education and training was a fundamental ideological belief behind the Conservative Government's project of incorporation. This included encouraging local bargaining on wages and conditions of service and the planned introduction of vouchers for all post-16 learners to allow price to enter the picture for the first time. There were also plans to create a common funding methodology for 16–19 year olds in school sixth forms and FE (DfEE, 1996).

At the time of writing there is a fundamental review of the funding methodology taking place, although incorporation itself is not being challenged. In the meantime some extra funds have been given to the sector, but the process of national convergence continues. The outcome of the review of funding and the 'marketisation' of FE is not yet known. At present many merger proposals are being considered, some involving HE, others involving mergers of existing FE colleges. Ministers in the New Labour Government are giving mixed messages, calling for a rationalisation and a more proactive approach to mergers, whilst at the same time warning against mergers that are motivated by the wish to make savings. Furthermore, the period of intense competition associated with the previous government is changing with a greater emphasis on collaboration, with the FEFC allocating some targeted funding to achieve this end. The hope is that the FEFC's regional committees will encourage such cooperation (Education and Employment Committee, 1998), although much of this still remains at the level of political rhetoric. Recently an 8.2 per cent cash increase for FE was announced by the Chancellor, with efficiency gains being held (with HE) at 1 per cent per annum (Crequer, 1998). It would seem that the experiment of the 'marketisation of FE' is being replaced by a new mixture of quasi-market involving a cocktail of the old methodology of the FEFC, alongside more state and regional planning. It is too early to evaluate the outcome of this new phase for FE, as the government gives FE a high priority in its plans for lifelong learning, welfare to work and social inclusion.

Difficulties in analysing the Further Education Funding Council's model of incorporation

The problem in analysing the effects of the movement from an historically local and variable level of funding to a standardised national system is trying to disentangle the variable effects of historical funding from the problem of meeting student needs which vary socially, geographically and financially. The FE sector has undergone the most rapid change in its history, yet, as outlined above, incorporation was not a clean break with the past and has many points of continuity. The FEFC's funding methodology may represent some important advances on past practice, but it is having contradictory effects on colleges (and departments) due to the dependence on quantitative expansion, national convergence and institutional competition. It is worth noting in the context of this section, that although this chapter focuses on the FEFC's model of funding, colleges receive finance from a number of other sources, such as the Higher Education Funding Council, the TECs, the European Social Fund and LEAs. Colleges generate income from fees, short courses, lettings and consultancy. It is estimated that at present the FEFC's funds constitute approximately 80 per cent of the income for the average college; although in some colleges it is as low as 35 per cent (Huddlestone and Unwin, 1997). Thus, in any analysis of the effects of funding on colleges difficulties are encountered because the experience of national funding systems varies from college to college depending on their average level of funding (ALF), the proportion of their budget which is funded by the FEFC, and also because the experience of funding has not yet fully worked through college systems.

Many of the colleges with higher ALFs are to be found in inner cities with student populations that require exceptional levels of support. They can also be colleges which have multi-sites and which are expensive to run. These colleges claim that the FEFC's image of the incorporated college is located somewhere in middle England and does not appear to take seriously the problems of colleges in urban areas. Chambers (1995) argues that this is a significant design flaw of the funding mechanism and that an Institutional Weighting Factor (IWF) should be introduced to produce a more level playing field on which FE colleges in quite different socio-economic contexts can compete. On the other hand, many colleges that have had to live with low levels of funding point to the inequities of historical funding and broadly welcome the funding mechanism and convergence. These differing experiences of incorporation, between high and low ALF colleges create difficulties for analysis. The recent House of Commons Report on FE (Education and Employment Committee, 1998) found college views on convergence divided, with low ALF colleges wanting convergence speeded up and high ALF colleges, often in the inner cities, wanting it slowed down and reconsidered.

Trying to be objective about the history of FE under LEA control also causes some difficulties. There is a temptation by those in favour of incorporation and the funding methodology to have a one-dimensional and oversimplified view of the experience of FE within LEA control. This view emphasises the paradigm shift of the FEFC's funding model from an 'allocation model' to an 'earning model' (Spours and Lucas, 1996). This underplays developments in the management of FE prior to incorporation, such as the devolution of budgets and management to governing bodies, local management of colleges, and the direct annual link between funding and student numbers all made in the 1988 Education Reform Act (ERA). At the other extreme, many lecturing staff look back on LEA control as a 'golden era', ignoring reports such as *Unfinished Business* and instead concentrating on their perceived deterioration in conditions of service.

Another problem of analysing incorporation is the changing sentiments about the FEFC's model now six years into its operation. Many in FE were originally well disposed towards incorporation. It was associated with a higher profile for the sector and seen as a means of rescuing FE from local control and cuts in resources that had been taking place in the early 1990s. In this climate of tension between colleges and LEAs, many in FE thought that there could be benefits under the FEFC's national organisation rather than under local political control. The initial positive disposition towards the FEFC was helped in the first year of incorporation, as budgets were relatively unaffected because the funding model was not yet operational. However, attitudes became more critical over the next few years as the resource implications of the funding model became increasingly evident. The hope that incorporation would simply be an extension of the LMC was soon lost, as the funding methodology itself worked its way through college systems. Furthermore, staff perceptions were being shaped by the bitter and protracted dispute about contracts, the problems of meeting growth targets, the impact of cost reductions and a wave of redundancies. This was particularly the case in those colleges with high ALFs. There appears to be an emerging feeling that the FEFC's model is in some form of crisis (quite apart from the recent demand-led element (DLE) incident), and that change is required to ease the financial pressure on colleges. The recent announcement by the Chancellor to hold FE growth at 1 per cent per annum and to inject an extra £225 million will certainly relieve the financial pressure on colleges. However, the 95 per cent of colleges supporting Option E during the FEFC's consultations on Circular 93/32 has certainly declined. According to one principal, the supporters who entered the 'Faustian bargain' with the FEFC and 'leaped smiling over the cliff' (Perry, 1997: 3) are now characterised by splits and divisions according to high ALF versus low ALF, high franchise versus low franchise, big versus small, urban versus rural and commercial focus versus community focus. In these circumstances, FE has moved beyond its traditional fragmentation to one of competition and division, as it scrambles to compete for units of funding to improve 'efficiency' and lower the ALF.

Trying to look beyond the current model is also difficult for a number of other reasons. Going back to LEA control is not on the political agenda of any party, and people associate incorporation and the FEFC's funding model as being synonymous. At one level the FEFC's approach demonstrates a strong and rationalising tendency and the funding model, despite its complexities, is regarded by many as intellectually sound. For some there may be the temptation to resist change because they have only just understood it, and are exhausted with the effort. Many find it difficult to foresee a change in the funding of 'Entry', 'On-programme' and 'Exit' which still has widespread support.

In any analysis of the FEFC's model of incorporation it is important to distinguish between two important things. First, there is the distinction between incorporation as a particular form of ownership and control and the actual funding methodology, which has given incorporation its particular form. It is theoretically possible to have incorporation of colleges with a different funding methodology. Also, conversely, it is possible for the form of ownership to change (perhaps back to LEAs or to a regional basis), but the funding methodology to remain. Second, consideration needs to be given to the distinction between the funding mechanism itself and the overall quantum. Cuts in public expenditure were already biting colleges prior to incorporation. Perhaps the 'efficiency gains' forced upon the sector are more important than the funding methodology itself. In other words, if the quantum were increased, as called for by the House of Commons 'Hodge Report' (Education and Employment Committee, 1998), it is likely that criticism of the methodology would decrease. Both the financial quantum and growth targets for FE were not set by the FEFC but by the government. Thus, any judgement of the FEFC should recognise these dimensions as important, because it distinguishes between political dimensions and funding aspects of incorporation.

An assessment of the Further Education Funding Council's model

The experience of the past few years would support the view that the choice and implementation of funding methodologies has a profound impact on the values and culture of colleges – certainly far more powerful than policy shifts from national or local government. In general, few supporters of incorporation realised that a move away from the benign control of LEAs would mean so much FEFC regulation and downward pressure as the new body attempted to create a national sector. Even those most critical of the past and most supportive of incorporation would now admit that alongside considerable gains, the funding methodology is proving to be far more problematic than was foreseen at the time of incorporation. These problems are not always apparent when judged by quantitative standards such as increases in the participation rate. However, when judged by qualitative and curricular criteria, worries emerge about the qualitative impact of cuts in courses hours, the increasing use of part-time teaching staff and the difficulty in funding part-time, partial achievement.

Within the judgement of strengths and weaknesses it is important to distinguish between problems caused by the FEFC and the problems resulting from an inadequate and shrinking quantum – this is often quite difficult. However, accepting the difficulties outlined above, the gains from the FEFC's model of incorporation can be summarised in the following way.

• Despite the pain experienced by FE staff since incorporation, the increasing number of people studying in the sector and an evaluation of exam results would suggest that, on balance, the service to students has improved. The emerging consensus seems to be that the funding mechanism has focused college attention on the processes of induction, tracking and information systems, special needs and student retention. In interviews and research amongst staff and students (Ainley and Bailey, 1997; Leney, Lucas and Taubman, 1998), acknowledgement of these gains were conceded by almost all those interviewed. Those best disposed to the new regime were managers and students, with main grade lecturers having a more negative view (although this was less so amongst new members of staff).

- The methodology can easily be steered at a national level to reflect the policies of government, such as encouraging colleges to offer courses which meet National Targets by funding them at a higher level. In the short time that it has been in operation, the funding methodology has proved to be surprisingly responsive to some important educational and social issues. For example, in implementing the Kennedy Report on widening participation, the idea of 'Kennedy students' being given extra funding via postcodes is being considered within the existing funding mechanism.

- Another example in favour of the methodology is the emphasis on units for additional learning support to assist those students with special educational needs and making available additional units for child care. The policy adopted by the FEFC effectively blocked the purely market driven funding that would have excluded certain 'expensive' categories of students with special needs (Cantor, Roberts and Prately, 1995). The benefits of identifying and costing students with learning support needs have improved initial guidance and screening at enrolment, particularly for literacy and numeracy. The funding mechanism for additional support has, despite some criticism, brought special needs provision into the mainstream of college work and provision.

- The consensus seems to be in favour of funding the process of learning in its three distinct parts. Entry units seem to have particularly beneficial effects on colleges' advice and guidance systems, legitimising good practice that had already started in some areas and systematising it. Leney, Lucas and Taubman (1998) found not only general improvements in advice and guidance systems, but also evidence that advice, guidance and induction was being done in hitherto neglected areas such as outreach work. The 'On-programme' funding units have certainly put more emphasis on retaining students on courses, although keeping students on course and cutting down 'drop out' is still a major problem facing many FE colleges and courses (FEFC, 1998).

• The experience of the last few years has showed that colleges are capable of being corporate, flexible bodies. Incorporation has lead to improved management systems and colleges capabilities. Since incorporation, tracking, recording and management information systems have improved. Whilst the initial impulse for tracking was the FEFC's funding and auditing demands, teachers and managers recognise (Leney, Lucas and Taubman, 1998) that this information is important for good teaching and curriculum development, a fact woefully overlooked by management in pre-incorporation days.

• Although there has been a serious decline in the provision of non-vocational adult education, the FEFC's funding has provided colleges with incentives to take the education and training of adults more seriously. With the levelling off of the spectacular rise in participation of 16–19 year olds, colleges are not only turning their attention to questions of retention and progression, but are also looking towards expanding their adult provision to meet future growth targets (Spours, 1995). The implications for a more flexible curriculum, teaching staff and college to cater for this growth in adult participation (see Chapter Three) are beginning to be addressed by some colleges.

The major criticisms of the FEFC's funding can be summarised into the following broad areas.

• The FE sector may now have a national profile and a national system of funding, but incorporation has not led to a national sector. The argument is that there is no national funding for 16–19 year olds (with schools given unfair advantages), part-time LEA-funded adult education is not on an even playing field, there is no national standard for inspection of 16–19 year olds or adults and there is no distinctive national role for the sector. Local or regional links that were developed under LEAs have often weakened and the sector has become even more fragmented. In the first few years of the new funding methodology, colleges struggled to survive and compete with other providers, such as other colleges, TECs, school sixth forms and universities. As the Hodge Report highlighted, there are too many bodies involved with funding, planning and delivering of post-16 education and training (Education and Employment Committee, 1998). Within the struggle to maximise units of funding, the debate about the distinctive national or regional role and a planned local curriculum has been marginalised.

- Although there have been improvements in qualification outcomes, quantity has been emphasised more than quality. In the process of efficiency savings and convergence designed to drive down unit costs, educational values and concerns with the quality of learning have been replaced by funding and financial considerations. According to the FEFC's Chief Inspector (FEFC, 1996), the 20 per cent efficiency gains achieved since incorporation have been brought about by reducing the number of taught hours rather than by increasing class size (which remains at an average of 11). A common criticism of the FEFC's funding methodology is that it has reduced colleges to a scramble for units and cost-cutting measures, detracting attention from the curriculum. Colleges report cuts in teaching hours of as much as seven hours on 'A' Levels and GNVQs. Some of today's full-time students would have been part-time in the past. Some of the cuts in teaching hours are made to accommodate the '16-hour rule' for those on benefit, but for most it is a cost-cutting measure. Although colleges are moving towards more resourced-based learning to compensate for the cuts in teaching hours, some categories of students, particularly those targeted for inclusion by the Kennedy Report, are being disadvantaged by these developments (Leney, Lucas and Taubman, 1998).
- The bureaucratic complexity of recording, which appears to be on the increase, is taking up far too much management time (FEDA, 1998) and is detracting from curriculum development. The paperwork being generated by GNVQs and the ISR is proving to be enormously problematic and is aggravated by software failings. Greater workloads are being created, particularly at lecturer and middle management level.

Data is absorbing valuable college resources due to the volume of data required and there are difficulties in identifying whether courses are full- or part-time (Derrick, 1997). The ISR is a feature of centralised management of the sector and as a symptom of the 'units logic', with detailed record-keeping on students to support funding rather than educational purposes. Recent research (Leney, Lucas and Taubman, 1998) found that colleges were complaining that the information and audit requirements demanded by the FEFC, were 'out of control'.

- The funding methodology is introducing more rigidities into course design. So far the funding mechanism has been unable to relate to modularisation/unitisation and credit accumulation because its view of achievement is based on a whole-course completion. Even where the funding methodology has proved to be responsive, as in the case of additional learning support, it has brought with it surprising rigidities, such as the high threshold in the number of hours to be offered before the unit funding can be triggered. This seems to reflect the view that there are 'normal students' and those with special needs. The ones which fall between these categories are left out of the equation, yet as participation increases and widens these students may increasingly be the norm – those who are relatively slow learners, but with a little extra support and attention could achieve progression thresholds. The funding methodology in its present form fails to recognise partial achievement, which is so important for those who have some learning difficulties. In this sense, the FEFC's funding is in need of reform if it is to meet the more flexible curriculum (see Chapter Eight) required by the recommendations of Kennedy (1997), Dearing (1996) and the DfEE's document *Qualifying for Success* (1997) or the government's policies on lifelong learning and social inclusion.
- Although colleges are concentrating on improving retention rates, some students are staying on courses when they should, in fairness to other students, have been asked to leave. The importance given to retention has pushed the funding allocated to achievement into second place. Achievement is still an important matter of professional pride, but it is not an important component of a college's funding consid-

eration. It also seems the case that TEC output-related funding appears to have put lecturers under pressure to distort objective judgements of quality (FEDA, 1998) and pass incompetent candidates doing NVQs so as to secure payment and promote future recruitment. It is openly acknowledged that although concrete evidence of abuse is scarce, the temptations and pressures are real and cannot be lightly dismissed (CGLI, 1995).

- Incorporation has seriously affected the morale and quality of FE staff, as they have gone through a bitter and protracted dispute with college employers. Faced with the need to save money, managers have been forced to make redundancies and to replace full-time posts with a growing number of part-time teachers. Very real concerns about the quality of teaching has been raised about the drift towards colleges being made up of a small core of full-time trained and a growing periphery of part-time, sometimes agency staff (Education and Employment Committee, 1998). Staff development has been marginalised and dominated by the short-term needs of management. Human Resource Development has been replaced by Human Resource Management (Guile and Lucas, 1996) and the whole question of the professional development and the quality of teaching and learning (see Chapter Nine) has been secondary to meeting the information demands and financial restrictions of the FEFC.

- The FEFC's funding mechanism is easy to 'manipulate' and hard to audit, despite the data demands of the FEFC. When auditing the large and complex world of FE, it is very difficult to verify the accuracy of registers at the census points. In its evidence to the Select Committee of the House of Commons, FEDA (1998) expressed concern not only about the amount of management time devoted to maximising revenue or 'tariff farming', but also that in many cases the distribution of funds was more sensitive to those that 'played the system' than to real growth and quality. The FEFC was urged by the Committee to ensure that 'the funding system does not create perverse incentives or reward behaviour which runs counter to the core aims of the FE sector' (Education and Employment Committee, 1998: 31). A proportion of the much applauded expansion of FE has been a result of franchising existing provision in the private sector, reclassifying work and 'unit farming' (sometimes called 'tariff farming', 'nesting' or 'additionality') in order to gain full funding advantage and lower the ALF of colleges (Gravatt, 1997). Unit farming is where funding units are increased without increasing student numbers. It is achieved by entering students on extra qualifications around the same course (nesting). According to Perry (1997) one college increased its unit total by 100 per cent whilst actually reducing student numbers. Taking a broader view of unit maximisation, it can be regarded as a form of unit inflation because as the units increase the value of the unit must be lowered, unless new resources are found.

• Franchising is being questioned by some principals, the FEFC and politicians. It is important in the controversy surrounding franchising to realise that it has been part of the FE landscape for some time, often representing genuine quality partnerships between employers and FE. However, recent criticism (FEFC, 1998) has focused on the dramatic increase in the last three years, during which the number of colleges involved in franchising has doubled from 2 per cent to 10 per cent of the FEFC's funding with only 20 colleges accounting for 58 per cent of the franchising units. Some colleges have registered dramatic growth and lowered their ALF through franchising courses and training that already existed in the private sector, thus diverting funds from mainstream FE work (Perry, 1997). This includes existing courses, such as SCUBA diving, St John's Ambulance training and private training where existing students become part of the college role, spectacularly lowering the college ALF, with the FEFC's funds subsidising costs of other providers (Gravatt, 1997). Now that the demand-led element (DLE) pool (which was a driver for growth) is capped by the DfEE, funds for future franchising must be found out of the FEFC's existing budget. Many colleges are calling for franchised and non-franchised provision to be separately allocated and identified and a fundamental review of franchising is being undertaken by the FEFC.

• The call for the harmonisation or convergence of funding criteria for schools, TECs and HE (AoC, FEDA, 1998) have been growing. FE, and particularly sixth form colleges, feel that the different and more generous funding for 16–19 year olds in school sixth forms is grossly unfair to the 16–19 year olds in FE. There is particular concern that 16–19 years olds are disadvantaged in FE by the cuts in course hours and the loss of additional or enrichment studies/activities. It is difficult to make accurate comparisons of costs as the FEFC and DfEE use different methods of calculation, but all figures show the FE sector disadvantaged. There is also concern about funding HE courses in FE which is currently funded at 75 per cent of the same provision in the HE (FEDA, 1998). Furthermore the different funding levels between LEA and FEFC part-time adult education, as well as the disadvantages faced by part-time students generally when compared to those of full-time courses has yet to be dealt with by the FEFC.

The funding methodology appears to be a complex mix of centralism and decentralisation and of high trust and low trust. It is highly centralist, insofar as the FEFC has created a model which can be very effectively manipulated to favour particular qualifications or to value particular services to students. This has the effect of making colleges immediately respond in order to maximise income. Although institutions have full responsibility for their income, it can nevertheless be regarded as a low-trust approach because there is the assumption that institutions will not have sufficient regard for quality without direct economic incentives. Despite the FEFC's aim to provide a measure of stability, this has not proved to be the case as there have been constant adjustments within the methodology and constantly changing criteria which have made it difficult for colleges to plan.

Challenges for the future

One way of understanding the FEFC's model of incorporation is by seeing incorporation not as a single process but as series of stages (Spours and Lucas, 1996). The first stage was a phase of independence from LEA control prior to incorporation when colleges were given devolved budgets.

Some principals look back on this as a short but golden era of freedom without centralised regulation. The second stage was the first year of incorporation, but without the effects of the funding mechanism. It was marked by the building of college corporations and organisational adjustments to the new regime. Even though there were some doubts about the FEFC's model, optimism was still high. This was followed by a third stage, in which the funding system began to impose its rigours on colleges with high growth targets as well as driving down unit costs within the convergence period. It was also a period marked by a damaging dispute over contracts, a wave of redundancies, massive increases in part-time teachers and a fracturing of consensus about the FEFC's model. During this third stage the FE sector changed internally in the drive for efficiency gains. This period ended with the DLE crisis in early 1997 and the fall of the Conservative Government in May of the same year.

The fourth period, which we are now entering, is one of cautious optimism tinged with uncertainty. Reform of the funding mechanism seems forthcoming. We do not yet know what form it will take, but it seems unlikely that the FEFC's funding mechanism will be radically changed. The FE sector has been given a high profile by the new government with over 80 per cent of the 500,000 additional students expected by the year 2002 allocated to the FE sector. Considerable extra funding has been found as the sector and growth rates have been held at 1 per cent per annum, in line with HE. The relentless 'efficiency savings' and worst aspects of the 'marketisation' of FE identified with the third period of incorporation seem to be over. This fourth period will be one of organisational change, with colleges having to respond to new initiatives by the government such as the 'New Deal'. This new period of incorporation could be marked by mergers and possible college closures if the drive to national convergence is pursued. The new recommended convergence targets are a 2.5 per cent band range achieved by the year 2002 (Education and Employment Committee, 1998). Some concern has been expressed by the FEFC (1998) that the trend of FE colleges merging with universities will cause 'academic or mission drift' and the further abandonment of the FE's vocational mission as mergers are sought on financial rather then strategic considerations.

In the present period of incorporation the difficult balance of reforming the funding mechanism is on the agenda. On the one hand, reform needs to take account of the major criticism of the present system's inability to fund different types of student differently and to recognise partial achievement. On the other hand, any reform needs to simplify the funding methodology to rescue colleges from the auditing demands and complications of the present system. The need to make the system sensitive to different needs, yet to provide stability and transparency is generally accepted, belatedly, by the FEFC. However, such a balance between responsiveness and rescuing colleges from the funding methodology's present complexity and the FEFC's overwhelming auditing demands requires a stepping back and a re-evaluation of what should be determined by funding and what should be influenced by other processes. The present FEFC's model is based on the dogma that everything can be controlled and influenced by funding. There is no evidence that this dubious assumption is being questioned. In a more balanced and less severe system the activity of providing guidance and learning support services could be regulated more by an inspection and development process linked to strategic plans rather than being directly influenced by funding. Recent evidence (Leney, Lucas and Taubman, 1998) suggests that funding encourages basic services to be put in place and quantitative targets to be met, but it does not sufficiently influence its quality.

Two options for change are being considered. The first option is a period of consolidation and adjustment of the present unit-based model rather than the further pursuit of high growth targets. The recent quantum increase and 1 per cent growth targets are evidence of this, as is the FEFC's proposal to consider more weighting being given to certain types of students following the recommendations of the Kennedy Report (1997). The basic argument for the consolidation of the current system is that FE colleges have gone through many painful adjustments. They are now more efficient organisations that have been squeezed financially, and with the slowing down of convergence and/or an increase in resources, the next period can coincide with a period of 'quality' with steady rather than rapid growth (Crowne, 1995). An adjusted model could also be applied to cover all 16–19 education, perhaps by requiring LEAs and school governing bodies to fund their sixth form provision by the FEFC's norms (Scott, 1995). The more likely scenario is the harmonisation of funding levels rather than establishing a common methodology for all post-16 education and training (Education and Employment Committee, 1998). This would mean the establishment of a 'common entitlement', including enrichment activities for all 16–19 year olds in school or college. The comparative cost of the same courses in HE and FE is at present under investigation by the Higher Education Funding Council – the details are not yet known, but a more level playing field between FE, schools and HE seems a likely outcome.

The second option, apparent in government policy discourse, is a shift towards a more collaborative, planned and coherent regional post-16 system. There are as yet no details of how this is to be achieved, although there has been a perceptible shift by the FEFC to concede that they have some responsibly for planning, and not just funding, a reversal of earlier statements. The Hodge Report (Education and Employment Committee, 1998) was concerned that too many bodies are involved in post-16 education and training and suggested that the FEFC and its regional committees should facilitate the establishment of regional and sub-regional partnerships. The role of Regional Development Agencies (RDAs) remains unclear, as do many details of the regional approach, although they would be based on social partnership and a more planned and supply-side direction linked to regional economic education and training and development. This scenario, if it were to be effective, would mean reforming the FE sector in the light of wider reforms of the post-16 education and training system. There could be the formation of regional planning and funding bodies, possibly under the auspices of the DfEE. Within the regional framework, representatives of different providers could meet to decide regional priorities and targets for participation, achievement and progression along with the development of new forms of provision. 'Healthy competition' could continue, but the dysfunctional aspects of the cut-throat market place could be avoided. Regional training and education targets could be set. Regional and local socio-economic factors could be taken into account when calculating average levels of funding or weighted funding and judging institutional effectiveness in terms of progression and retention. It is too early to make any certain judgements, but the general direction seems clear.

The two scenarios outlined above, the adjustment of the FEFC's model and the creation of a regional model, should not be seen as mutually exclusive. They could be viewed as steps and stages with institutions being recognised as independent entities but encouraged to cooperate rather than to compete. The first step would involve adjustment of the funding mechanism to encourage internal planning and inter-institutional cooperation. The main aim would be to stabilise FE colleges and create a level playing field with schools and other providers. There would also have to be moves to bridge the 'democratic deficit' (Scott, 1995) at a local level by giving more LEA and local community representation; this is already proposed in the Green Paper *The Learning Age* (DfEE, 1998). The second step could be the formation of local frameworks for the exchange of institutional plans and to decide priorities for development. Participation in these could be financed by a new Institutional Development Fund at a local level. These forums would involve colleges, schools, TECs and other training providers. A further stage could be the formation of a regional planning framework to integrate the providers involving the devolution of the FEFC's responsibilities to a regional level and the merging with regional government offices and the TEC structures.

In considering the scenario described above, there is a case for re-evaluating the virtues of a modified approach to Full-time Student Equivalent (FTE) in the light of the experience gained from the present funding methodology. I would not like to be prescriptive about FTEs, but it is important to balance the present debate that sees units of funding as the only option. I would suggest that FTEs can be a means of funding, although it is not being actively considered by policy makers. I would submit that this view is not necessarily backward looking and may produce more stability and less bureaucracy than a system based on units of funding. A more flexible FTE system could fund the three FEFC stages and have an institutional weighting factor which could be far less complex then the current funding methodology. An FTE could be modified by being socially weighted, adjusted to take account of additional learning support, course weighted, weighted more in favour of part-time participants and take account of work-based trainees or those on alternating patterns of participation. The FTE could be supplemented by a 'bonus element' for successful course completion and achievement. This would be sufficient to encourage institutions not to focus simply on 'bums on seats'. The balance between the weighted FTE and the bonus element could be altered according to policy priorities. Both the weighted FTE and the bonus element would follow actual students and replace the complicated and bureaucratic system of units attached to learning activity and the consequent generation of units without necessarily increasing student participation.

I started my analysis by suggesting that the FE sector had moved from LEA control to a national and bureaucratically regulated marketised sector under the auspices of the FEFC. As Chapter One of this book argues, the FEFC's model of funding may have created a centralised national system of funding, but it has not lead to the creation of a national sector. The crisis facing FE is not just financial, but one of strategic drift. There is a policy vacuum concerning FE's contribution to developments in the 14–19 curriculum, welfare to work, modern apprenticeships and government initiatives on lifelong learning and social inclusion. The FEFC was until quite recently 'educationally agnostic' (Scott, 1995), seeing itself as a funding council not a planning council. With the election of the New Labour Government, a new phase of incorporation has opened up. Although the details are not yet firm, it would seem that the next stage for FE could represent a shift from a 'national bureaucratic' model to a 'regional strategic' one. Within the regional strategic phase, it is difficult to be prescriptive about a new funding methodology, because the focus of such a debate should extend beyond the boundaries of this book towards a broader consideration of a tertiary sector spanning 16–19 year olds in schools and colleges as well as adults in transition between college, work or HE. There are many steps and stages in the movement towards a harmonisation of funding and of regional coherence and strategic planning, but a starting point must be a recognition that the present arrangements are no longer adequate for a further education system for the twenty-first century. A discussion concerning the realignment of FE takes place in Chapter Ten.

References

Ainley, P. (1993), *Class and Skill: Changing Divisions of Knowledge and Labour*. London: Cassells.

Ainley, P. and Bailey, B. (1997), *The Business of Learning. Staff and Student Experiences of Further Education in the 1990s*. London: Cassells.

AOC (1998), *Evidence to Sixth Report of the House of Commons, Education and Employment Committee*, Vol. 2, 19 May. London: The Stationery Office.

Atkinson, D. (1995), *The Dan Quayle Guide to FEFC Recurrent Funding*. Bristol: Coombe Lodge Report.

Audit Commission/OFSTED (1993), *Unfinished Business: Full-time Educational Courses for 16–19 Year Olds*. London: Audit Commission/OFSTED.

Ball, S. (1993), 'Market Forces in Education', *Education Review, 7(1)*, 8–11.

Carlton, E. and Nash, Ian (1998), 'Driving Lessons Offer Accelerates Unease', FE Focus. *Times Educational Supplement*.

Cantor, L., Roberts, I. and Prately, B. (1995), *A Guide to Further Education in England and Wales*. London: Cassells.

CGLI (1995), *NVQs/GNVQs: Continuity or change?* FE Forum Series, London: City and Guilds London Institute.

Chambers, R. (1995), *Lewisham not Lewis! Profligate Colleges or Penalised Students*. Praxis Papers No. 1. London: Lewisham College.

Crequer, N. (1998), 'Colleges Hit the Jackpot', FE Focus, *Times Educational Supplement*, 17 July.

Crowne, S. (1995), *The Marketing Network*. Conference Speech, 21 November, Bexley Heath, London.

Dearing, R. (1996), *Review of Qualifications for 16–19 Year Olds*. London: SCAA.

Derrick, J. (1997), *Adult Part-time Learners in Colleges and the FEFC*, Working Paper No. 21, Post-16 Education Centre. London: University of London Institute of Education.

DES/ED (1991), *Education and Training for the 21st Century*, Vols 1 and 2, Department of Education and Science / Employment Department. London: HMSO.

DfEE (1996), *Funding 16–19 Education and Training: Towards Convergence*. London: Department for Education and Employment.

DfEE (1997), *Qualifying for Success*. London: The Stationery Office.

DfEE (1998), *The Learning Age: A Renaissance for a New Britain*. London: The Stationery Office.

Education and Employment Committee (1998), *Hodge Report, the Sixth Report of the House of Commons Education and Employment Committee*, Vols 1 and 2, 19 May. London: The Stationery Office.

FEDA (1998), *Evidence to Sixth Report of the House of Commons, Education and Employment Committee*, Vol. 2, 19 May. London: The Stationery Office.

FEFC (1996), *Quality and Standards in Further Education in England*. Coventry: Further Education Funding Council.

FEFC (1998), *Evidence to Sixth Report of the House of Commons, Education and Employment Committee*, Vol. 2, 19 May. London: The Stationery Office.

Gleeson, D. (1996), 'Post-compulsory Education in a Post-industrial and Post-modern Age'. In J. Avis, M. Bloomer, G. Esland and P. Hodkinson (eds), *Knowledge and Nationhood*. London: Cassells.

Gravatt, J. (1997), *Deepening the Divide: Further Education and the Diversion of Public Funds*, Praxis Paper No. 6. London: Lewisham College.

Green, A. (1995), 'Exam Sitting Targets', *Times Higher Educational Supplement*, 17 March.

Guile, D. and Lucas, N. (1996), 'Preparing for the Future. The Training and Professional Development of Staff in the FE Sector', *Journal of Teacher Development, 5(3)*.

Huddleston, P. and Unwin, L. (1997), *Teaching and Learning in Further Education. Diversity and Change*. London: Routledge.

Kennedy, H. (1997), *Learning Works: Widening Participation in Further Education Colleges*. Coventry: FEFC.

Le Grand, J. and Bartlett, W. (1993), *Quasi-Markets and Social Policy*. Basingstoke and London: Macmillan.

Leney, T., Lucas, N. and Taubman, D. (1998), *Learning Funding: The Impact of FEFC Funding, Evidence from Twelve FE Colleges*. London: NATFHE/University of London Institute of Education.

Perry, A. (1997), *A Pencil Instead. Why We Need a New Funding System for Further Education*. London: Lambeth College.

Scott, P. (1995), *A Tertiary System, Report for the Society of Education Officers*. Leeds: Leeds University.

Spours, K. (1995), *Post-16 Participation, Attainment and Progression*, Working Paper No. 17, Post-16 Education Centre. London: University of London Institute of Education.

Spours, K. and Lucas, N. (1996), *The Formation of a National Sector of Incorporated Colleges: Developments and Contradictions*, Working Paper No. 19, Post-16 Education Centre. London: University of London Institute of Education.

3 'Flower Arranging's Off but Floristry is On': Lifelong Learning and Adult Education in Further Education Colleges

Lorna Unwin

Introduction

Seven years after the passing of the 1992 Further and Higher Education Act, which divided the responsibility for adult education between colleges and local education authorities (LEAs), the further education (FE) sector is still struggling to define its role within a diverse yet fragmented community of adult education providers. This chapter will explore the challenges facing FE colleges in seeking to serve the needs of adult students.

Figures for 1996–1997 show that in England 80 per cent of students on FEFC-funded courses are aged 19 and over; of these 92 per cent are studying on a part-time basis (FEFC, 1998). Statistics for adult participation in FE are problematic, as they may include double counting and some courses for adults only last a few weeks (Steedman and Green, 1996). However, it is a fact that adult students form the majority population in FE colleges. This may be a surprise to many people whose impression of the FE sector is dominated by the debates of the 1980s and 1990s around the reform of post-compulsory education and training (PCET) provision for 16–18 year olds. Many initiatives in the last 20 years have had a significant effect on the structure, activity and funding base of FE colleges, and most of them have been targeted at young people rather than adults (for example, the Technical and Vocational Education Initiative (TVEI) in 1982; the Youth Training Schemes (YTS) in 1983 and 1986; Training (later Youth) Credits in 1991; General National Vocational Qualifications (GNVQs) in 1992; and the modern apprenticeship in 1994).

Whilst many organisations might be very happy to have a youthful image, their close association with teenage students poses problems for colleges seeking to clearly distinguish themselves from other post-compulsory providers. Put simply, school sixth forms and sixth form colleges concentrate their provision on 16–18 year olds, and higher education (HE) institutions, whose numbers of adult students have grown considerably, are distinguished in terms of the level and nature of the courses on offer. Colleges of FE compete for the 16–18 year old market and also have a sizeable stake in the HE market (for example, franchised and two plus two degrees, access courses and Open University tutoring). FE colleges start to take on a very different complexion from their post-compulsory rivals in two fields: first, the provision of vocational education and training for government-sponsored schemes; and, second, the provision of vocational and non-vocational courses for adults. It is in deciding the nature and scope of their adult provision that colleges have the means to forge a more distinctive identity.

Defining adult education: the 1992 Further and Higher Education Act

The passing of the 1992 Further and Higher Education Act, which transferred control of colleges from LEAs to the new FEFC, made the provision of adult education a statutory requirement for both FE colleges and LEAs. The Act enshrined the proposal of the 1991 White Paper *Education and Training for the Twenty-first Century* (DES/ED, 1991) that colleges should be funded to provide only those courses (listed under Schedule 2 of the Act) deemed to be vocational or work-related in nature and which led to a recognised qualification. The provision of non-vocational adult education (non-Schedule 2) became a statutory requirement of LEAs which were to receive government funding for this purpose. Colleges could provide courses not included under Schedule 2, but students would be expected to pay fees. The proposals to separate adult education courses into vocational and non-vocational courses was met with widespread opposition at the time of the 1991 White Paper and continues to cause problems for colleges and students today. Bradley (1997) discusses how the critics of the proposals came from a surprising range of backgrounds and all shades of political opinion, including the National Federation of Women's Institutes, the Association of County Councils, the Association of Metropolitan Authorities, peers in the House of Lords and backbench MPs. Of prime concern to these critics was what they saw as the arbitrary division which the White Paper sought to create between, on the one hand, so-called vocational courses and, on the other hand, so-called leisure courses. They pointed out that many non-vocational courses actually developed important 'vocational' skills and increased the learning capacity of adults. Although the subsequent Act maintained the divide, it did make one compromise to public opinion by announcing that LEAs would receive government funding to provide leisure courses.

The seemingly streamlined framework of the 1992 Act envisaged two clearly defined and locally delivered types of adult education; one offered by FE colleges and the other by LEAs. (It is worth noting here that a third group of providers, the Training and Enterprise Councils (TECs), had arrived on the scene in 1991 and were charged with managing the government-sponsored youth and adult training programmes.) In the real world, however, the capacity and willingness of the FE colleges and the LEAs to deliver adult education as seen by the drafters of the Act has been seriously called into question in the intervening years.

There are two key reasons for this. First, the requirement that LEAs should provide non-vocational (or leisure) courses coincided with a political climate in which the LEAs' powers were being diluted and local authorities more generally were coming under severe financial pressures. Adult education suffered badly as local authorities sought ways to make their diminishing budgets pay for essential services. In 1998, in its response to the Green Paper, *The Learning Age*, the National Institute for Adult Continuing Education (NIACE) complained that the statutory requirement for LEAs to provide 'adequate facilities' for adults' FE had, for too long, 'been treated as if it were discretionary, with the tacit support of government' (NIACE, 1998: 8). NIACE called upon the New Labour Government to agree with the Local Government Association 'a mechanism to identify clearly the adult education element in standard spending assessment allocations' in order to secure 'a minimum platform of provision' (NIACE, 1998: 8). At the same time, NIACE emphasised the need for the government to clarify the FEFC's role *vis-à-vis* the funding of adult education. This brings me to my second reason for questioning the gap between the rhetoric of the 1992 Act and the realities of providing a coherent, appropriate and fundable service for adult learners.

Following the Act, colleges were required to work within the strict parameters of the FEFC's funding methodology. In order to receive FEFC funding, a college now had to ensure courses led to qualifications and had vocational relevance. This struck at the heart of the FE sector's long-standing informal curriculum which included subjects such as flower arranging, pottery, conversational French, art appreciation, photography and car maintenance, none of which was certificated but which attracted substantial numbers of adult students to both daytime and evening classes. In order to maintain, and hopefully increase, its numbers of adult students, and to continue the tradition of supplementing LEA provision, colleges were forced to review their adult education curriculum and engage in some particularly creative thinking. Rather than dismantling the rich tapestry of their adult education curriculum, many colleges have been battling to make it fit into the FEFC's rigid frame, and in some areas, colleges and LEAs have worked together to overcome the impoverished vision of the 1992 Act. In the Manchester area, for example, South Trafford College has formed a partnership with the local Workers Educational Association (WEA).

It is worth noting that, at the time of writing, FE colleges are likely to be asked to support even more partnership activity as the government clearly believes there is room in the crowded adult education marketplace for yet more providers. Two initiatives suggest this. First, the government has called for local partners, including traditional education providers and community groups, to bid for a share of its Adult and Community Learning Fund (maximum grants of £50,000 are available) because:

> We want to support activities that will take learning into new sectors of the community not reached by traditional educational organisations,

> providing opportunities that are relevant to the people involved and
> delivering them in ways that will interest and attract the people who are
> hardest to reach. (DfEE, 1998a: 3)

This fund will not support provision that can be funded from other
sources (for example, the FEFC, the Higher Education Funding Council,
'New Deal' and local authority social services). Second, colleges are also
expected to support the government's desire to raise adult participation in
education and training by becoming involved in the University for Industry (UfI). The UfI has two strategic objectives: to stimulate demand for
lifelong learning amongst businesses and individuals; and to promote the
availability of, and improve access to, relevant, high-quality and innovative
learning, in particular through the use of information and communications
technologies (DfEE, 1998b).

The UfI's prospectus outlines a vision of a national network of UfI
learning centres, many of which 'will be based on existing facilities in
workplaces, colleges, universities, schools and libraries' (DfEE, 1998b:
29). The UfI has been designed to be 'the hub on a national learning
network...coordinating and accelerating the nascent market' (Hillman,
1996: 3). It will not be a provider as such, but will act in the way the
'Open Tech' was supposed to work, that is developing strategy, commis-
sioning materials, bringing providers together, kite-marking work-related
learning provision and exercising a quality monitoring function. FE colleges
might argue, with much justification, that they have been operating as the
'hub on a national learning network' for many years through their
involvement with the Open Tech, the Open University and Open College
of the Arts.

Both the UfI and the Adult and Community Learning Fund are consequences of the 1992 Act, which sought to put FE colleges, and hence
PCET more generally, in a marketplace where providers would compete
for customers. Gleeson's (1996) analysis of the Act is pertinent here.
He asserts that that as well as making colleges 'competitive, independent
and entrepreneurial', incorporation also had 'much to do with deregulat-
ing post-16 arrangements, making them more responsive to a business,

industrial and commercial infrastructure which they are expected to serve' (Gleeson, 1996: 87). It remains to be seen whether making colleges compete for parts of a PCET cake which is being further divided will result in attracting the four-fifths of the adult population whom Steedman and Green (1996) remind us do not engage in any form of education or training. What is certain, is that these two initiatives will result in large amounts of precious and scarce time being spent on negotiating partnerships and writing funding bids by college staff.

Adults and colleges: reasons for a relationship

Before this chapter examines the ways in which colleges have responded to the FEFC challenge, it is important to explore the reasons why colleges should provide courses for adult learners. I would suggest there are three reasons worth exploration:

- to respond to the government's economic agenda (as disseminated via a series of White Papers and Education Acts in the 1990s and the FEFC's funding methodology) in order to improve the basic and intermediate skill levels of adults and increase their participation in education and training;
- to fulfil their role as the main provider of PCET at local level; and
- to continue to provide a wide-ranging curriculum which bridges the vocational/non-vocational divide.

These reasons are not, necessarily, contradictory, but selecting any one as its main *raison d'être* will determine how a college then identifies, packages and ultimately delivers its curriculum. There will be consequences for the teaching and support staff as well as for the local community. Research by Ardley (1994) showed that college managements had to listen carefully to their staff when developing their mission statements and marketing policies and understand 'that institutions are not simple systems, but a complex array of different subjectivities, with competing interpretations of reality' (Ardley, 1994: 12).

Chris Hughes, former principal of Gateshead College and from September 1998 Chief Executive of the Further Education Development Agency

(FEDA), suggests that although colleges should certainly concentrate on their adult customers, those customers should be studying for qualifications and, hence, he aligns himself to the economic agenda (as encapsulated in the first reason listed above):

> Above all, we have to get to grips with our core business. This is, I would argue, to help adults become qualified. Not a grand statement and not a fashionable one, but the word 'qualification' resonates with esteem, success, progress, progression and value added. We in FE should champion qualifications (although less rigidly defined) as a means of creating a learning society. And we should concentrate on adults because they are our core constituency. (Hughes, 1997: 6)

In contrast, Chris Jude (the Director of Lifelong Learning at Lewisham College in London) believes that in order to serve the needs of a diverse range of adult students, many of whom are suffering extreme financial and cultural hardship, Lewisham has had to transcend the FEFC's straight-jacket and provide 'space for the extra or hidden curricula aspects of people's lives, for those aspects of identity for which, in this increasingly legislated world, education has no script' (Jude, 1997: 201). By doing this, Jude asserts that the college has had to overcome the body of opinion which 'casts further education as the most instrumental of education providers' and goes on to say:

> Adult education is neither homogeneous nor unitary. It is not the preserve of any one kind of organisation or institution. What we have done is to take those elements from the adult education curriculum which involve participation, creating learning agendas from people's experience, the desire to know, understand and explore other areas of experience and wed them to the FE curriculum. In doing this we have consciously sought to extend what is best in the adult education tradition to new audiences. We have also acknowledged that located within that tradition is a set of involvements and processes which are inspired both by the politicising, radical wing of adult education as well as its liberal curriculum and that these form the essence of an enriching and, we trust, empowering education process. (Jude, 1997: 202)

Although both Hughes and Jude present seemingly polarised agendas in regard to the service colleges might offer to adults, they appear to share the view summed up in the second reason listed above – that colleges should be the main providers of PCET at local level. Part of that provision includes creating and supporting adult students with learning difficulties and disabilities (FEFC, 1996).

Harris and Hyland (1995) have suggested that one way in which the FEFC's funding methodology has had a positive effect on adult students is through the requirement for colleges to provide students (on entry, during the course and at exit) with all necessary support to achieve their qualifications. This, they assert, has enabled colleges to increase their learning support for the large numbers of adults who need to improve their basic skills, particularly in terms of literacy and numeracy (see Ekinsmyth and Bynner, 1994, for research on young adults and basic skills). Whilst any help of this kind is to be welcomed, there is a danger that basic skills are improved for the purely instrumental and short-term reason to ensure that the adult student achieves a qualification which then unlocks FEFC funding for the college. In other words, basic skills improvement becomes 'the act of showing people how to work within a system from the perspective of people in power' (Delgado-Gaitan, 1990: 2). For radical adult educators, basic skills, and particularly literacy, are the key to unlock far more than government funding: 'To be literate is to continually "read" one's world (understand social, cultural, political aspects), to write and rewrite it, and thereby transform one's relationship to it' (Holland, Frank and Cooke, 1998: 12). This emphasis on the transformative powers of education echo the views of the late Paolo Freire, who wrote:

> The conception of education which I am defending…centres around the problematisation of the human being and the world, not the problematisation of the human being isolated from the world, nor the world isolated from the human being…. Of fundamental importance to education…is the problematisation of the world of work, products, ideas, convictions, aspirations, myths, art science, the world in short of culture and history which is the result of the relations between human beings and the world. (Freire, 1974: 152)

Freire's views necessarily pose enormous challenges to all providers of adult education, but they have a particular resonance for those in colleges who seek to balance instrumental and short-term educational goals with the desire to provide space for longer-term personal growth. Elliott's (1996) research with FE college lecturers shows the difficulty they have in finding and maintaining that balance and that they are 'fearful of a shift in the core business and focus of colleges, from the development of students' potential to a preoccupation with balancing the budget' (Elliott, 1996: 13).

One group of colleges that could claim to have kept the spirit of Freire alive are the eight UK adult residential colleges of which there are six in England, one in Wales and one in Scotland. They provide long-term residential courses as well as short and part-time courses for adults and have a long history of links to trades unions and political and community-based activism. However, these colleges have been criticised for their 'geographical isolation...their cloistered, "stately home" setting and... the remedial paternalism of (their) hidden curriculum' (Iphofen, 1996: 66). Ironically, as Iphofen argues, the colleges have sought to promote the 'remedial paternalism' aspect of their work in order to find favour with government whilst, at the same time, attempting to maintain their image as schools for class activism in order to maintain 'trade union and local community support' (Iphofen, 1996: 67). Fryer rejects the criticisms of residential colleges and argues that they have 'given opportunities to thousands of people who otherwise may not have fulfilled their true potential and built up the self-esteem and confidence of many wrongly regarded as educational or social failures' (Fryer, 1997: 145). He further argues that the residential aspect is vital, as it allows for 'focused and undisturbed study, the likelihood of accelerated learning, the use of specialist facilities and access to expert learning support, [and] the chance to engage in team-building and develop other essential social skills' (Fryer, 1997: 145).

Curriculum change: flower arranging to floristry

In order to construct and receive funding for a curriculum and the necessary learning support infrastructure which meets the needs of adult learners, colleges have been busy redefining and re-packaging courses whose names do not fit the FEFC's curricular guidelines. This make-over of the FE curriculum has been aided by, and some would say become totally dependent on, the development of unitisation, whereby subjects are broken down into small chunks of study, each of which can be separately accredited. Central to this development has been the growth of Open College Networks (OCNs), which were first established in the late 1970s, and the National Open College Network, which was founded in 1987. Wilson notes that: 'Collectively, OCNs are now the fourth largest vocational awarding body in the UK (according to the DfEE) and, by some considerable margin, the largest awarding body for adult learners in the FE sector and beyond' (Wilson, 1997: 241).

The Derbyshire Regional Network is an OCN comprising five FE/ tertiary colleges and the University of Derby, and submits its curricular units to the North East Midlands OCN for accreditation. This means that students in any of the six participating institutions can gain credit for small chunks of study and transfer credits between the institutions. The Director of Curriculum at one of the colleges described this structure as a 'lifelong learning pathway' (Unwin, forthcoming). The OCN curriculum is classified into 10 curriculum groups:

- humanities;
- basic education;
- social studies;
- creative arts and media;
- sciences;
- engineering;
- construction;
- health and community care and beauty therapy;
- hotel and catering, travel and tourism, and leisure and recreation; and
- business.

A unit equates to 30 hours of study usually taken over a six-week period, daytime or evening. To get accreditation, units have to be written according to the OCN guidelines and they can then be made available across a number of courses. For example, the Derbyshire OCN explains that 'a unit entitled Marketing may form part of a Business GNVQ, a Business BTEC, or stand alone as a short course to offer to a small local firm or form part of a customised pathway for an individual learner' (Derbyshire Regional Network, 1998).

Re-defining and re-naming curriculum options requires, as was noted earlier, considerable creative skills on the part of college staff and is a process which is particularly necessary if colleges want to protect their non-vocational adult education provision. Hence, one college lecturer explained, 'flower arranging is off, but floristry is on because we can get that accredited and, even better, link the units to an NVQ' (Unwin, forthcoming). Similarly, popular classes in stencilling and other interior design techniques have been re-classified under the heading 'decorative paint techniques'. Parents who want to learn more about how young children learn to talk can now study this as a unit in 'child acquisition of language', which forms part of the 'A' Level in English Language. The impact of this activity on college lecturers is worthy of serious research in order to explore the extent to which applying creativity to the curriculum has led to greater creativity in teaching and learning methods.

Holland, Frank and Cooke make the useful point that: 'Providers of education need to be able to understand and to model critical thinking strategies in order to enhance these skills in learners' (1998: 82). Many in FE would say, however, that the pressures under which staff now have to work militate against creativity and have, in effect, led to the de-professionalisation of lecturers. Randle and Brady comment that 'in order to significantly expand FE, while simultaneously reducing unit costs, it has been necessary to intensify work' (1997: 237). Furthermore, they argue that through students being re-defined as 'customers', the customer has 'taken on the role of manager in the classroom, being in a unique position to monitor and evaluate the hidden and indeterminate aspects of the lecturer's role' (1997: 238).

At Lichfield College in Staffordshire (first established as the Lichfield School of Art in 1879), one departmental head describes how she and her colleagues engaged in 'lateral thinking' to find ways to meet the FEFC requirements without 'sacrificing the integrity of the course content' (Churchill, 1997: 246). The college has arranged its art and design, crafts, textiles and languages courses on a grid with a common core and Churchill explains: 'It is an approach which provides great flexibility and benefit to students as it removes the label of "recreational" or "vocational" from courses and allows a student simply to be a student' (Churchill, 1997: 246).

The college has also joined forces with Staffordshire University, Tamworth College and Staffordshire County Council with funding from the European Union (EU) to try to further bolster the provision of non-Schedule 2 courses and build a 'learning community' (Birch, 1998: 8).

There are growing concerns, however, that this constant re-defining and re-naming of the adult education curriculum may, in the end, be overtaken by instrumentalism:

> Ironically, just at the time when Open College Networks had done so much to facilitate better links between informal adult learning and mainstream provision, which benefited both types of provision, they began to marginalise informal provision by imposing on it criteria devised primarily for mainstream provision.... What is deeply worrying about the changing approach to quality assurance is that it represents a radical shift from a credit system designed around meeting the actual needs and situations of adult learners, to awarding credits only if the needs and situations of adult learners are compatible with the accreditation system. (Maxwell, 1996: 112)

A more optimistic view is that people who care about adult education will triumph as 'adult learning is irrepressible, with or without the state' (Harvey, 1997: 219). This view is echoed in a study of adult education in inner London following the demise of the Inner London Education Authority in 1990: 'This exercise has revealed that adult education in inner London is bruised and fractured, but not dead. It may have been marketised and commoditised, tariffed and truncated, but it remains an important part of the lives of many Londoners' (Cushman, 1996: 31).

Individual adult education tutors in colleges continually demonstrate their determination to fight, as Fuller illustrates with her study of metal-work classes in Nottingham:

> Class activity depends on facilities available, and maintenance, replace-ment and provision of equipment was poor in many cases. Many resources in terms of tools and equipment were the tutors' own and not provided by the centres… . At one Nottingham college a tutor had single-handedly hauled a number of anvils into a workshop to rescue them from destruction! (Fuller, 1998: 13)

If and when college staff do tire of trying to save a broad-based adult education curriculum, they could revert to one of FEDA's suggested strategies which is to offer GNVQs to adults (Pettitt, 1996). FEDA believes that GNVQs 'combine characteristics of both academic and job-specific qualifications, enabling students to keep their options open' (Pettit, 1996: 1).

Barriers to adult participation in further education

As was noted in the introduction to this chapter, we need to be cautious when considering the statistics on adult participation in FE. Steedman and Green (1996), referring to studies by Maguire, Maguire and Felstead (1993) and McGiveney (1994), note that participation is related to age, social class, gender, and educational and occupational level. They add: 'The more an individual engages in learning the more that person is likely to continue learning, so that learning is very unevenly distributed among the adult population with some groups almost completely excluded' (Steedman and Green, 1996: 13).

A range of factors acts as barriers to adult participation for those who want to study full-time or part-time. Such factors include the lack of adequate educational and vocational guidance and financial support to cover child care, transport and course equipment. For adults who are in full-time employment, there are the additional problems of finding the time to study and the lack of employer support. There has been some improvement in the provision of guidance for adults in FE colleges, although Payne and Edwards (1996) point out that this means institution-based provision as opposed to that supplied by independent guidance services. Traditionally, Careers Services have been funded to work with school pupils but, as Warner (1998) explains, since they too became quasi-privatised, they are beginning to realise the potential of the adult guidance market. To what extent the adult learner about to enter or already within an FE college can find access to an appropriate guidance service is still open to debate. Indeed, NIACE (1998) highlighted the 'absence of clear proposals for developing adult guidance' as being 'the most conspicuous gap' in the government's Green Paper, *The Learning Age*. Payne and Edwards (1996: 161) raise the following important questions.

- Is impartial guidance more likely in colleges or on courses that have a high demand?
- Can impartiality be assured without active guidance networks with independent services at their centre?
- Does the lack of outreach guidance already result in a partiality towards certain social groups in terms of access and participation?

Conclusion

This chapter has explored a range of issues related to the provision of adult education in FE colleges and the promotion of the lifelong learning agenda. Part of the ongoing dynamism of the FE college environment is the continued struggle to meet the needs of the diverse and fragmented community surrounding the college. FE colleges' origins lie in being responsive, but I would suggest, in the late 1990s, that responsiveness now dominates college life disproportionately. Adult education should be provided in FE colleges as they are the key education and training institutions serving local and regional communities. If, however, college staff spend too much time battling to make their adult education cur-riculum conform to a bureaucratic framework and writing bids to secure relatively small amounts of funding in competition with other providers, then there may be too little time available to develop and deliver properly an innovative curriculum and provide the levels of support which adult learners need.

References

Ardley, B. (1994), 'College Marketing and the Management of Change', *Journal of Further and Higher Education, 18(1)*, 3–13.

Birch, C. (1998), 'New Centre, New Opportunities', *Adults Learning, 10(1)*, 8–9.

Bradley, D. (1997), 'Influence, Compromise and Policy Formulation: The Further and Higher Education Act and Adult Education', *Studies in the Education of Adults, 29(2)*, 212–221.

Churchill, A. (1997), 'Flexibility and Funding', *Adults Learning, 8(9)*, 246.

Cushman, M. (1996), *The Great Jewel Robbery? Adult Education in Inner London since the Break up of the Inner London Education Authority.* London: National Association for Teachers in Further and Higher Education.

Delgado-Gaitan, C. (1990), *Literacy for Empowerment.* London: Falmer Press.

Derbyshire Regional Network (1998), *Unitisation of the Curriculum Within a Credit Framework: A Practical Guide.* Derby: University of Derby.

DES/ED (1991), *Education and Training for the Twenty-first Century.* London: HMSO.

DfEE (1998a), *Adult and Community Learning Fund: Prospectus.* Sudbury: Department for Education and Employment Publications.

DfEE (1998b), *University for Industry: Pathfinder Prospectus.* Sudbury: Department for Education and Employment Publications.

Ekinsmyth, C. and Bynner, J. (1994), *The Basic Skills of Young Adults: Some Findings from the 1970 British Cohort Study.* London: ALBSU.

Elliott, G. (1996), 'Educational Management and the Crisis of Reform in Further Education', *Journal of Vocational Education and Training, 48(1)*, 5–23.

FEFC (1996), *Student Voices: the Views of FE Students with Learning Difficulties and/or Disabilities.* Coventry: Further Education Funding Council.

FEFC (1998), *Student Numbers, In-Year Retention, Achievements and Destinations at Colleges in the Further Education Sector and External Institutions in England in 1996–97*, Press Notice, 28 July. Coventry: Further Education Funding Council.

Freire, P. (1974), *Education: The Practice of Freedom.* London: Writers and Readers Publishing Co-operative.

Fryer, B. (1997), 'Lifelong Learning, Exclusion and Residence', *Adults Learning, 8(6)*, 144–145.

Fuller, S. (1998), 'Making in Metal', *Adults Learning*, 9(6), 12–14.

Gleeson, D. (1996), 'Post-Compulsory Education in a Post-Industrial and Post-Modern Age'. In J. Avis, M. Bloomer, G. Esland, D. Gleeson and P. Hodkinson (eds), *Knowledge and Nationhood*. London: Cassell.

Harris, S. and Hyland, T. (1995), 'Basic Skills and Learning Support in Further Education', *Journal of Further and Higher Education*, 19(2), 42–48.

Harvey, L. (1997), 'Identity and the Role of the State', *Adults Learning*, 8(8), 219–221.

Hillman, J. (1996), *University for Industry: Creating a National Learning Network*. London: Institute for Public Policy Research.

Hudleston, P. and Unwin, L. (1997), *Teaching and Learning in Further Education: Diversity and Change*. London: Routledge.

Holland, C., Frank, F. and Cooke, T. (1998), Literacy and the New Work Order. Leicester: National Institute of Adult Continuing Education.

Hughes, C. (1997), 'FE's Future: Strategic Alliances in a Learning Market', *College Research*, Further Education Development Agency, Summer, 6–7.

Iphofen, R. (1996), 'Aspirations and Inspirations: Student Motives in Adult Residential Colleges', *Studies in the Education of Adults*, 28(2), 65–68.

Jude, C. (1997), 'Community and Identity', *Adults Learning*, 8(8), 201–202.

Maguire, M., Maguire, S. and Felstead, A. (1993), *Factors Influencing Individual Commitment to Lifetime Learning*. London: Employment Department.

Maxwell, B. (1996), 'Open College Networks, Are They Still for Adult Learners?', *Adults Learning*, 7(5), 111–112.

McGiveney, V. (1994), *Wasted Potential: Training and Career Progression for Part-time and Temporary Workers*. Leicester: National Institute of Adult Continuing Education.

NIACE (1998), *Realising the Learning Age: A Response to the Government Green Paper from NIACE*. Leicester: National Institute of Adult Continuing Education.

Payne, J. and Edwards, R. (1996), 'Impartial Guidance in Further Education Colleges', *Adults Learning*, 7(7), 160–161.

Pettitt, A. (1996) *Adults and GNVQs*, FEDA Report, 1(4). London: Further Education Development Agency.

Randle , K. and Brady, N. (1997), 'Further Education and the New Managerialism', *Journal of Further and Higher Education*, 21(2), 229–239.

Robson, M., Goodchild, G. and Gray, J. (1996), 'Wasted Potential, Career Progression for Part-time Staff and Students', *Adults Learning*, 7(7), 178–179.

Steedman, H. and Green, A. (1996), *Widening Participation in Further Education and Training: A Survey of the Issues*. London: Centre for Economic Performance, The London School of Economics and Political Science.

Unwin, L. (forthcoming), *Creativity and the Curriculum: FE Colleges and the Pressures of Funding*.

Warner, B. (1998), 'Gateways, Guidance and Getting Together', *Adults Learning, 9(10)*, 15–16.

Wilson, P. (1997), 'National or Local? Which Future for Open College Networks?', *Adults Learning, 8(9)*, 240–241.

4 Further Education and Higher Education: The Changing Boundary

Anna Paczuska

The current line drawn between FE [further education] and HE [higher education] is irrational and cannot be sustained for much longer than five years because it essentially divorces FE from its mainstream function of preparing people for technician-level roles in tomorrow's workplace. (Shackleton, 1995)

Introduction

Some argue that the convergence of FE and HE is inevitable and that a formal merger between the sectors is simply a matter of time. Lesley Wagner, Vice Chancellor of Leeds Metropolitan University, is one. Accordingly, his university has just merged with Harrogate College. Jenny Shackleton, principal of Wirral College, has also outlined a future in which the FE/HE relationship grows much closer, but her view stopped short of institutional merger. She envisaged a relationship that develops along collaborative lines, in which FE colleges link with different HE institutions to provide university education locally to a wider range of students (Shackleton, 1995). Her view is widely reflected in current trends. According to recent reports, the FE sector is poised to take a big slice of the proposed expansion in HE (*THES*, 1998a). John Brennan, Director of Development at the Association for Colleges, has said that up to 35,000 of the expected 80,000 new HE students will end up on HE courses in FE colleges.

Recent moves to mass higher education and widening participation have extended HE provision into FE institutions, but the separate status and function of universities is still vigorously defended. Early in 1998 new government legislation was introduced to limit the use of the title 'university college' by FE and HE colleges. The reason given for the legislation is to avoid confusion (*THES*, 1998b), but it is difficult not to see it as a sign that some sections of HE feel a need to differentiate themselves clearly from other degree providers in the face of an expansion of HE provision in settings outside traditional universities.

In FE, closer relations with HE are often viewed with scepticism. Partnership arrangements still involve only a minority of college staff and HE links are often seen as attempts by some FE lecturers to enhance their individual status by working on HE courses. The higher status of HE work is often quoted as one of the main benefits for FE arising from FE/HE partnerships (Bird, 1996; Rawlinson, Frost and Walsh, 1997; Shackleton, 1995), although the view that FE is simply being used to provide HE on the cheap is widespread.

That differences of opinion exist is not remarkable. What is remarkable is that there is a relationship between FE and HE to discuss. Traditionally the FE and HE sectors were separate with a well-marked boundary between them. The divide was shaped by 'the highest school leaving qualification' (Hall, 1994) and indicated a difference between training and education, between vocational courses and academic courses, between part-time, day-release students and full-time, grant aided students. The culture of the two sectors was as different as was the assumed distinction between skill and knowledge. The FE/HE divide supposedly protected the superior status of HE and was reinforced by the selectivity and elitism of HE itself.

Now the boundary has become blurred. Joint activity, collaboration and partnerships (including access arrangements, franchising of HE provision to FE colleges, joint delivery of courses and associate college arrangements) have produced a complex interleaving of provision across the FE/HE divide. Over 13 per cent of HE is now delivered in FE colleges. Some FE/HE partnerships have resulted in merger, and more mergers are likely. In June 1998 the *Times Higher Educational Supplement* listed 19 current proposals for institutional mergers; 11 were between FE and HE (*THES*, 1998c). Although the impetus for this joint activity came from individual institutions and partnerships operated mainly at local level, the government is now apparently moving towards a national policy of cross-sector partnership (Bird, 1996).

These radical changes in the relationship between FE and HE have been brought about by government policy on skills. For the last 10 years government policy on education and training has been directed towards securing a greater skills element in both FE and HE courses. The publication of a report by the Skills Task Forces, *Towards a National Skills Agenda*, in September 1998 alongside the plan to channel funds into even more skills training in FE and HE continues this trend.

The focus on skills in the curriculum has had two main outcomes for the FE/HE relationship. First, the drive to a more skills-based curriculum established a trend towards similar developments, such as the inclusion of key skills in the curriculum, in both FE and HE. Second, the expansion of both FE and HE to enable more people to gain high-level skills, coupled with the introduction of targets in terms of student numbers, increased collaboration between FE and HE to open up progression routes. This provided FE with exit routes for their students and HE with the recruits. The 'new' students who came into HE as a result of HE expansion came through a variety of mainly FE routes and brought a diversity of learning experiences with them. HE has had to respond by developing new approaches to teaching and learning to cater for their differing learning needs. These changes have further reinforced the trend towards curriculum convergence between the two sectors and have helped to establish what Shackleton called a 'common operating environment' in FE and HE (Shackleton, 1995).

Most recently the introduction of the lifelong learning policy, with its aim of making post-school education available as widely as possible, calls for even more FE/HE collaboration to develop access to a breadth of higher level provision in a variety of settings. The Green Paper, *The Learning Age* (DfEE, 1998), makes a clear call to universities to work with FE colleges to provide access courses and also encourages FE/HE partnerships in general.

Viewed as a whole, provision across both sectors is developing towards an interconnected network of vocational and academic qualifications at different levels, delivered in different ways. This marks the first moves towards a new landscape for post-compulsory education, which brings together current notions of FE and HE into a single new concept of life-long learning. *The Learning Age* sees this relationship between FE and HE as providing the basis for a new kind of HE and creating a culture of lifelong learning which attracts mature people and students from groups who would not traditionally have thought about continuing their education or progressing to HE. The development of such a culture clearly requires continuing collaboration, at least at the interface. Regardless of whether the sectors remain formally separate or not in the immediate future, and regardless of whether individual institutions merge or not, the prospect is one in which partnerships will continue to develop both locally and regionally to ensure continuous and complementary post-compulsory provision is widely accessible.

Skills and further education

Skills policy and the skills agenda in education grew out of ideas first developed during the youth training initiatives of the 1980s. These initiatives were originally an attempt to solve the problems of youth unemployment. Their aim was to provide unemployed and poorly qualified young people with skills for employment. The youth training policy was developed by the Manpower Services Commission (MSC). The argument was that promoting the right attitudes and skills among young people would help them to find jobs. Employers identified flexibility and adaptability as two of the qualities important for employability (CBI, 1989).

'New vocationalism' was an educational idea that grew up in the context of the policy to promote employability. It aimed to prepare students for 'the world of work as a whole' (Chitty, 1991: 108). The purpose was to enable young people to progress to a variety of workplaces equipped not just with subject-specific knowledge but with a range of new high level skills for employment. New vocationalism was interpreted in different ways, sometimes as a narrow substitution of training for education, alternatively as a broad concept not confined simply to 'skills training' but encompassing personal development and as an idea which should 'respect the arts and humanities in the vocational preparation' (Pring, 1990: 226). Although the exact balance between education and training in the 'new vocationalism' has never been defined precisely, the idea was important popularising new ideas about skills for employment and their importance to education.

Ideas about new kinds of skills needed for new kinds of work were very different from old ideas about skills. They incorporated a knowledge element. In the past skills and knowledge were two separate concepts. Skill was associated with qualities linked to manual dexterity and technical abilities. Knowledge was built up of abstractions associated with ideas and intellectual abilities. Knowledge was not generally seen as a practical ability, but was based on the accumulation of facts gained on academic courses (such as those offered by schools and universities). New ideas of skills combined elements of old ideas of skills and knowledge and have been described as 'intellective skills' – the skills needed for work in new technology environments (Zuboff, 1989).

New ideas of skills and the importance of learning them were not confined to the policy agenda for poorly skilled or unemployed young people. They soon spread to other sectors of education and just as it was argued that unemployed young people were lacking skills for employment, so in the 1980s a number of surveys suggested that graduates in the UK were also under-equipped for employment (Assiter, 1995). Skills that were said to be lacking included numeracy and information technology (IT) abilities, and written communication and oral presentation skills. The claim was that not only did graduates need to be more skilled, they also needed to be more flexible and adaptable. The conclusion was that future courses in HE should not simply enable students to become knowledgeable in the traditional sense, but should also help them acquire skills that can be transferred to employment.

A series of government reports published in the late 1980s and early 1990s argued for the need to increase links between school, college, education and employers and also for HE to be more closely linked to employment. This was really the beginning of a common skills agenda for FE and HE. As in schemes designed to find jobs for young unemployed people, the HE argument was that graduates should be more mobile in a highly competitive economy that is constantly being changed by technical innovation. It was also argued that there was a need for new kinds of high-level skills and that future HE qualifications should imply that graduates have gained skills that can be transferred to employment (Assiter, 1995).

Developments in HE ran parallel to those in FE. FE expanded and numbers in HE doubled as part of the effort to equip more people with more high-level skills. The government's Enterprise in Higher Education Initiative (EHE) in the early 1990s, a kind of TVEI initiative for HE, set out to encourage the development of 'enterprising people' who are adaptable and resourceful as well as creative and dynamic. As in the school and college curriculum, transferable skills were identified as desirable generic outcomes for HE, providing skills and abilities, which promote 'enterprise' in graduates. Transferable skills, which have also been called 'core skills' and, more recently, 'key skills' have now become common elements in the HE curriculum as they already are in FE.

Skills and higher education

Creating a curriculum centred on skills for employment resulted in massive changes right across education, but in some ways meant more extreme changes for HE. For FE the emergence of a national educational agenda for equipping students with skills for employment resonates at least partly with the vocational agenda it had 20 years ago. Such an idea would have been unimaginable for HE then. Even where degree courses equipped people with skills for work in science or technology, the prime aim of a university was pursuing the liberal notion of 'education for education's sake'. Not surprisingly the introduction of ideas about skills for employment into the debate about the future of HE provoked a great deal of reaction.

There were many critics of the new interpretations of skill in HE coupled with opposition to the idea that HE should follow the route of post-16 education and, increasingly, be concerned with practical abilities and enabling graduates to acquire skills for work. Many staff were horrified at the prospect of what appeared to be the emergence of a 'national curriculum for HE' and attacked the idea that the purpose of HE should be dictated by the requirements of employers. Typically Barnett opposed the whole employment-led agenda and argued that the work agenda is a threat to the liberal aims of university education which will 'reduce the scope available to fulfil the emancipatory potential in the ideal of higher education' (Barnett, 1994: 61).

Many in the old universities agreed with Barnett and tried to resist changes in curriculum or outcome. As a result, many schools and faculties in old universities have hardly been affected by new ideas of skill (Ainley, 1993). Their stand is possible because their elite status guarantees their graduates find employment regardless of whether their degrees specifically equip them with the skills for employment or not (Brown and Scase, 1994).

New universities, however, have moved much more towards educational processes, which emphasise not only the acquisition of knowledge but also transferable skills and the use of knowledge. This is leading to the evolution of a university curriculum, which aims to enable students to acquire the skills for employment. It is also designed to enable wider access to HE by providing continuity of provision and learning support for students progressing from the qualifications offered by FE.

So far, the new skills-based curriculum has not been able to guarantee employment to graduates from new universities. It has been argued that this is because many recruiters are 'looking for clones of themselves' and as many went to old universities 'they they will feel most at home with their products' (Haselgrove, 1994: 9). It is a real issue for the organisers of current FE/HE collaborations who are supporting 'new students' progressing through very different kinds of FE and HE programmes than the students who progressed to traditional university courses from 'A' Level courses.

'New students' and the 'new curriculum'

'New students' are those who made up most of the increase in university numbers during the expansion of HE. Much of the growth in HE in the late 1980s and early 1990s was due to an increase in the numbers of adult students and to increased participation by women. Women are now over-represented relative to their population size. Ethnic minority groups have also been significant in the expansion, and are also over-represented relative to their respective population size: Caribbeans by 43 per cent, Asians by 162 per cent and Africans by 223 per cent (Mirza, 1995).

New students generally progress to HE from FE rather than schools and often progress to new universities who are generally more open to admitting students with the variety of qualifications offered by FE students. In spite of the general HE expansion based on 'new' students, old universities have by and large continued to admit students from those social groups they have always admitted: 'the more elite institutions and courses continue to recruit a large proportion of middle-class, white males, despite commitment to equal opportunities' (Brown and Scase, 1994: 38).

This differentiation in the intake of different HE institutions is partly a result of decisions by academic staff and partly due to the decisions by students themselves. It is reinforced by links and partnerships between FE and HE institutions. Staff define the academic criteria by which student achievement is judged and give applicants strong messages about who they welcome through their admissions decisions. The message given to 'new' students by old universities is that they prefer 'A' Level applicants. Thompson (1997) argues that this does not necessarily mean university admissions tutors actively discriminate against non-'A' Level applicants, but standard 'A' Level admissions procedures are recognised and easy routines. Admissions decisions involving other qualifications take more time and may lead to a preference for selecting students with 'A' Levels if admissions tutors can select from a range of well-qualified applicants.

Link agreements and progression agreements between FE and (mainly) new universities usually help to promote progression for non-'A' Level candidates. They spell out clearly to intending HE applicants where qualifications such as GNVQs, access and BTECs are most likely to be welcome. If students apply to linked institutions it also lessens the chance of making an application that will be rejected. Students also select themselves into courses and institutions where they think they will be most likely to be accepted and in which they will be most likely to succeed (Ainley, 1993: 30).

Teaching and learning

HE link agreements with FE institutions not only promote progression to selected institutions, they also indicate institutions which may have developed skills-based curricula and approaches to teaching and learning which are accessible to students progressing from access, GNVQ or BTEC courses. Traditional university courses were designed on the assumption that people coming on the courses would offer the skills and qualities developed on 'A' Level programmes.

New students have often progressed from courses that have developed skills, interpersonal and non-academic qualities as well as subject area knowledge. They may be familiar with portfolios and coursework and alternative modes of assessments. They are more likely to have been on modular programmes and programmes designed to cater for a range of learning styles and experiences. These learning experiences may be an additional reason for choosing to apply to new universities.

In 1997, 100,000 of the 275,000 new entrants to HE offered alternative qualifications (*Education Guardian*, 1998) and went mainly into new universities. This is commonly interpreted simply as an indication that 'better' students (those with 'A' Levels) choose old universities in preference to new universities. It can also be taken to mean that new students apply to new universities because these institutions are familiar with their qualifications and cater for their learning needs. They can do so because they have developed programmes for students with a range of skills profiles on entry and offer support them in making up learning in areas where skills may be lacking.

Such an interpretation of student destinations means acknowledging that different qualifications are not necessarily either 'better' or 'worse' than one another, may be generally equivalent for the purposes of admission to HE, but equip students with different skills and abilities. Each student has been judged able to progress, but on the basis of different qualifications and so tends to find different areas of 'match' and 'mismatch' between the skills they have already gained through whichever qualifications route they have already followed, and the skills needed for success on their chosen course in HE.

The tendency to 'mismatch' among some students may be reinforced by their learning histories. Students offering GNVQ, BTEC or other qualifications often choose these routes because they offer the opportunity for immediate progression in spite of poor results in English or mathematics at GCSE (Payne, 1995) early on in their learning. Whatever their other qualities and abilities, these students enter university classes alongside students who have acquired much higher general levels of skill in English and mathematics because they progressed through other routes such as 'A' Level.

Traditional teaching and learning styles promoted in HE accentuate such differences among students. Formal approaches to teaching with large lectures, large group seminars and little or no individual tutorial support also favour those who come from educational backgrounds such as 'A' Level. Traditional approaches to assessment based on exams disadvantage students from educational backgrounds where assessment has been based on coursework and practical demonstrations. Large class sizes make the problem worse.

Acknowledging these needs and these differences, universities who accept significant numbers of new students have been among the first to modify and change their curriculum to enable all students to identify areas of match and mismatch between their skills and abilities on entry and the qualities needed to succeed on their courses. Students are then given the opportunity to strengthen their skills in weaker areas. This should not be viewed as 'remedial' education, but as an approach to supporting a body of students with a wide range of skills profiles on entry. It may include enabling students from courses such as 'A' Level to gain skills in group work and making presentations as well as providing learning support in mathematics for students from vocational programmes.

Learning support and study skills programmes, resource-based learning, modular programmes and new modes of assessment all provide flexibility in approaches to learning which cater for a diversity of learning histories. The approach is new to HE, but mirrors what was developed earlier. It is perhaps an inevitable consequence of widening access and drawing in new kinds of students: 'when the majority of students are in their late twenties, do not have 'A' Levels but do have children, changes occur' (Corrigan, Hayes and Joyce, 1995: 32).

Curriculum convergence

The increasing diversity of student skills profiles in FE and HE and the focus on skills in the curriculum has led to similar developments in teaching and learning right across the curriculum of the two sectors. Davies (1997) identifies six areas of curriculum convergence:

- student-centred learning;
- flexible curricula;
- assessment methodologies;
- learning processes;
- resource allocations; and
- accessibility and openness.

The move to modularity is also important. This new form of learning has appeared in both FE and HE. It can be argued that it is just a device to deliver more courses to more people, without spending significantly more money. However, modularisation is not just a reorganisation of the way syllabus content is arranged and presented, it represents an approach which enables the student to build a profile of skills and abilities, flexibly in different institutions, if necessary, and at their own pace. Modularisation may have been spurred by financial considerations, but it has led to a focus on course design, content and outcomes which clarifies the learning process and helps students to make choices about the learning which will suit them best. The focus on learning resources and the ability to use them goes alongside the policy need to develop people who have the skills to search for facts and information and process them appropriately, rather than acquire knowledge by rote. The opportunity provided by modularisation for a student to accumulate credit and gain qualifications incrementally also means people can work towards qualifications in a way that suits them throughout their lives.

Lifelong learning and local access

The blurring of the FE/HE curriculum boundary is not just the result of a growing need to promote progression from FE to HE from a variety of routes. It is also promoted by the policy of lifelong learning which aims to involve more and more people in continuing education, whatever their age or previous educational history. For funding reasons, and because older students have more domestic commitments, it is increasingly likely that post-compulsory provision will be made accessible to local communities. To eliminate travel to a distant FE or HE institution, which may become an obstacle to participation, facilities for all levels of post-compulsory education have to be made available locally. This has been described as making provision a 'local, even a very local offering' (Shackleton, 1995) and implies integrating HE and FE provision in local institutions and establishing an expectation of being able to progress to HE level courses as an integral part of local post-compulsory community education: 'a college established as the main provider in post-compulsory education and training for a local community and labour market, could not fulfil its mission of mass recurrent learning by drawing a line below higher education as defined in the UK' (Shackleton, 1995: 28).

This emphasises the need for physical links between FE and HE in terms of making them available in close proximity to one another. It also calls for curriculum links between FE and HE to ensure continuity of learning. For an FE college the logic of more local HE provision is to build on existing FE provision and extend it to HE programmes. Common curriculum elements, which include core studies, learning frameworks, modularity and CATs, widely accessible computer networks and student information, advice and guidance, are all central to this development and reinforce new trends developing in HE.

This poses a new model of HE, which is quite unlike that of the traditional universities and very much more like FE. It is partly based on the needs of 'new' students who want to study very close to home, and also establishes new kinds of relationships between FE and HE, students, teachers and the community from which the students are drawn.

Further education/higher education partnerships

Both curriculum links and progression routes between FE and HE were a practical response to the skills agenda and were established as a response to government policy to create new routes into HE, to cater for a diversity of students and to make HE more available locally. Although links and partnerships go back as far as the 1960s, the main growth of joint activity was in the 1980s and 1990s alongside the expansion of HE. In the 1970s only 11 per cent of FE colleges had links with HE. By the 1990s this figure had risen to 50 per cent (AfC, 1994).

Links and partnerships helped ensure recruitment for HE, gave linked HE institutions direct access to the new students coming into HE, extended HE provision beyond existing HE institutions and helped universities to work towards missions which were increasingly expected to cater for communities local to their institutions (Rawlinson, Frost and Walsh, 1997). For FE the main reasons for joint work were to provide access and progression routes to HE for their students, to use and develop staff expertise and resources more fully, to promote the status of their institutions through links with HE and also to diversify funding sources (Rawlinson, Frost and Walsh, 1997).

The exact extent of activity across the FE/HE boundary is difficult to estimate, as there is no single source of information and what exists is not always an index of activity as a whole. It has been estimated that 50,000 students are now engaged in 'off campus' HE (Abramson, Bird and Walsh, 1996). This number, however, does not present the true significance of FE/HE relationships or how far the sectors are coming together on a range of issues.

There are many different types of partnership and joint work, and details vary according to regional and local circumstances. Three main approaches to describing the relationships have been used in recent literature. They are not mutually exclusive and, indeed, there is a degree of overlap between them. Rawlinson, Frost and Walsh (1996) describe how partnerships or collaborations between FE and HE fall into two main categories: associate college and preferred partnerships. Bird (1996) summarises four main areas of activity: franchising, associate college arrangements, validation and accreditation arrangements, and access courses. The High Education Quality Council (1993) identifies five categories of work: articulation, joint provision, validation, franchising and subcontracting. These are summarised in Table 1.

Table 1: Types of further education/higher education partnerships

Rawlinson (1997)	Bird (1996)	HEQC (1993)
Associate college arrangements	Franchising	Articulation
Preferred partnerships	Associate college arrangements	Joint provision
	Validation and accreditation arrangements	Validation
	Access courses	Franchising
		Subcontracting

Franchising

Franchising is the most common FE/HE activity and like everything else across the FE/HE boundary, definitions differ according to institutions and the precise form of the arrangement. It is used as a general term to describe academic partnerships and in the context of FE and HE work it usually describes an arrangement whereby an FE institution teaches a degree or similar course designed by an HE institution and for which the HE institution as the franchiser has overall responsibility. The CVCP describes it as: 'a whole course, or stage of a course, designed in one institution (the franchiser, such as an HEI) and delivered in, and by the staff of, another institution (the franchisee, such as an FE college); overall responsibility for the quality of the course and the assessment of the students resides with the franchising institution (Opacic, 1996).

Franchising is the oldest form of partnership between FE and HE. Early franchising agreements established relationships, which were dominated by the HE partners and in which the FE partners were 'subcontractors' of provision. The agreements emphasised the need to ensure students following a HE course in an FE institution would gain the same outcomes of learning as those following a traditional course in an HE institution. In later arrangements there was a shift to a focus on the student experience and on the quality of that experience regardless of the setting in which the learning occurred. This marked a change of attitude, which accepted that HE provision could be different in different settings, but that quality could be equivalent whatever the setting (Brownlow and Eggins, 1994).

Later developments in franchising also included a move away from the use of the word 'franchising' to the use of the word 'partnership'. This was an attempt to get away from early models of activity dominated by HE, to a more equal relationship in which the roles and interests of both partners were considered equally. It is doubtful whether true equality is possible given the superior status of HE, the different working conditions of staff in the two sectors and that funding for franchised courses is obtained from the Higher Education Funding Council (HEFCE) and handed down FE providers by the HE partner.

The superior status of HE in franchising partnerships has been the focus of much resentment by FE. It often focuses on the financial dealing. This is clearly illustrated by a workshop report from a conference on franchising (Brownlow, 1994) in which the FE participants identified 'openness' as something they wanted more of from HE:

> It was, however, recognised that currently it was a scarce phenomenon, especially when it came to HE institutions disclosing the level of resourcing received in respect of students who were taught by FE institutions. Even anecdotally it was apparent that there were considerable variations in the total of available funding passed to the FE institutions which called into question the quality of the learning experience. (Brownlow and Eggins, 1994: 30)

However, the discussion about partnership in franchising has led to an understanding of some of the issues, and in particular an understanding that FE and HE are different but that neither is better or worse than the other – they have different strengths and weaknesses.

Evaluating these different strengths and weaknesses can be a complex process. In general, HE delivered in FE benefits students by providing learning that takes place in small groups, provides good contact with staff and access to good counselling and guidance. This does not necessarily benefit part-time students on HE courses in FE institutions who on the whole have poorer experiences than students on comparable courses in HE institutions (Haselgrove, 1994). HE institutions, on the other hand, have better library, laboratory and student union facilities than FE institutions, although this must be weighed against the disadvantages of large student groups and more formal approaches to teaching and learning.

Access courses

Access courses were also established to provide progression to HE for students who would not traditionally have gone on to study in HE. Access courses provided the basis for joint FE/HE work in many areas, but unlike franchising, involved HE only in the agreement to admit students progressing from designated FE courses. HE generally played no part in funding, validating or delivering the courses. Nevertheless, access courses more than any other joint activity formed the relationship between FE and HE and helped staff to understand issues facing practitioners in different sectors. Once established, these relationships formed the basis for other relationships which then developed in different ways.

The first access courses were set up in 1978 and numbers expanded greatly in the late 1980s. By 1996, there were nearly 1,200 access courses catering for about 30,000 students (UCAS, 1997). Early initiatives were based on close links between FE providers and individual HE institutions. Today a national framework for the recognition of access courses provides multi-exit routes from most courses, although some access courses still have specific links with individual HE institutions. Access courses cater for adults and mainly for groups traditionally under-represented in HE, such as women, members of ethnic groups, the unemployed and members of socio-economic groups who do not traditionally go to university. They aim to recruit mature students lacking formal qualifications and vary a great deal in both content and settings. Students study mainly humanities and social studies.

As with franchising, the benefits of access are broad. The benefits to HE lie primarily in recruitment. Access courses establish progression routes that guide students from particular access courses to particular HE courses. In general the success rates are good – 52 per cent of access students gain HE places. With a low student-teacher ratio, the courses are expensive to run and are unlikely to make significant amounts of money for FE colleges. The benefit of running them is not financial and apart from providing employment for FE lecturers their main function for FE is to provide good exit routes for FE students.

Associate college arrangements

Associate college arrangements describe a collaborative approach to HE course provision in FE and indicate common understandings beyond the need simply to promote progression and make HE more accessible.

Stennet and Ward (1996) outline how for them associate college status is a way of indicating that there is joint responsibility for quality in course planning. The arrangement does not mean an exclusive arrangement between a particular FE college and a single HE institution, but it consolidates the notion of partnership and common curriculum development that may be missing from the idea of franchising.

There are also broader interpretations of associate college arrangements that may use the term to cover any kind of joint course planning and provision. Alternatively, the term may specify joint bidding for funding and resources, or even joint delivery where one institution on its own could not deliver the programme.

Preferred partnerships

Preferred partnerships are similar to associate college agreements, but the term is generally used to mean an HE institution which has close links with a smaller number of FE colleges than the wider network which may exist in associate college arrangements. Preferred partnerships relate both to progression and to course development and curriculum issues.

Validation and accreditation arrangements

Validation and accreditation arrangements describe arrangements in which one or both institutions develop and deliver different parts of a course that is validated and accredited by the HE partner. Typically this includes so-called 'two plus two' arrangements, where two years of a course are completed in FE and two years in HE. (This includes a foundation year 0.) Another arrangement is 'two plus one', where two years are completed in FE and one in HE.

The HE institution's role is to consider whether the resources, accommodation, teaching and learning provision and assessment arrangements for the proposed courses ensure the same quality of provision, and the HE institution requires its own degrees or diploma programmes. When it agrees to validate a course or programme, the HE institution takes responsibility for ensuring quality and standards are maintained in the same way as for its own programmes. The FE college has to pay for this and also for assessment and exams.

Students on validated courses are counted as FE college students. Although the HE institution monitors quality as a part of the validation service, the FE college takes responsibility for quality assurance. Programmes are funded by HEFC and this can be on a tuition fees basis or on a core plus tuition fees basis. The costs charged to the FE college by the HE institution vary a great deal, and a larger portion probably goes to the HE institution than in franchising arrangements.

It has been estimated that franchising is the main partnership arrangement between FE and 'new' universities whilst most validation arrangements are between FE colleges and 'old' universities (Eade, 1997).

Articulation

Articulation agreements describe arrangements that enable students completing a higher level course in an FE college to gain direct access onto a degree course in an HE institution. Most commonly an HNC or an HND course gives access to a degree in a linked HE institution. In many cases the articulation agreement is a formal arrangement which may include the guarantee of a place on a degree course for students successfully completing a particular HND or HNC programme. In some cases an articulation agreement specifies extra material to be studied or extra work to be undertaken by the student before progression to the degree programme. The amount and nature of this extra work depends on the measure of equivalence between the HND or HNC programme and years one and two of the degree programme.

In other cases agreements are informal and are the result of relationships between staff in the FE college and in the HE institutions. One problem that frequently arises is that students on FE courses where the equivalence with the degree programme is poor may find they have 'lost' a year when they attempt to progress because of the poor 'match' between courses. More formal agreements which result in a closer match between the material to be learned in the FE and HE programmes, or which designate 'top up' study clearly have an advantage over informal agreements here.

Joint provision

Joint provision, like articulation arrangements, takes many different forms. In some cases it involves joint development and delivery of degree programmes, or it may be like a pre-planned articulation agreement where an HE institution designs and delivers a third year degree programme built on existing HNDs. The HE institution validates the degree programme, but quality depends on recognition of the process within the FE institution and on joint agreement of quality criteria.

Benefits of links

The different arrangements benefit FE and HE in different ways according to the type of link and its complexity. Franchising and access courses are usually relatively simple arrangements compared with more sophisticated arrangements, such as associate college agreements. Despite payment of franchise fees, franchising is unlikely to bring the HE partner any significant financial gain. Indeed, it has even been suggested that HE institutions generally make no money at all from franchising: 'it is likely that most HE institutions make no direct financial gain from FE partnerships, and that those which take quality assurance and administrative structures seriously may be running at a direct financial loss' (Abramson, 1996: 9). FE, however, has a cynical view of the financial arrangements on which franchising is based: 'it is presumed that the HE institutions use the substantial difference between the total funds they receive for the programme and that which they pay to the FEC partner to subsidise their other provision' (Eade, 1997: 275).

More recent developments in the FE/HE relationship, and mergers in particular, are notably dominated by finance and resource issues and the logic of the quasi-market in education: 'mergers, take-overs and acquisitions are different agendas to collaboration. The trouble with mergers is that they are very aggressive – it is a highly competitive commercial model' (*THES*, 1998c). These differences between early HE-dominated relationships and later, more complex links, often with sharper financial agendas, have led to attempts to distinguish between different types of FE/HE relationships. These have been described as first- and second-generation relationships (Bird, 1996). Bocock and Scott (1994), however, prefer to designate them mode one and mode two relationships, because this does not imply that the relationships are sequential. Secondary or mode two links are not primarily about franchising or progression, but mark a qualitative change in joint activity and focus on curriculum issues and more equal links between FE and HE: 'a small number of genuinely equal "second generation" partnerships are now emerging, which thrive on a two-way flow of ideas, experience and expertise, and which extend the concept of partnership to embrace strategic planning, research, staff development and curricular merger' (Abramson, 1996: 2).

Partnerships for what?

HE recruitment needs have been a central feature of all link activity. Joint work and subject links cover all subject areas, but 'hard to recruit' areas (such as science and technology) are frequent targets for work, although collaboration is not confined to these difficult areas. The most common subject areas for collaboration are business studies, engineering, maths and computing. Efforts increasingly concentrate on the whole range of provision – on HNC/D links, professional qualifications and small amounts of degree work. Franchising also covers all levels from preparatory courses or foundation courses to postgraduate programmes (Rawlinson, Frost and Walsh, 1997).

These links and partnerships are educational policy initiatives that evolved as a pragmatic response to government policy. This 'bottom up' development of educational initiatives is not unusual and, as Bird points out, shows how policy evolves through practice: 'the history of FE/HE partnerships provides a picture of education policy in the making' (Bird, 1996: 22).

Broadfoot describes a similar process at work in the evolution of National Records of Achievement from local and regional profiling schemes for school students (Broadfoot, 1986). Yet as with profiling, so with FE/HE relationships, calls for national standards and criteria are emerging. The Dearing Report, for example, made a number of recommendations about franchising arrangements between HE and FE institutions, which included the suggestion that the QAA should in future specify criteria for franchising arrangements, and that there should be periodic reviews to ensure franchising arrangements are operating according to these criteria.

Current funding arrangements and assessment methodologies in the different sectors are widely seen as barriers to further collaboration (Dearing, 1997). The needs of progression and of wider opportunities for lifelong learning require not only more and wider links between institutions to consolidate current provision, but also closer links to 'improve the range of individual requirements' (Dearing, 1997: 260).

Local joint FE/HE provision benefits both FE and HE institutions and also benefits students. Opacic (1996) has described these benefits to students in some detail. Her work draws on research carried out by the National Union of Students (NUS) which shows that students appreciate local HE provision on franchised courses for four main reasons: accessibility, cost effectiveness, an intimate atmosphere and flexibility of attendance (Opacic, 1996: 74). Franchising provides easy access to HE via local colleges, which makes HE accessible for those who cannot travel away from home to attend HE, typically mature, adult returners with family and child-care responsibilities. Studying close to home can also reduce costs and financial pressures. Franchised students also mention that they appreciate the teaching approaches in FE, which enable lecturers to vary their approach and provides students with appropriate attention, as they need it (Opacic, 1996). This means students' needs can be more readily met and students take away an impression of a supportive and friendly atmosphere which builds a positive attitude towards learning. Finally, franchised students find the flexibility of attendance offered by franchised course – part-time and evening courses are common – and appreciate the facility which fits in with their other commitments.

Conclusion

FE and HE are no longer separate. Responses to the skills agenda have resulted in joint FE/HE activity mainly between FE and 'new' universities but also between FE and 'old' universities. Joint activity has opened up new routes to HE for students from a wide range of backgrounds. This happened through access courses, franchising, joint provision and collaboration, all of which made HE more widely accessible and more widely available. Now the lifelong learning agenda is promoting further partnerships and links.

The government's latest plans for widening participation require even more FE/HE collaboration and partnership. They also hint at the possibility of project links between the two sector funding councils – a sign that there may be moves to address the funding issues which currently form a barrier to greater collaboration between the sectors. Funding will also make more HE places available in FE institutions and there are plans to make progression between sectors easier. These plans focus on the experience of transition from FE to HE and on developing a progression curriculum. As David Hussey (HEFCE spokesman) said, 'we can make most progress in the area of enhancing progression from FE to HE. Linked to that is the need to support students during transition' (*THES*, 1998d).

As an increasing number of HE students are home-based, it is likely that HE and FE collaborations will continue to evolve to provide students with a greater range of HE programmes in local institutions. This may lead FE to develop more extensive relationships with HE institutions. Where the physical resources to provide local access may be limited, IT offers the opportunity to bring higher level learning within everybody's reach through collaboration between sectors by computer. A recent link-up based on partnership between the University of Derby and five local colleges provided virtual learning centres in a number of Derby towns through an Internet-based access-to-learning scheme. This could provide a possible pattern for future developments.

One problem at the heart of current trends towards greater partnership is that in spite of the experience of collaboration and cross sector activity, former differences between FE and HE have remained in institutional and sector cultures. Pay and conditions are different across the sectors. Working hours and time allocated for research and scholarship vary widely. These reinforce differences in status. The status of HE staff is still generally higher than that of FE staff, which reflects the traditional superiority and exclusivity of the HE sector as a whole and leads to continuing inequalities in partnership relations between the two sectors.

Old attitudes and the tendency of old universities to admit mainly 'A' Level students means moves to a shared post-compulsory agenda may also be limited by cultural factors. Although the results of HE expansion and a focus on skills in the curriculum have established a trend towards parallel developments in the sectors, further developments may be beyond the control of the sectors themselves because they rely largely on whether funding is available.

In some places the two sectors have become almost inextricably linked across the boundary and this has led to joint agendas and joint planning of initiatives. Developments, such as changes in approaches to teaching and learning, have been consolidated into sector practice. How far this continues depends on the agenda set for each sector. HE is increasingly reliant on FE to provide the student numbers needed to meet government targets. FE has student numbers, status and the potential of a more stable financial base to gain through developing sub-degree provision and becoming the sites for lifelong learning.

Existing FE/HE partnerships are leading to the development of a new and distinctive kind of HE provision based in FE colleges. This provision has been shaped by the widening participation agenda and has been successful in attracting students 'from those categories usually most underrepresented because local provision of higher education overcomes the major barriers to access such as time, distance, cost, cultural dislocation and unease, domestic difficulties and fear of the unknown' (Eade, 1997: 275). This has considerable potential for the future.

Catering flexibly for local needs and a diversity of student experiences is what colleges do well. In the light of the lifelong learning agenda this poses a future for FE/HE relationships, in which FE will continue with its local brief, developing easily accessible programmes of higher level studies for the community through FE/HE partnerships as well as providing progression routes to regional HE institutions. This could mean that FE will become the main arena for developments in lifelong learning, while HE continues to cater for students on a wider regional or national level. HE institutions will almost certainly continue as the sites for academic research while at the same time evolving curricula which are increasingly influenced by the needs of 'new' students entering HE through routes provided by an evolving variety of FE/HE partnerships.

References

Abramson, M, (1996), 'Partnership Imperatives: A Critical Appraisal'. In M. Abramson, J. Bird and A. Stennet (eds), *Further and Higher Education Partnerships*. Buckingham: SRHE/Open University Press.

Abramson, M., Bird, J. and Stennet, A. (eds) (1996), *Further and Higher Education Partnerships*. Buckingham: SRHE/Open University Press.

AfC (Association for Colleges) (1994), *Nature and Extent of Higher Education Provision Offered by Colleges of Further Education*. London: Association for Colleges.

Ainley, P. (1993), *Degrees of Difference: Higher Education in the 1990s*. London: Lawrence Wishart.

Assiter, A. (ed.) (1995), *Transferable Skills in Higher Education*. Buckingham. SRHE/Open University Press.

Barnett (1994), The Limits of Competence: Knowledge, Higher Education and Society. Buckingham: Open University Press.

Bird, J. (1996), 'Further and Higher Education Partnerships: The Evolution of a National Policy Framework'. In M. Abramson *et al*. (eds), *Further and Higher Education Partnerships*. Buckingham: SRHE/Open University Press.

Bobcock, J. and Scott, P. (1994), 'HE/FE partnerships: Redrawing Boundaries'. In S. Brownlow (ed.), *Equal Outcomes, Equal Experiences?*, Medip Papers No. 59. Bristol: SRHE/Staff College.

Broadfoot, P. (1986) *Profiles and Records of Achievement: A Review of Issues and Practice*: Eastbourne: Holt, Rinehart and Winston.

Brown, A. (1994), *What Messages do Higher Education Admissions Policies Send to Applicants?*. Surrey: Department of Education Studies, University of Surrey.

Brown, P. and Scase, R. (1994), *Higher Education and Corporate Realities*. London: UCL Press.

Brownlow, S. and Eggins, H. (1994), 'Introduction'. In S. Brownlow (ed.), *Equal Outcomes, Equal Experiences?*, Medip Papers No. 59. Bristol: SRHE/Staff College.

CBI (Confederation of British Industry) (1989), *Towards a Skills Revolution*. London: CBI.

Chitty, C. (1991), 'Towards New Definitions of Vocationalism'. In C. Chitty (ed.), *Post-16 Education: Studies in Access and Achievement*. London: Kogan Page/ London University Institute of Education.

Corrigan, P., Hayes, M., and Joyce, P. (1995), 'A Modernist Perspective on Changes in Higher Education'. In A. Assiter (ed.), *Transferable Skills in Higher Education*. Buckingham: SRHE/Open University Press.

Davies, D. (1997), 'From the Further Education Margins to the Higher Education Centre', *Education and Training, 39(1)*.

Dearing, R. (1997), *Higher Education in the Learning Society: Report of the National Committee of Enquiry into Higher Education*. London: HMSO.

DFEE (1998), *The Learning Age*. London: HMSO.

Eade, D. (1997), 'Higher Education in Further Education', Appendix 34. In Education and Employment Committee, *Sixth Report of the House of Commons Education and Employment Committee*, Vol. 1, 19 May. London: The Stationery Office.

Education Guardian (1998), 'Students Say it Can be Done', 28 July.

Haslegrove, S. (1994), 'Setting the Scene'. In S. Brownlow (ed.), *Equal Outcomes – Equal Experiences*? Bristol: Staff College/SRHE.

Hall, V. (1994), *Further Education in the United Kingdom*. London: Collins Educational/Staff College.

HEQC (High Education Quality Council) (1993), *Some Aspects of Higher Education Programmes in Higher Education Institutions*. London: HEQC.

Mirza, H. (1995), 'Black Women in Higher Education'. In Morley and Walsh (eds), *Feminist Academics*. London: Taylor Francis.

Opacic, S. (1996), 'The Students Experience of Franchising'. In M. Abramson *et al.* (eds), *Further and Higher Education Partnerships*. Buckingham: SRHE/Open University Press.

Payne, J. (1995), *FE/HE Progression Project: Final Report*. London: Employment Department/South Bank University.

Pring, R. (1990), 'The Curriculum and the New Vocationalism'. In G. Esland (ed.), *Education, Training and Employment*, Vol. 2. Addison Wesley.

Rawlinson, S. (1997), *The FE/HE Interface: A UK Perspective*, Report to the CVCP. Institute of Employment Studies.

Rawlinson, S., Frost D., and Walsh, K. (1997), *The HE/HE Interface: A UK Perspective*, Report No. 316. Brighton: Institute for Employment Studies.

Schuller, T. (ed.) (1995), *The Changing University?*. Buckingham: SRHE/Open University Press.

Shackleton, J. (1995), 'The View From Further Education'. In T. Schuller (ed.), *The Changing University?* Buckingham: SRHE/Open University Press.

Stennet, A. and Ward, S. (1996), 'Smaller but Beautiful'. In M. Abramson *et al.* (eds), *Further and Higher Education Partnerships*. Buckingham: SRHE/Open University Press.

THES (1998a), 'Colleges Good Report Backs Expansion Bid', 8 September.

THES (1998b), 'Tighter Rules on Title Use', 12 June.

THES (1998c), 'Hitches of Getting Hitched', 26 June.

THES (1998d), 'FE Teaching Increases', 21 August.

Thompson, A. (1997), 'Gatekeeping: Inclusionary and Exclusionary Discourses and Practices'. In J. Williams (ed.), *Negotiating Access to Higher Education*. Milton Keynes: SRHE/Open University Press.

UCAS (1997), *Access Provision Briefing for Higher Education*. London: UCAS.

Zuboff, S. (1989), *In the Age of the Smart Machine: the Future of Work and Power*. London: Heinemann.

5 Information and Learning Technology: The Implications for Teaching and Learning in Further Education

David Guile and Annette Hayton

Introduction

The power and potential of information and learning technology (ILT) to transform teaching and learning has become one of the great educational orthodoxies of our time in all areas of education and training. A popular consensus exists amongst UK politicians and many educationalists that the development of the Information Superhighway and ILT will be a socially liberating and educationally rejuvenating experience. It is claimed that students will be afforded access to a vast range of information as well as the chance to interact with people around the globe, while teaching will be enhanced through the availability of the most significant educational tools ever to emerge.

Such views about the potential of ILT reflect a traditional trust and belief that technological systems can by themselves enhance teaching and learning, yet as the history of educational technology indicates such 'technological utopianism' can be sorely misplaced. Certainly, official policy reports from both government departments and government agencies often give the impression that the use of ILT in teaching and learning is purely a technical question. In other words, they imply that all the problems will be solved once reliable networks are installed, PCs are widely available throughout colleges and teachers have gained a key skill in ILT.

The primary aim of this chapter is to examine how ILT can enhance teaching and learning in further education (FE). Using ILT to enhance teaching and learning in FE, or for that matter any other sector of education, is not as straightforward as it may appear. We would argue that it involves the recognition that learning is fundamentally a social activity and certainly not solely an individual act of sitting a student in front of a screen or with a book. Indeed, teachers know this implicitly from their own practice, but current orthodoxies leave little space for developing these ideas. Furthermore, as with any other educational resource, it is essential that the use of ILT is firmly grounded in an understanding of how students learn and a consideration of how different types of ILT may support different types of learning.

We begin by locating the discussion of ILT in terms of the changes in FE provision over the last 25 years and the concurrent development and introduction of new technology in FE. We then review some of the changes in approaches to teaching and learning which took place over this period, exploring in particular the concept of 'learner-centredness', the way it developed and its limitations. We then go on to look at the pressures to introduce ILT into the FE curriculum and consider how these, coupled with the commitment to 'learner-centred' education, have influenced thinking about the use of ILT as a resource for teaching and learning in FE colleges. Finally, we conclude by arguing that if teachers and colleges wish to develop ILT's potential to enhance creativity and develop new knowledge, then they will need to take a more explicit account of different types of learning and the various ways ILT can be used to support those types of learning.

The further education curriculum and technology

The changing context of teaching and learning
As Green and Lucas argue in Chapter One, there have been substantial changes in the organisation, curriculum and ethos of FE Colleges over the last 25 years. In the 1970s the range of courses could be divided fairly clearly into two main areas: vocational and technical education, and academic and general studies. Although the vocational and academic strands were quite strictly divided there were a number of similarities in approach. Although most academic programmes were full-time, both areas had a tradition of part-time provision (through day-release and

evening provision) and also an ethos focused on the self-motivated adult. In terms of teaching and learning, there was a general acceptance that there was a 'body of knowledge' which needed to be 'transmitted' to students. This relatively stable picture soon changed as FE sought to come to terms with the economic, social and cultural changes of the late 1970s and 1980s.

The demise in the 1980s of the manufacturing and engineering base of the UK economy had important consequences for FE. First, it led to a decline in apprenticeship and the loss of the traditional 'day-release' FE student. Second, in an effort to respond to unemployment, particularly youth unemployment (Finn, 1991), the vocational education and training (VET) curriculum was considerably broadened to include new pre-vocational programmes such as the Certificate of Prevocational Education (CPVE) and training initiatives such as the Youth Training Scheme (YTS).

During this period there was also a cultural and social shift in the way that FE and HE were regarded. Participation rates in FE increased markedly as more young people stayed on in education (Hodgson and Spours, 1997) and the number of 'adult returners' increased. Consequently, as Green and Lucas suggest, the main purpose of FE became provision of 'second chance' education and training either for 16-year-olds leaving school with few or no qualifications or for adults returning to study. Taken in combination, these changes resulted in a much more diverse student population, which required new courses, increased flexibility of delivery and new approaches to teaching and learning. As a result, the sector had to consider how to integrate new curriculum programmes alongside its traditional academic and vocational courses as well as developing strategies to support the learning needs of its new clientele (Huddleston and Unwin, 1997).

Further education and information technology
In addition to the economic and cultural changes taking place during the 1980s and early 1990s there was rapid development in 'new technology'. Three main factors were responsible for these technological changes:

- the development of digital technologies, which enabled all forms of data (i.e. financial, scientific) to be encoded and transmitted via telecommunication networks;
- the internetworking of telecommunication and computer networks, which made possible global links between individuals, organisations and societies; and
- information technology (IT) which started to provide new resources for working and learning as well as enabling new sites for learning to emerge.

The introduction of IT had four main strands which were linked to the core elements of the college curriculum offer (FEU, 1984). To begin with, as in schools and universities, most colleges introduced IT as a separate subject, for example 'O' Level and 'A' Level Computer Science and BTEC Computing. However, the sector's close links with industry also meant that many colleges made considerable efforts to ensure that they reflected current technical developments in the workplace by introducing IT applications, for example Computer Aided Design (CAD) and Computer Aided Manufacture (CAM) into such mainstream VET courses as Ordinary/Higher National Diploma (O/HND) Engineering, and word-processing and spreadsheets into Business Studies. In addition, IT was included as a key element in the increasing number of general education and basic skills programmes on offer. Finally, a number of colleges made attempts to provide cross-college provision to support teaching and learning through learning resources sections.

The pattern of development during the 1980s and early 1990s was very uneven (FEU, 1984). However the curricular links which many FE colleges had with business and industry ensured a readiness to adopt new technology not often found in other sectors. Despite local innovations and a number of development projects, there was no national policy for IT in FE. The first attempt to initiate a national response to the use of IT in the FE sector did not occur until after incorporation in 1993.

The Higginson Report (FEFC, 1996) was the first national policy initiative primarily concerned with developing a more strategic approach towards the use of ILT in the FE sector. This Report, *Teaching and Learning with*

Information and Learning Technology, was the final Report of the Learning and Technology Committee (LTC) established by the Further Education Funding Council (FEFC) in 1993. Higginson noted that many colleges had already been highly imaginative in their strategies to capitalise on the potential of ILT to enhance access to diverse learning pathways. However the LTC urged more investment from the colleges and government in order to ensure that the FE sector would be in a pivotal position to use ILT to meet the needs of its diverse client groups.

'Learner-centred' education and training

The full implications of the challenge of teaching 'second chance' populations and harnessing the benefits of IT slowly began to be felt within FE in the mid 1980s. One of the first attempts to conceptualise the new challenge posed by the changing student profile and introduction of IT was provided by Shackleton (1989). She characterised the required change in philosophy as a shift from a 'curriculum-led' focus (i.e. allowing course requirements and teacher expertise to determine the construction of learning programmes) to a 'learner-led' focus (i.e. identifying learners needs and building learning programmes from that basis).

The move to develop a more 'learner-centred' pedagogy within the FE sector was pursued by the Further Education Unit (FEU) throughout the 1980s. Four ideas contributed to the development of the currently accepted concept of 'learner-centred' education and training:

- the idea of experiential learning, which arose from a specific branch of cognitive psychology that is concerned with cognitive processes (Kolb, 1984);
- the idea of andragogy, which was developed within the field of adult education to identify the key characteristics of adult learning needs (Knowles, 1995);
- the idea of competence-based assessment through the outcomes model, which is strongly associated with the work of the National Council of Vocational Qualifications (Jessup, 1990); and

- the idea of flexibility of access to the curriculum, which is a key principle within Open and Distance Learning (ODL) (Field, 1994).

We will examine each of these ideas below.

Experiential learning

Kolb's ideas were based on the central importance of experience to learning, often referred to as 'learning-by-doing'. They were perceived as consistent with the burgeoning interest in FE to combat the disaffection of many 'second chance' students from the academic models of general education they had experienced during their schooling and to help them to develop a sense of purpose for their post-16 studies (FEU, 1988a). One of the chief attractions of Kolb's 'learning cycle' was that it appeared to provide an active role for learners in applying knowledge and reflecting upon what they had learnt (Huddleston and Unwin, 1997; Cowham, 1995).

Andragogy

The idea of andragogy was originally developed by adult educators. Andragogy is based upon two assumptions. The first is that the basis of adult learning is a sense of 'self-directedness'. This sense of independent purpose is regarded as a feature of all adult learners and it assumes that all adults wish to become autonomous learners and accept responsibility and control for their own learning. Second, andragogy assumes that the process of learning should be determined through collaboration and shared authority between learners and teachers about what will be learnt, how it will be learnt and how it will be evaluated. Viewed from the FE sector's interest in developing 'learner-centred' education and training, andragogy appeared to provide the basis of a more egalitarian conceptualisation of the student/teacher relationship than the relationship many students had experienced in secondary education.

Outcomes model

The 'outcomes' model first surfaced in FE at the beginning of the 1980s after the publication of *A New Training Initiative: A Consultative Document*

(ED/MSC, 1981), which advocated a system of vocational qualifications based on competence statements. The original idea of occupational competence, however, gave way to the 'outcomes' approach which had its foundation in behaviourist psychology and the use of behavioural objectives which had been developed in the 1950s and 1960s (Mager, 1962; Bloom, 1956). The 'outcomes' approach was a key feature of the National Council of Vocational Qualifications' (NCVQ) model of education and training (Jessup, 1990), and National Vocational Qualifications (NVQs), designed in terms of units and elements of competence, represent one of the 'purest' form of this approach. Modified forms of this approach, which used the broader concept of 'learning outcomes' rather than the notion of competence and which aimed to increase autonomy and flexibility, are now integral to most recent learning programmes (Ecclestone, 1999).

Flexibility and Open and Distance Learning
Finally, the idea of flexibility has also been a significant factor in development of 'learner-centred' education and training. In this context, the word 'flexibility' has usually referred to the delivery of learning programmes rather than the development of a flexible curriculum. Many FE colleges turned to the field of ODL to gain inspiration and ideas. ODL has a tradition of placing the learner at the centre of educational practice and providing a set of methods for flexible delivery of knowledge and skills (Field, 1994). As well as reinforcing FE's interest in making education and training more accessible, flexible and learner-centred, it also provided the rationale for freeing learners from their dependence on teachers or fixed class hours. This led to the pioneering of resource-based teaching and training in FE (FEU, 1988). As with the outcomes approach, much of the theoretical literature on the development of ODL packages is based on a behaviourist approach to learning and advocates the use of instructional objectives in the design of materials. This tradition also provided the basis for the development of computer-based 'programmed learning', an approach which is used today in many commercially produced learning packages.

The limitations of the 'learner-centred' approach

The move towards a more 'learner-centred' approach to education and training was, in part, a radical response to the demands of a new clientele (i.e. 'second chance' students) and a new economic and cultural context. However, the notion of 'learner-centredness' coincided with the demise of youth labour markets in the UK and with the introduction of new approach to training by the then Conservative Government. The government, through the activities of the Manpower Services Commission (MSC) generated a number of new schemes and courses, such as CPVE and YTS. These were all competence-based schemes that were firmly based in the behaviourist tradition. They laid the foundations for the creation of NVQs, and later GNVQs, which have come to dominate the vocational curriculum. The impact of this new 'outcomes' approach on the VET curriculum, however, led to a particular interpretation of 'learner-centredness' gaining ascendancy. The idea of a 'learner-centred' approach has come to mean flexible access for individuals to a wide range of programmes which are built around achieving competence in certain areas, in particular processing information.

As Young and Lucas (1999) point out, there have been two notable consequences of this development. First, the significance of the actual context of learning was totally marginalised. 'Learner-centred' approaches normally conceive of learning simply as an individual act of processing information. As a result, little account is taken of how social and cultural factors influence interaction between students and between teachers and students. In addition, collaborative processes between students are not accorded sufficient attention, despite their importance in mediating student experiences and developing some worthwhile knowledge from their studies. Second, the actual content of what has to be learnt and for what purposes has been played down. Learning has often been reduced to simple descriptions about individual processes such as gathering and evaluating information and so on. As a result, little attention has been given to the need for teachers to develop an appreciation of the relationship between different types of learning (i.e. processing information and developing critiques) and to consider the extent to which all learning is inevitably shaped by the context in which it occurs (Young and Lucas, 1999). Unfortunately, it appears that this highly individualised conception of 'learner-centredness' has been carried over into much of the sector's approach to the use of ILT, as we shall see below.

Teaching, learning and information and learning technology

The desire to exploit ILT's potential as a learning resource and to transform colleges' capacity to deliver education and training has become a key policy objective for the New Labour Government. It has clearly signalled in the Green Paper, *The Learning Age* (DfEE, 1998), that the FE sector is expected to make a major contribution to realising the aims of a 'learning society'. The Green Paper assumes that a clear link exists between access to information via ILT and increased interest in learning and attainment of qualifications. Thus, it explicitly highlights that FE colleges should use ILT to widen participation amongst those sections of the population which are currently excluded from education and training as well as a resource to ensure that learning becomes a lifelong process, not limited by age, gender, ethnicity, or by access or status. Furthermore, the Green Paper also assumes that colleges have a key role in supporting the objectives of the University for Industry (UfI), as any investment in ILT will enable them to work in partnership with local employers and bring education and training more directly into the workplace.

The 'pressures' to introduce information and learning technology into the further education curriculum
Broadly speaking it is possible to identify three main pressures upon the FE sector to extend the use of ILT within the curriculum. These pressures have reflected the policy imperatives of both the last Conservative Government and New Labour. They can be classified as the economic, equity and democratic pressures. Each one presupposes a quite different rationale for advocating the use of ILT as a resource for learning in FE.

The economic rationale has stressed that national economies will be unable to compete successfully in the emerging 'digital economy' until

all members of society have an opportunity to acquire information processing skills (DfEE, 1997). Thus, it has been argued that FE colleges
must use ILT to ensure all students, irrespective of which learning pathway they elect to follow, acquire the skills that will prepare them for this
new world of work (FEDA/AoC, 1996). Those who champion equity
arguments have argued that using ILT can inspire and motivate students
disillusioned with traditional teaching methods and also has the potential
to provide them with direct access to information and resources which
they have been unable to utilise fully in other ways (Kennedy, 1997).
Finally, those who advocate the use of ILT to meet political goals argue
that it will be the critical 'tool' to enable people to participate more fully
as citizens in the new 'information world' – for example by on-line voting
(DfEE, 1998). Consequently, the FE sector, along with primary education,
secondary education and HE, is now expected to provide all students
with opportunities to develop their 'network literacy' (NCET, 1997).

Oversights and omissions within current policy and approach
There can be little doubt that concern with economic, equity or political
issues and the imperative to provide access to resources are inescapable
elements of public policy for ILT in any sector of education. Certainly,
these considerations spurred the FEFC to form the Learning and Technology Committee in order to try to develop a more strategic approach to
using ILT as a learning resource. The developments that have occurred
in the FE sector, however, have taken place without the support of a
coherent, national strategy for investment in ILT and, to a lesser extent,
staff development. As a result colleges have tended to prioritise the issues
of access and implementation and a number of key issues in the debate
about the need to rethink teaching and learning prior to using ILT have
been neglected. We develop the implications of these points below.

To begin with, the economic case that students need to acquire
information-processing skills has to be tempered by the current realities
for most FE colleges. Since incorporation, the sector has been increasingly
concerned with 'cost-cutting' (Young and Lucas, 1999). Consequently, there
is a genuine perception amongst many FE teachers that providing students

access to on-line and other multimedia resources is primarily a way of reducing staff costs rather than enhancing the quality of teaching and learning (Leney, Lucas and Taubman, 1998). Indeed, the belief that the individualised, technological approach to delivery is a cheap option appears to be prevalent. This is despite the fact that research into the effectiveness of ODL courses has consistently demonstrated that high-quality provision of this kind is not a cheap option (Rowntree, 1992).

In addition, although access to ILT for all students and using ILT to encourage student autonomy is an important consideration (Burford, 1996; Kennedy, 1997; FEDA/AoC, 1996), the concentration on access alone has tended to obscure how certain educational uses of ILT may, in fact, result in the emergence of new forms of social and educational divisions. As Wasser has argued passionately about the United States' experience, 'it is not enough that high and low achieving students all have access to ILT in classrooms, if high achievers use ILT as a tool for communication and collaboration, while low achieving students only use it for drill and practice' (Wasser, 1997: 5).

Research from the UK and the United States is increasingly demonstrating that ILT is not, by itself, a vehicle for assisting people to become acquainted with new ideas or for enabling them to think in theoretically informed ways (Bates, 1995; Mergondollar, 1996). Instead, research is indicating that the effective use of ILT involves teachers rethinking the relationship between the process of learning and their role in supporting such learning (Laurillard, 1995; Sandholtz, Ringstaff and Dwyer, 1997).

Therefore, it is important that there is clarity about the purposes of learning and the potential of ILT to support those purposes. If colleges and FE teachers wish to take full advantage of the potential of ILT to enhance learning, they will have to consider ways in which ILT could support students to reflect, analyse and conceptualise in new and challenging ways. Furthermore, it involves them actively working together to deepen understanding and produce new knowledge and not simply accessing information and returning to learning by rote, albeit with the aid of a computer.

These concerns are not specific to the UK or to the FE sector. They are in fact increasingly reflected in the wider global educational debate about the relationship between learning and ILT (Windschildt, 1998; Owston, 1997; Mergondoller, 1996). As Windschildt has observed, it is quite misleading to claim that ILT helps students to learn simply by connecting them to the world of information, let alone to guarantee the creation of 'on-line' learning societies or communities.

The limitations of 'learner-centred' approach for information and learning technology

In the aftermath of the Higginson Report, many colleges have made substantial investment in ILT, sometimes with the support of external agencies and funding. Furthermore, the FEDA, in conjunction with British Education Council for Technological Advancement (BECTA), has set up the Quality in Information and Learning Technology (QUILT) to try to foster the use of ILT within the sector. QUILT is a national staff development programme designed to offer ILT-related training to FE teachers. However, it is clear from the various FEDA/QUILT publications that the idea of 'learner-centredness' has informed much of the work of the development work. This can be illustrated in a number of ways.

First, FEDA has tried to extend the 'learning-by-doing' tradition by raising the profile of Honey and Mumford's work on individuals 'learning styles' (Honey and Mumford, 1995). Honey and Mumford's work has been presented in FEDA/QUILT publications as both complementary to the objectives of 'learner-centred' education and training and as providing a useful way of understanding teaching and learning ILT (Lockitt, 1997).

Honey and Mumford derived their idea of 'learning styles' from Kolb's 'learning cycle' (Kolb, 1984). They use the term 'learning styles' to refer to the ways individuals respond cognitively to such external stimuli as access to web sites, computer simulations, and data banks in order to organise and process information. The 'learning styles' inventory, therefore, reinforces the idea that learning is an individual and active process, as it stresses that individuals' preferred ways of learning should be taken into consideration by teachers when they design students' learning programmes.

Second, it has been claimed that colleges can use Honey and Mumford's 'learning styles' inventory as the basis of a framework which will help them match 'learning styles' to particular types of ILT (Lockitt, 1997). Lockitt has argued that once such a framework is in place, teachers could use their knowledge of a student's preferred 'learning style', and their knowledge of which type(s) of ILT support that style, to offer advice on how to achieve specific learning outcomes. Students, for example, could be advised which ILT to use to help them achieve specific technical 'outcomes' (i.e. manipulate a spreadsheet program) or information-handling 'outcomes'.

Finally, several FEDA/QUILT publications have suggested that if the idea of 'learning-by-doing' and 'learning styles' are combined, they can be used as the basis of a generic approach to learning that reflects the andragogic principle of self-direction and the ODL principle of flexible learning (Cowham, 1995; Lockitt, 1997; Foster, Howard and Reisenberger, 1997). By increasing access to ILT, individuals can explore and assimilate information at their own pace and in accordance with their own learning style. Such a development is perceived to have two possible benefits. It is suggested that it might enable colleges to overcome the barriers that have often deterred many people from recommencing their studies, and moreover, enable them to deliver 'customised' education and training to any client group.

The FEDA/QUILT literature has presented a rather one-sided conceptualisation of the relationship between teaching and learning with ILT (Beaumont, 1996). It has maintained the highly individualised approach to learning, that we have noted was a feature of 'learner-centred' education, and thus tended to overlook how the social and cultural factors shape 'nattering on the net' (Spender, 1995). Moreover, although the literature has recognised that different types of ILT have different functional attributes, it has not considered the pedagogic implications of these differences. By stressing that learning is primarily a matter of processing information, the FEDA/QUILT literature has inadvertently implied that learning is purely a technical question of the 'fit' between individual's learning style and specific type of ILT. There are, however, two quite different types of ILT. Both types of ILT have a specificity of their own and raise profoundly different questions about how they should be used as a teaching and learning resource (Bates, 1995).

Types of information and learning technology and their pedagogic implications

One type of ILT is primarily a computerised system. It can usefully be distinguished by the following terms: Multimedia (i.e. CD-ROM) and Integrated Learning Systems (ILS). Multimedia and ILSs can either be used by learners to access information, or to provide students with access to free-standing teaching and learning materials which contain pre-set tasks and which monitor and assess their performance. The other main type of ILT is primarily a resource for communication and collaboration over networks. They are often referred to as Computer Mediated Communication (CMC). Some of the most notable examples are video-conferencing, e-mail systems, multimedia interactive bulletin boards, remote shared computer screens and annotated screen transfer.

Most commercially available multimedia and ILS systems, however, are characterised by a pedagogically determined learning process as instructional objectives have already been built into software programs. These instructional objectives often restrict users to responding within pre-determined boundaries. Hence, they can constrain the development of users' capabilities to personalise and apply their learning (Bates, 1995). Although there is every indication that even more sophisticated ILSs, involving greater degrees of self-pacing and virtual reality, will soon be more widely available, it is still unclear how far their basic instructional approach will differ greatly from existing multimedia.

Nonetheless, various writers have drawn attention to the paradox of multimedia (Laurillard, 1995; Windschildt, 1998). They argue it is generally regarded as both 'user-friendly' and 'interactive', but that these assumptions are under-explored and that as a result some important issues are overlooked. First, the assumption that interactive media allows learners to control the process of learning is deeply flawed, as the content of the package and the pathways through it are previously defined. Laurillard, for example, highlights the critical role of the teachers' pedagogic knowledge and the development of 'conversational styles' which assist students to explore concepts and ideas presented to them when they use multimedia or ILSs (Laurillard, 1995). Laurillard, along with many other writers, also points out that students require opportunities to work collaboratively with other people (students, on-line contributors and teachers) to test out their understanding of new ideas if they are to personalise their learning (Sandholtz, Ringstaff and Dwyer, 1997).

Similar conclusions about the social basis of learning and the critical role of the teacher supporting such learning can also be drawn about the use of CMC. CMC can provide any organisation (educational or business) with more flexible range of resources which can be used either to support dialogue between different colleges, subject-matter experts, local communities, etc., or self-directed learning (e.g. access to especially designed learning materials). However, depending upon the goal of the learning activity, there are quite different models for using CMC. If the primary aim is to engage students in scanning the Worldwide Web for information on a particular subject, the crucial pedagogic issue is often perceived as assisting students to formulate those questions which will delimit the focus of their search (Brown, 1993), enabling them to verify evidence and identify bias (Owston, 1997) and learn to work collaboratively with students either in the same classroom or on-line to produce new text (Windschildt, 1998).

On the other hand, if the aim is to develop wider human and social communication through interaction through the computer to distributed communities, there are two quite different pedagogic approaches (Paulsen, 1997). One model – the open-conferencing model – is designed to link all the members of different on-line communities to one another, the other – the Learning Circle model – groups on-line communities in terms of specific curriculum foci (Riel, 1992). Irrespective of which model is adopted, CMC can only be used effectively if teachers and learners shape, through negotiation and collaboration, the goals of the teaching and learning process and take more explicit account of how social and cultural factors influence on-line learning and the production of knowledge as much as they influence other types of learning (Fetterman, 1996; Harrisim, 1993).

Reconceptualising teaching and learning with information and learning technology

Throughout this chapter we have argued that the idea of 'learner-centredness' has cast a shadow over much of the thinking in FE about teaching and learning *per se* and teaching and learning with ILT. As a result, highly individualised accounts of learning, including learning with ILT, have gained ascendancy. We outline below an alternative approach to teaching and learning with ILT that takes account of the social and cultural dimension of learning.

The social dimension of learning

One way of avoiding many of the limitations of 'learner-centredness' is to think of learning as a social process that takes place in 'communities of practice' (Lave and Wenger, 1991). Lave and Wenger have argued that if learning is viewed as a 'situated' process, it is possible to take more explicit account of the context of learning (i.e. the 'community of practice') as well as the process of social interaction between people. Lave and Wenger introduce the idea of 'legitimate peripheral participation' to encapsulate the processes by which people learn in 'communities of practice'. By this they mean having opportunities to work collaboratively and hold discussions with other people. It is their contention that theories of learning which reduce learning to some special mental process or unique 'learning style' miss what is distinctively human about learning. Lave and Wenger argue that learning is always a social process, for example, and that the role of conversation and debate or the use of mediating resources such as television or books are always critical to learning. The concept of 'community of practice' is particularly helpful when it comes to considering the implications of learning with ILT. It can be used to throw light on the link between colleges' policies for learning and their policies for ILT. This connection highlights two important pedagogic issues.

First, colleges (as well as other organisations) need to place learning and the opportunity to participate in a 'community of practice', rather than learners, subjects or learning programmes, at the centre of their concerns about how to use ILT. This is a totally different issue from the question of matching ILT to individuals' 'learning styles'. A 'community of practice' denotes a locus for both understanding the social and historical basis of different types of practice (i.e. understanding how a historian analyses documents) and for trying out new ideas in practice with other learners. Second, colleges need to recognise that teaching and learning with ILT is a complex process with the potential to foster creativity and encourage the production of new knowledge. From Lave and Wenger's perspective, such knowledge will be built up through a process of interaction and negotiation, in the case of ILT – via e-mail or video-conferencing – between learners and teachers in different contexts. Thus, FE teachers will need to come to terms with the tacit knowledge (i.e. opinions and views) that is embedded in the different 'communities' of which they are members, as well as being able to develop new codified knowledge about specific developments in disciplinary or multi-disciplinary fields (Young and Lucas, 1999).

Types of learning and contexts of learning

One of the great strengths of Lave and Wenger's work is that it sensitises educationalists to the idea that learning, including learning with ILT, takes place in a context (Seeley, Brown and Duguid, 1993). Nonetheless, it is important not to lose sight of the extent to which learners need to be supported to understand how extra-contextual factors, such as alternative ideas about teaching and learning, may shape learning that takes place in specific contexts. This indicates that it may be important for colleges and FE teachers to think carefully about different types of learning, prior to considering how ILT may be used to support them.

One of the most interesting attempts to spell out the implications of different types of learning is provided by Engestrom (1991, 1995).

Engestrom distinguishes between three types of learning: 'adaptive learning', 'investigative learning' and 'expansive learning'. He suggests that the differences between them can be explained in the following way. 'Adaptive learning' entails students discovering existing knowledge and acquiring existing skills. 'Investigative learning', however, entails providing students with opportunities to personalise concepts, ideas and skills and it may lead to them developing new knowledge. 'Expansive learning' involves students being encouraged to use ideas that exist independent of existing knowledge and skill to develop a critical perspective about them. Engestrom suggests that only when this occurs is new knowledge produced. He clarifies the different relationships between learner and context that are presupposed by each one. His ideas have a number of uses for any college that aspires to use ILT in a less individualised and behaviouristic way.

To begin with, Engestrom's typology of learning represents a continuum reflecting the extent to which learning is related to but separate from discovery. He argues that although 'adaptive' learning is valuable, it does not lead to new knowledge being produced because it takes contexts, in other words subject boundaries, examination requirements, as given and unchangeable. Engestrom does not, however, suggest that teachers should automatically reject 'adaptive' learning, as he recognises that it has often formed the basis of how most education and training systems have taught students and assisted them to gain qualifications. He argues that it needs to be placed alongside other types of learning.

Engestrom contrasts 'adaptive' learning with 'investigative' learning. He argues that the latter, (for example, using the Internet to investigate how sampling technology enabled hip hop music to develop) does generate discoveries. Nonetheless, he reinforces Lave and Wenger's argument that this is only likely to occur so long as opportunities are provided for students to participate within on-line and college-based 'communities of practice'. In other words, it is not merely a matter of students acquiring information from the Internet; they must transform that information into worthwhile knowledge by clarifying their thoughts, ideas and opinions, and gain feedback from teachers and others. Engestrom, however, suggests that such opportunities that are likely to generate discoveries are inevitably bounded by two factors which help to shape their production. He urges teachers to take more explicit account of the context of learning (i.e. college access to the Internet), and the 'community of practice' in which the learning occurs (i.e. Internet 'Chat Line', Web Site).

'Expansive' learning, the third category in Engestrom's typology, implies that there may be a need for teachers to think about how to plan learning programmes which enable teachers to go beyond the immediate context in which their students are located. Engestrom argues that 'expansive' learning only takes place when two conditions prevail. They are: first, when 'investigative' learning is unable to deal with the problems experienced by those in a particular context; and, second, when there is a need to challenge the context within which the learning is located. From Engestrom's perspective, this implies that 'communities of practice' (i.e. learners in college and groups of FE teachers) should be encouraged to use ideas that are external to their immediate context to question, criticise or reject some aspects of accepted 'learner-centred' practice and existing wisdom and ultimately, to postulate alternatives to such practice. For example, just as many FE teachers originally developed the idea of 'learner-centred' learning as a way of addressing the perceived rigidities of transmission learning, the idea of 'expansive' learning may provide a new way of thinking about the relationship between the context and content of learning with ILT.

Understanding that learning is a situated process, and that different types of learning generate different types of outcomes, raises the following two questions. First, how can FE colleges develop 'communities of practice'? Second, what skills do 'communities of practice' need if they are to use ILT as a resource for 'adaptive', 'investigative' and 'expansive' learning?

The organisational challenge of introducing information and learning technology

One way to approach the above questions is through the work of Zuboff (1988), who argued that it is important to distinguish between the possible use of technology and the skills associated with different uses. This led her to study the experiences of companies in the paper and steel industries.

In contrasting the possible ways that IT might be used, Zuboff first described the use of IT to replace or control existing patterns of work within an organisation as an 'automating' approach to technology. In other words, the change and improvements brought about by IT took place at the level of work flow, through enhancing the capacity of existing organisational technology (i.e. machines). Put simply, effort had been made to make machines faster, more powerful and smarter. Nonetheless, as Zuboff demonstrated, irrespective of the extent of the restructuring or the technological innovation, it became clear that smart application of IT did not inevitably result in smarter workplace performance.

On the other hand, she used the word 'informating' to describe the potential of IT to provide members of an organisation with the opportunity to communicate with one another and to develop greater understanding about the consequences of their work. Zuboff however went further. She recognised that the different uses of IT in the workplace require workers to have different and new sorts of capabilities. Therefore, she made a distinction between 'action-orientated' skills (i.e. tacit skills about how processes are based on feelings and experience); and 'intellective' skills (i.e. the ability to hypothesise, identify and solve problems, conceptualise and try out new ideas). Consequently, Zuboff highlighted that the introduction of IT involves changes to the management and control systems within organisations and also changes in the knowledge, skills and capabilities which individuals need to fully exploit the potential of IT as a resource for working.

A parallel can be drawn between Zuboff's insights about the introduction and use of technology in workplaces and the use of ILT to support the introduction of new pedagogies in FE (or for that matter any other educational institution). Those colleges that only perceive the value of ILT in terms of its 'automating' functions are likely to use ILT merely to enhance their existing approaches to teaching and learning. Thus, they will be far less likely to see the need to rethink the relationship between the process of learning and the use of ILT, or to develop a policy for learning with ILT as opposed to a policy for ILT. In many ways, this is hardly surprising. As Armundsen (1993) has argued, the debate about making learning and not learners the central focus of attention is only slowly beginning to happen in such fields as Open and Distance Learning (ODL), a field of study that has devoted considerable time and resources to exploring how ILT can be used as a resource for learning. Furthermore, colleges that adopt an 'automating' approach are more likely to view staff development issues purely as a question of ensuring that all staff acquire a key skill in ILT to ensure they are technically competent to use ILT. They will be less likely to recognise that teachers actually need time to rethink the process of teaching and learning with ILT and to develop new pedagogic approaches to ensure the benefits of ILT are fully realised (Sandholtz, Ringstaff and Dwyer, 1997).

It follows, however, that if the potential of ILT to 'informate' learning is to be maximised, and if colleges are to develop an approach to learning which helps staff and students to develop 'intellective' skills, they will need to rethink both their ideas about teaching and learning generally as well as what is involved in teaching and learning with ILT.

We would suggest that this will involve colleges seeing themselves as learning organisations. This is an important step for colleges to take because it is clear that they will confront the following dual challenge as they seek to develop learning with ILT. First, they have to develop their own internal practices regarding, for example, curriculum delivery, strategies to enhance student motivation, student expectations and widening participation. Second, they will also have to create new partnerships and alliances within colleges to support new developments in teaching and learning (see Chapter Nine); and, they will have to establish new forms of collaboration between themselves, other schools, colleges, universities and other organisations who have already taken learning through ILT seriously. Given the focus of this chapter, however, we only address the first of these two challenges.

'Informating' learning and developing 'intellective' skills
'Informating' learning and developing 'intellective' skills will involve ensuring that teachers have opportunities to rethink the process of learning

with ILT, prior to introducing ILT to students. There are a number of issues that will require careful consideration. First, colleges will need to ensure that FE teachers have the opportunity to participate in new 'communities of practice'. These may consist of other FE teachers, university staff or representatives from the business community who are actively using ILT as part of their human resource development strategy. One such example of a 'community of practice' is the Post-16 Centre's 'Distributed Learning Community' project. This involves the Post-16 Centre, Andersen Consulting and seven FE colleges in examining how on-line communities can work collaboratively on college-specific projects.

Second, colleges and FE teachers must clarify the goal of participating in new 'communities of practice'. Is it to support 'adaptive', 'investigate' or 'expansive' learning, or even a combination of all three? These are not abstract distinctions as the following illustration makes clear. If the primary goal was to support 'expansive' learning, FE teachers might use the new ideas about the design, delivery and evaluation of the use of ILT that emerge from collaborating and networking within a 'communities of practice' to fundamentally rethink the idea of a 'learner-centred' approach to using ILT. On the other hand, if the goal were to ensure that a college's approach to the use of ILT was consistent with practice elsewhere in the sector, it would not necessarily involve any fundamental rethinking of their approach to teaching and learning with ILT.

As different types of learning presuppose different uses of ILT, another important issue will be gaining a greater understanding about how to develop the type of capabilities (i.e. 'intellective' skills) students will need in order to fully exploit the opportunities provided by ILT. Addressing this issue will require, for example, senior management within FE colleges to recognise that key skill development, for either teachers or students, is not merely a matter of the acquisition of information and skills gained in one context and applied in another. It is complex process of interaction and negotiation, which may involve the production of new knowledge as well as using existing knowledge in new contexts. This is only likely to materialise when the design and delivery of learning activities take account of the content and context of learning. In other words, teachers and students will need to have the opportunities to pose hypotheses and to try out new ideas within their current staff development or learning programmes, and prepare themselves to subsequently use ILT in other contexts.

Conclusion

This chapter was stimulated by two issues, one theoretical and one practical. Theoretically, it is an attempt to overcome the limitations of current conception of 'learner-centredness' that dominates FE. Practically, it has attempted to provide a framework which FE teachers and colleges can use if they are to explore the pedagogic implications of using ILT as a resource for teaching and learning. We have argued that exploiting the learning potential of ILT will involve policy makers as much as colleges (and, for that matter, schools and universities) recognising that learning is a social process and rethinking their ideas about learning and pedagogy as well as developing a more critical approach to the potential of on-line learning. Furthermore, it has suggested that if young people are to develop the new kinds of skills and knowledge that are emerging as essential to a learning society, they will need to be able to use ILT as a resource both to access information as well as to collaborate with others within 'communities of practice' to produce new knowledge. Developing such capabilities does not automatically occur through providing access alone, nor will it occur if ILT is perceived to be a substitute for teachers.

References

Armundsen, C. (1993), 'The Evolution of Theory in Distance Learning', 61–79. In D. Keegan (ed.), *Theoretical Principles in Distance Education*. London: Routledge.

Bates, A.W. (1995), *Technology, Open Learning and Distance Education*. London: Routledge.

Beaumont, D. (1996), *Learning with IT – A Preliminary Literature Review*. London: FEDA.

Bloom, B. (1956), *A Taxonomy of Cognitive Objectives*. New York: McKay.

Brown, A. (1993), 'Expertise in the Classroom'. In G. Saloman (ed.), *Distributed Cognition*. Cambridge: Cambridge University Press.

Burford, J. (1996), 'Widening Participation Using Telematics'. In FEDA/AoC, *Creating Connnections*. Bristol: FEDA Publications, Coombe Lodge.

Cowham, T. (1995), *Information and Learning Technology: A Development Handbook*. Bristol: FEDA Publications, Coombe Lodge.

DfEE (1997), *Excellence in Schools*. London: The Stationery Office.

DfEE (1998), *The Learning Age: A Renaissance for a New Britain*. London: The Stationery Office.

ED/MSC (1981), *A New Training Initiative: A Programme for Action*. London: Employment Department and Manpower Services Commission, HMSO.

Ecclestone, K. (1999), 'Empowering or Ensnaring?: The Implications of Outcome-based Assessment in Higher Education', *Higher Education Quarterly, 53(1)*: 29–45.

Engestrom, Y. (1991), 'Towards Overcoming the Encapsulation of School Learning', *Learning and Instruction, 1(1)*, 49–59.

Engestrom, Y. (1995), *Training for Change*. London: International Labour Office.

FEDA/AoC (1996), *Creating Connnections*. Bristol: FEDA Publications, Coombe Lodge.

FEU (1984), *Information Technology in FE*. London: Further Education Unit.

FEU (1988a), *Learning by Doing*. London: Further Education Unit.

FEU (1988b), A Basis for Choice. London: Further Education Unit.

Fetterman, D.M. (1996), 'Video-conferencing On-line: Enhancing Comunication over the Internet', *Educational Researcher, 25(4)*, 23–27.

Field, J. (1994), 'Open Learning and Consumer Culture', *Open Learning, 9(2)*, 3–11.

Foster, P., Howard, U. and Reisenberger, A. (1997), *Adult Learning in a Learning Society*. Bristol: FEDA Publications, Coombe Lodge.

FEFC (1996), *Teaching and Learning with Information and Learning Technology*. Coventry: Further Education Funding Council.

Finn, D. (1991), 'The Great Debate on Education, Youth Employment and the MSC'. In G. Esland (ed.), *Education, Training and Employment, Vol. 2: The Educational Response*. Wokingham: Addison-Wesley and the Open University.

Hodgson, A. and Spours, K. (1997), *Dearing and Beyond: 14–19 Qualifications, Frameworks and Systems*. London: Kogan Page.

Harrisim, L. (1993), *Global Networks*. Cambridge, Mass.: MIT Press.

Honey, P. and Mumford, A. (1995), *Manual of Learning Styles*. Maidenhead: Honey Publications.

Huddleston, P. and Unwin, L. (1997), *Teaching and Learning in Further Education*. London: Routledge.

Jessup, G. (1990), *Outcomes: The Emerging Model of Education and Training*. London: Falmer Press.

Knowles, M. (1995), *Andragogy in Action: Applying Modern Principles of Adult Learning*. San Francisco Jossey Bass.

Kolb, D. (1984), *Experiential Learning*. USA: Prentice Hall.

Kennedy, H. (1997), *Learning Works: Widening Participation in Further Education Colleges*. Coventry: FEFC.

Laurillard, D. (1995), 'Multimedia and the Challenge of the Learner', *British Journal of Educational Technology, 26(1)*, 179–189.

Lave, J. and Wenger, E. (1991), *Situated Learning*. Cambridge: Cambridge Press.

Leney, T., Lucas, N. and Taubman, D. (1998), *Learning Funding: The Impact of FEFC Funding, Evidence from Twelve FE Colleges*. London: NATFHE/Institute of Education University of London.

Lockitt, B. (1997), *Learning Styles: Into the Future*. Bristol: FEDA Publications, Coombe Lodge.

Mager, R.F. (1962), *Preparing Instructional Objectives*. Palo Alto, C.A.: Fearon.

Mergondoller, J.R. (1996), 'Moving from Technological Possibility to Richer Student Learning: Revitalised Infrastructure and Reconstructed Pedagogy', *Educational Researcher, 25(8)*, 43–46.

NCET (1997), *Preparing for the Information Age: Synoptic Report of the Education Superhighwats Iniative*. Coventry: NCET/DfEE.

Owston, R. (1997), 'The World Wide Web: A Technology to Enhance Learning?' *Educational Researcher, 25(8)*, 43–46.

Paulsen, M. (1997), *The Online Report on Pedagogical Techniques for Computer Mediated Communication*. http.www.nki.no/-morten/

Rowntree, D. (1992), *Exploring Open and Distance Learning*. London: Kogan Page.

Riel, M. (1992), 'A Functional Analysis of Educational Technology: A Case Study of Learning Circles', *Interactive Learning Environments, 2(1)*, 15–29.

Sandholtz, J.H., Ringstaff, C. and Dwyer, D.C. (1997), *Teaching with Technology*. New York: Teacher College Press.

Seeley, J., Brown, J. and Duguid, P. (1993), 'Stolen Knowledge', *Educational Technology*, March, 10–15.

Spender, D. (1995), *Women, Power and Cyberspace*. Melbourne: Spinifax Press, Australia.

Shackleton, J. (1989), *The Professional Role of the Lecturer. Planning and Curriculum*. London: Further Education Unit.

Young, M. and Lucas, N. (1999), 'Pedagogy and Learning in Further Education: New Contexts, New Theories and New Possibilities'. In P. Mortimore (ed.), *Pedogogy and its Impact on Learning*. London: Sage.

Wasser, J.D. (1997), *Reform, Restructuring and Technology Infusion*, Http://ra.terc. edu.alliance/TEMPLATE/alli

Windschildt, M. (1998), 'The WWW and Classroom Research; What Path Should We Take?', *Educational Researcher, 27(1)*, 28–33.

Zuboff, S. (1988), *In the Age of the Smart Machine*. New York: Basic Books.

6 Inclusive Learning: From Rhetoric to Reality?

Lesley Dee

Introduction

Inclusion as an ideal applies to all potentially socially excluded groups. However, some have argued that only since the growth of movements of, rather than for, disabled people have the rights of people with disabilities and learning difficulties begun to be addressed within the inclusion debate (Lipsky and Gartner, 1996). The disability movement emphasises a socially constructed model of disability where the barriers facing disabled people are located within society rather than stemming from an individual's impairment. The report of the Further Education Funding Council's (FEFC) committee on learning difficulties and disabilities, *Inclusive Learning* (FEFC, 1996), is based on this concept and, in so doing, conflicts with many of the social policy reforms of the 1980s and 1990s.

The committee, chaired by Professor John Tomlinson, collected evidence from a wide range of interest groups and produced five reports in all. The main report, *Inclusive Learning*, made over 80 recommendations to the FEFC and colleges about the future direction of the provision in further education (FE). Many of its recommendations are linked to those of Dearing (1996) on the 16–19 curriculum and Kennedy (1997), whose report *Learning Works* addressed participation in FE.

The report of the FEFC's committee, known generally as the Tomlinson Report, can be distinguished from these and other recent documents by the importance given by the committee to understanding the processes of learning as a basis for making provision. The Report argues that by understanding more about students' requirements, including how students learn best and their learning goals, colleges can then achieve a better match or fit, in other words they should create a learning environment that is 'fit for its purpose'. In addition, the Report argues that by responding effectively to the needs of individuals, which may be shared with others, these changes 'act as prompts to the process of improvement' (Sebba and Sachdev, 1997: 6), and in so doing benefit all learners. Many of the ideas challenge the inherent purposes of FE vested in the current legislation by, for example, arguing for an alternative definition of progression to the one used in the 1992 Further and Higher Education (FHE) Act. Perhaps most importantly the Report reasserts the importance of the teaching process and the professionalism of teachers and concludes, like Stenhouse in 1975, that there can be no development without staff development.

The Report was warmly welcomed not least because it finally acknowledged and gave direction to a significant but long neglected aspect of FE provision. However, many of the ideas contained in the Report are underresearched and there is little information about how they might work in practice. Bradley, Dee and Wilenius (1994), in their review of literature prepared for the Tomlinson Committee, cite Macchialora (1989) who pointed out that most developments in special education are characterised by implementing changes first and then encouraging academics and practitioners to investigate what works later. Sebba and Sachdev (1997) argue, however, that literature which describes ideology and opinion helps to set the agenda and create the vision for the future. Both are needed to move the agenda forward. Therefore, what the Report provides is a series of starting points for the development of practice and for systematic research into some of the more significant ideas. However, the extent to which the ideas can be realised within a policy framework based on free market principles is open to debate.

In his introduction to the Report, Tomlinson remarks that: 'We want to avoid a viewpoint which locates the difficulty or deficit with the student and focus instead on the capacity of the educational institution to understand and respond to the individual learner's requirements' (FEFC, 1996: 4). The intention of this chapter is, first, to explore the factors that are both supporting and inhibiting the capacity of colleges to realise the rhetoric of *Inclusive Learning,* and, second, to suggest what could be done to build their capacity.

Inclusion and inclusive learning

Before considering the capacity of the sector to respond to the Tomlinson proposals, it is important to try to understand what is meant by inclusive learning. In his introduction to the Report, Tomlinson defines inclusive learning as 'the greatest degree of match or fit between the individual learner's requirements and the provision that is made for them' (FEFC, 1996: 26), implying the need for changes to the learning context to meet the learner's needs rather than expecting the student to fit into existing arrangements. Such changes, the Report argues, will have knock-on effects throughout the system with implications for teachers' understanding of the learning process, colleges' values and systems and the FE sector's approach to funding.

Many commentators on inclusive education now draw a distinction between integration and inclusion and Tomlinson notes 'Inclusive learning is not synonymous with integration. It is a larger and prior concept' (FEFC, 1996: 5). In this context, integration is used to describe a way of organising provision whereby people with disabilities and learning difficulties learn alongside others without disabilities in mainstream settings, that is fitting into the existing provision. However, Pijl, Meijer and Hegarty point out that some definitions of integration already came very near to definitions of inclusion by arguing that 'integration is about fitting schools to meet the needs of all their learners' (1997: 2). This confusion over definitions is mirrored in practice, as despite the distinction drawn by Tomlinson and others, some colleges do see inclusion as synonymous with integration and are making wholesale changes to the organisation of their provision on this basis.

It is important to understand and fully appreciate the underlying ideas and debates without letting terminology confuse or cloud the issues. The fundamental basis for Tomlinson's proposals are a rejection of the psycho-medical model of disability, which focuses on remedying individual deficits, in favour of an interactive model of disability defined by Bradley, Dee and Wilenius as a match between 'the characteristics of individuals and the organisational and curricular arrangements available to them' (1994: 4). The definition adopted in *Inclusive Learning* acknowledges both the need for colleges to understand the different requirements of individual learners and then to respond by 'reconsidering and restructuring...curricular organisation and provision and allocating resources to enhance equality of opportunity' (Sebba and Ainscow, 1996: 9).

In understanding how institutions can build their capacity to become more inclusive, we also need to recognise that inclusion is a process and not an absolute state. Colleges can aim to become more inclusive, but they will never achieve a position where there is a perfect match between all learners' requirements and the curriculum. It is an ideal to which each college can aspire, but all will have different starting points along the road. Many of the ideas associated with inclusive learning are complex. Furthermore, the Report was produced by a committee on students with learning difficulties and/or disabilities. Old attitudes die hard and some will find it difficult to move beyond the disability label to hear the wider messages. Yet, equally, the notion of inclusion must not become a doctrine with its own lore and language. It is important that connections are made with this and other initiatives and ideas, linking with the existing priorities and experiences of colleges and the sector.

The implications of inclusive learning

The act of realising inclusive policies has far-reaching implications and consequently the scope of such a discussion is potentially limitless. Tomlinson identifies three aspects of provision where changes are required: across the FE sector as a whole, in colleges and in classrooms. However, Young and Spours note that in any successful reform it is necessary to recognise the 'interdependence of qualifications, funding and institutional capacity' (1997: 93). These two perspectives offer the basis for exploring some of the implications of *Inclusive Learning* and Table 1 attempts to combine the various factors into a single model.

Table 1: Implications of inclusive learning

Provision	Sector	College	Classroom
Dimension			
Curriculum	Schedule 2/ qualifications framework	Curriculum offer	Curriculum development at classroom level
Funding	Methodology	Management of resources	Teaching time
Capacity	Legislative framework Staffing Quality	Organisational capacity	Teacher capacity

Note: An amendment to Schedule 2, giving the FEFC the power to fund courses, has been included in the Teaching and Higher Education Bill currently passing through Parliament.

The first aspect of this model is that of curriculum. The word 'curriculum' has been used in preference to 'qualifications' as the issues as they relate to inclusive learning are more easily addressed through this broader concept. Indeed, McCrea, Maguire and Ball (1997) have argued that problems in implementing inclusive policies arise because the curriculum is framed on the basis of individual achievements rather than the need for social equity.

The second dimension refers to funding. Schedule 2 of the 1992 Act lists the courses that qualify for FEFC funding and, in so doing, provides both a curriculum framework for FE and a means of controlling resources. As Leney, Lucas and Taubman (1998) point out in their study of 12 colleges, the relationship between the funding methodology and the curriculum operates at several inter-connected levels, which has had both positive and negative effects.

Third, capacity refers to the conditions that are required in schools and colleges to enable them respond to change. Developed, among others, by Ainscow *et al.* (1994), institutional improvement is regarded as a dynamic and constant process of reflection, analysis and action. An improving organisation is one which responds to external pressures for change whilst retaining a sense of its own internal priorities, using one to support the other. However conditions for change do not stop at managerial arrangements, they also have implications for the whole sector and for the processes of teaching and learning and the environment in which learning takes place. This model of change is helpful, not least because it shifts the focus away from a purely managerial response to change to one which engages with the learning of students, teachers and organisations as the basis for progress.

Having described a possible model for considering the implications of *Inclusive Learning*, I turn now to exploring the framework in more detail, beginning with the FE sector as a whole.

The further education sector

First, the implications of each dimension for the roles and responsibilities of policy makers and the FEFC are discussed in turn, and consideration is given to the extent to which these factors support or hinder the realisation of a more inclusive sector.

Curriculum policy

Schedule 2(j) of the 1992 FHE Act attempts to rationalise the plethora of programmes for students with learning difficulties by describing them as 'independent living and communication for those with learning difficulties which prepare them for entry to courses listed above'. Unlike the rest of Schedule 2, this definition not only describes the content of courses and the progression routes which are acceptable to the FEFC, but also the kind of students for which the courses are designed.

There has been considerable confusion in colleges over the interpretation of Schedule 2(j). First, the FEFC's stated intention was to require external accreditation for all FEFC-funded programmes, including 'Entry' level. The expectation that programmes should be accredited has helped to raise expectations of students' achievements and added direction to a curriculum which was sometimes lacking. It also led to the development of a proliferation of qualifications, as colleges became concerned that funding would be stopped. As a result, the Chief Inspector observed: 'Many college managers believe, incorrectly, that provision must be accredited in this area in order to receive funding. This misunderstanding has led to a failure to address the learning needs of some students' (FEFC, 1997a: 45). The FEFC's Report, *Basic Education* (FEFC, 1998a), also notes that many students are now following inappropriate forms of qualification, a fact which supports the assertion of McCrea, Maguire and Ball (1997) that the current FE curriculum is based on an exclusive rather than inclusive model.

A second source of confusion has been the requirement that courses will enable students to progress to another course, at a higher level. This blanket requirement failed to take account of the complexity of students' learning and in any case seemed to ignore the apparent contradiction that courses to support independent living were fundable, but moving on to live an independent life was not regarded as an acceptable outcome! A consequence of this requirement has been a fall in numbers of students accepted onto programmes, particularly students with severe and complex learning difficulties, for whom the potential to progress to another course is difficult to demonstrate. To tackle this problem, Tomlinson offered an alternative definition of progression, loosely based on the work of Cameron, Owen and Gee (1986). This argued that the maintenance of skills could reasonably be included as evidence of progression and students demonstrating this were therefore eligible for funding. However, the committee did not recommend that the Schedule should be altered, only that it should be interpreted differently.

Third, the Schedule neglects wider and more holistic educational purposes. The concern to increase the nation's competitiveness has led to an emphasis on basic skills and vocational training at the cost of some traditional routes into continuing education, such as non-vocational adult programmes. The purpose of the curriculum should, as Tomlinson notes, support people with disabilities in the achievement of adult status. It should also enhance their quality of life. The quality of life approach advocates supporting individuals in defining their own value base and determining the course of their own lives. To support this, FE and adult education must explore ways of offering a more holistic curriculum, of listening to individuals and collaborating with other agencies to realise students' aspirations.

As it stands, the FE curriculum is not based on inclusive principles which seek to match the provision to the requirements of learners, but on determining the curriculum and then selecting students to fit courses. As Dyson and Millward (1997) argue, the curriculum must be formulated in such a way that all can participate and that such participation is a right. If FE is to become truly inclusive then the fundamental purposes of FE and continuing education must be revisited and the basis of the curriculum redrawn.

Funding the sector
The targeted funding mechanism which provides support to individuals in part explains the increase in numbers of students with disabilities and/ or learning difficulties from approximately 42,000 in 1987 to 75,000 in 1995 (Institute of Employment Studies, 1997), although different definitions of what constitutes a learning difficulty or disability make comparisons difficult. Individually targeted funding poses several dilemmas. It makes colleges potentially more accountable for how the money is spent, particularly in times of funding constraints, by safeguarding the resources needed by individuals. On the other hand, the FEFC (1998b) is clear in stating that the support must be given directly to the student. This is inconsistent with an interactive model of learning difficulties, which regards investment in the wider learning environment, such as support for staff, as a means of reducing students' difficulties in learning as well as enhancing the quality of teaching for all students. A model of provision that recognises the interactive nature of learning requires both the individual and the institution to be funded.

Capacity of the sector

The capacity of the sector is circumscribed by the legislative framework, the supply and quality of teachers and the standards that are set by the FEFC for monitoring the quality of provision. The impetus for the Tomlinson Report came from the implementation of the 1992 Act. The Act strengthened the 'marketisation' of post-16 education by promoting competition and introducing an outcome-led element to the funding mechanism. The FEFC was charged with making sufficient provision for those under 19 and adequate provision for those over 19 and, in so doing under Section 4(1)–(3), 'to have regard to the requirements of people with learning difficulties'. A learning difficulty is described as 'a significantly greater difficulty in learning than the majority of persons of his [*sic*] age or [where] he [*sic*] has a disability which either prevents or hinders him from making use of facilities of a kind generally provided by institutions within the further education sector... ' (Section 4(6)–(7)). This was the first time that people with learning difficulties and/or disabilities within the FE sector had been acknowledged by law although the definition failed to recognise that learning difficulties are not located solely within the individual but are interactive. The committee was set up to examine the impact of the general changes in the FE sector on provision for people with learning difficulties or disabilities. It was made clear at the outset, however, that there was to be no new legislation, thereby both limiting what the committee might recommend and placing a significant responsibility on the sector to respond.

Successive governments have adopted a hands-off approach to staffing in FE. Nationally there has been a history of under-funding of staff development in FE and adult education as well as a 'benign neglect' (Young *et al.*, 1995) of any kind of policy development. Tomlinson identified the need for a comprehensive and coherent programme of staff development as the key to promoting inclusive learning and improving quality. However, the £5 million allocated by the FEFC to kick start the process will defeat this long-term objective if the ideals of *Inclusive Learning* do not influence other national staff development initiatives and providers. For example, an attempt is being made to create a Further Education National

Training Organisation (FENTO) to set standards for FE staff. Schools, however, are to have a General Teaching Council and higher education (HE) an Institute. These different titles are important in what they say about how the role of teacher is regarded. In schools and universities the titles seem to emphasise the professional nature of teaching, whereas the FENTO suggests a skills-based model of training. If teachers in FE are to respond to the increasing diversity of learners' needs in the ways envisaged by Tomlinson and Kennedy, then a model of teacher education is required that acknowledges the professionalism and growing complexity of the FE teacher's role.

Since the FEFC introduced systematic inspection procedures, more information is now available about what is happening in colleges. There has been a realignment of emphasis in the process towards the curriculum and teaching and away from management, in line with the aims and concerns of inclusive learning. Furthermore, the standards in 97/12 (FEFC, 1997b) are generally compatible with what could be regarded as a college that is striving to become more inclusive. On the other hand, it is perfectly possible for a college to receive high grades for teaching, but still not be regarded as inclusive. Selective sixth form colleges provide good examples of this. It is, then, the way in which the standards are interpreted and the nature of the supporting evidence that seem to provide information about the extent of a college's inclusivity.

This suggests that the reluctance on the part of the FEFC inspectorate to assess the inclusivity of colleges, unless expressly stated in their strategic plans, is misguided, as this implies that being inclusive is a state rather than a process. Becoming more inclusive is about having the capacity to change and improve and it is to these characteristics of colleges that I now turn.

Colleges

The college curriculum offer
Both Tomlinson and Kennedy identified the need for colleges to improve access for disadvantaged groups. As already argued, the curriculum offer in FE defines who participates and the FEFC's statistics for 1995–1996

(FEFC, 1997c) show that while 23 per cent of students were on 'other' entry level or foundation programmes only 1.6 per cent were on foundation level GNVQs and NVQs. It is reasonable to assume that most of these 'other' courses were entry level. This gap between entry and intermediate level qualifications constitutes a major barrier both to increasing participation and progression and has led to some students being placed on inappropriate courses because no alternative was available.

A further barrier to improving participation in FE has been the reduction in school/college link programmes which support individuals in making the transition from one phase of education to another. These courses provide guidance about available opportunities, broaden the curriculum offer and give colleges a chance to assess an individual's needs. Despite various official pronouncements about their value, the introduction of charges to schools since incorporation has lead to a dramatic decline in their availability.

Funding
Most colleges in Leney, Lucas and Taubman's study (1998) welcomed the introduction of the additional support units which can be claimed for students with disabilities and/or learning difficulties, although how these resources are allocated internally is left to individual colleges. The FEFC has responded to some of Tomlinson's recommendations and has made some modifications to the system.

More generally, one of the main aims of the reforms introduced by the 1992 FHE Act was to make colleges both more efficient and effective. Bassett-Jones and Brewer (1997) have identified two broad types of managerial response to this imperative which have implications for a college's capacity to become more inclusive.

The first response the researchers describe as core-periphery. Colleges adopting this approach have a relatively small number of full-time staff with good conditions of service and a large number of part-timers who are employed on a casual basis. This allows colleges to be responsive to changing patterns of recruitment and the demands of the market place. Colleges are able to respond to a wider range of needs much more

rapidly, for example to people with profound and complex learning difficulties or with mental health problems. However, having a large numbers
of part-time staff who are often not employed directly by the college but
through an agency means that colleges have much less control over the
quality of their staff. In addition, many part-time staff do not participate
in planning or training activities. Consequently, the quality of work may
suffer.

The second approach is described as differentiated. In this case almost
all staff are on full-time, permanent contracts. These colleges tend to
offer a much narrower curriculum, focusing on a particular market, such
as academic sixth form colleges and vocationally specific colleges. This
strategy is seen as a way of sustaining the quality of provision and thus
continuing to attract the best students. The obvious advantage of this
model is that students are more likely to be taught by highly qualified and
well-trained staff able to achieve the kind of 'match' envisaged by Tomlinson between the teaching and the learner's requirements. However,
they are less likely to achieve wider participation by under-represented
groups and, therefore, are less likely to become more inclusive in their
recruitment even though they may provide high-quality education for
those students who are accepted. Arguably then, the drive for efficiency
and effectiveness is not necessarily compatible with equity.

As a way of responding to a more diverse range of student needs than
is currently possible under Schedule 2 Regulations, some colleges make
use of other sources of funding. For example, Macadam and Sutcliffe
(1996) found that 44 per cent of colleges also used LEA funding and 36
per cent use social services funding. Negotiating this funding can be time
consuming and is one of the many management tasks that are taking
experienced full-time staff away from the classroom.

Capacity of colleges

Ainscow *et al.* (1994) have identified six components for increasing the
capacity of organisations to manage and support internal reform: use of
internal data; planning; co-ordination; leadership; linking organisational
and staff development; and the involvement of key stakeholders. All

colleges are now required by the FEFC to produce a strategic plan, but will only be inspected on their inclusivity if it is mentioned as part of the plan. In any case, Fullan (1993) argues that vision often follows rather than leads action and, this being so, many colleges are more likely to begin by making small changes to their practice rather than undertaking wholesale strategic changes.

Nevertheless, in judging a college's capacity to become more inclusive, it is worth considering its approach to strategic planning, as some have argued that the process of planning is more important than the outcome (West, 1998). Drodge and Cooper (1997) for example, found in their study of three colleges that although the FEFC promotes a collaborative model of strategic planning, the leadership style of the principal and the culture of the college are key determinants in how the plan is produced. If, as Fullan argues, vision follows rather than leads action then the status of staff involved in developing a more inclusive approach to teaching and the extent to which they are actively involved in the production of the strategic plan is likely to affect how far the ideas penetrate the college's long-term strategic thinking.

The centrality of leadership in moving organisations forward has been reiterated time and again in educational literature and *Inclusive Learning* states clearly that without the public commitment of principals little will change. Tomlinson attempted to appeal to college managers by arguing that inclusive policies benefit the whole college, including improvements in retention and achievements. Leadership is important, not only in creating organisational structures to support the implementation of policies, but in creating a culture responsive to change and development. Bennett and Hagan (1997) have carried out one of the very few studies into the relationship between the culture of colleges and change and concluded that organisational culture was central to implementing external curricular reforms. However, college managers have to choose between a range of competing priorities and it is unlikely that they will become fully committed to the principles and ideals of *Inclusive Learning* without a strong steer from the FEFC through the funding methodology and the curriculum framework.

The extent to which students, their families, the wider community and other outsiders are involved in the organisation has also been identified as important in facilitating organisational change. Listening to and valuing the student perspective was one of the defining features of the Tomlinson Report and most colleges now ask students to evaluate their courses, while many follow up the reasons behind student drop out. The extent to which this data is genuinely used to inform planning and improve practice is less clear.

Although the views and involvement of stakeholders are recognised as important, many colleges, particularly those in competition for the same students, have become more insular – a move often lead by governing bodies and principals. This reduction in opportunities for managers and staff to learn from each other has resulted in a loss of innovation and what Fullan and Hargreaves refer to as 'balkanisation', a sector consisting of competing groups 'jockeying for position and supremacy like loosely connected city-states' (1992: 71).

Staff development as the key to promoting inclusive and effective schools was highlighted by Rouse and Florian (1992) in a comparative study of provision in the United States and England. The Tomlinson Report also reasserted the professionalism of teachers by emphasising the need for all teachers in FE and continuing education to understand the processes of teaching and learning. Following incorporation, the FEFC adopted an outcomes approach to staff development, arguing that it was the Council's job to monitor student achievement and the responsibility of colleges to ensure that students were taught by competent staff and to manage their funds accordingly. As a consequence, the importance attached to staff development by individual colleges varied and led the Chief Inspector (FEFC, 1997a) to report an over-reliance on part-time staff without adequate teaching skills or qualifications. Yet, as colleges struggle to respond to budgetary constraints, it becomes increasingly difficult to release staff to attend courses and it is hard to see how colleges can improve the qualifications of part-time teachers without substantial investment in their terms and conditions of service.

Finally, the move towards college self-assessment has the potential to promote organisational improvement as the process should support colleges in becoming more self-critical, increasing their capacity to change by identifying and owning their own weaknesses. Central to the process is classroom observation, but the basis on which many observations are conducted still lies mainly in a model of inspection rather than a collaborative model of peer support, professional dialogue and mutual problem solving. Some of the most interesting and pioneering work has involved training staff from other colleges to review each other's practice (Furniss and Nicholls, 1998). Staff from similar disciplines act as critical friends to colleagues within the same specialism but from a different college. This approach acknowledges the professionalism of teachers and the capacity of individuals to learn from their own and each other's practice as well as contributing to the overall development of the organisation.

Professional practice in the classroom

The final aspect where change is required is in teachers' professional practice. The Tomlinson Report reasserted the importance of teaching and learning for colleges. In their concern to become self-managing organisations and in response to the demands of the FEFC, college corporations focused their attention on financial and administrative matters rather than teaching, reflected for example in the make up of many senior management teams. The Chief Inspector in his 1996–1997 annual report notes: 'Since incorporation, curriculum managers have generally assumed greater responsibility for managing staff and budgets' (FEFC, 1997a: 18). Due in part to the concern to improve retention rates, there has now been a revival of concern and interest in what happens in classrooms and in the processes of teaching and learning.

There is a good deal of agreement between West (1998) on the characteristics of effective classrooms and, for example, Iverson (1996) on inclusive classrooms. They describe these as engagement in classroom level curriculum development; establishing genuine relationships with students; negotiating appropriate ground rules and expectations; using a wide range of teaching methods; reflection on practice; and, finally, collaborative working with other teachers on teaching.

Yet the implementation of these principles must be placed in the context of the funding regime and the reductions in course hours. There has, for example, been an increase in resource-based learning which relies heavily on students own motivation, but Leney, Lucas and Taubman (1998) note that widened participation is likely to bring in students who require more, not less, teaching. Thus, although inclusive learning suggests the need for highly skilled teachers with time to listen to students and each other, colleges are under pressure to cut back in ways that will reduce opportunities for this to happen.

At the level of practice, the emphasis on vocational training and the need for specified learning outcomes has led to higher expectations about the facilities colleges should provide and the achievements of students with learning difficulties and/or disabilities. The need for all students to acquire key skills has, at least theoretically, created a more inclusive curriculum framework. However, one of the main disadvantages of the emphasis on outcomes has been the tendency for some teachers to use the outcomes as a syllabus, teaching to the assessment criteria and using a limited range of teaching methods.

Listening to a student helps a teacher to understand how the student is approaching a particular task and to evaluate his or her way of working. This is the basis of the relationship between the teacher and learner. Tomlinson emphasised the need for teachers to take time to understand the students with whom they are working and how those students learn best. He stressed the importance of dialogue between teachers and learners and suggested that we must 'move beyond bullet points and inventories to the complexities and contestedness of negotiations, dialogue and discussion' (Fielding, 1996: 96). For teachers in FE this presents a particularly difficult challenge as direct contact with students is diminished.

As a wider diversity of students continues to enter FE, teachers will need to adopt more sophisticated classroom management strategies. Of course, what constitutes challenging behaviour in one context may not be seen in the same light elsewhere. Indeed, FE is traditionally seen as a way of re-motivating disillusioned school pupils by offering vocational options and the numbers of pre-16 students in FE has grown exponentially, many of whom have either been excluded from schools or have dropped out. A survey carried out by the Further Education Development Agency for the DfEE in 1997, showed that over two-thirds of colleges reported their numbers of disaffected students had increased over the last three years, including pre-16s (Reisenberger and Crowther, 1997). Working with these learners requires particular responses which need coordination, time and staff development.

Inclusive Learning emphasises the need for teachers to identify and accommodate students' individual learning styles in their teaching. Following on from Kolb's work (1984), there has been a growing interest in learning styles across all phases of education, but despite this interest there has been little empirical research into the application of these ideas, particularly in working with pupils and students with learning difficulties and/or disabilities. There is then some naivety in the Report's recommendation to colleges that they should assess and use students' individual learning styles without signalling the need for much more research and development work particularly with older and more diverse learners.

Self-review and reflection by teachers was neglected by the Tomlinson Report, yet it is an essential part of teaching, as it is during these times that teachers often learn most about their own practice. The increased pressure experienced by college staff now makes these opportunities harder to find and yet the link between teacher's capacity to learn and organisational learning and change is self-evident. Fullan and Hargreaves (1992) in writing about organisational change observe that effective teachers reflect 'in, on and about action' and argue the need for reflection based on the systematic collection of evidence. Above all, they argue for teachers to be believed in and trusted as professionals, committed to the improvement of practice, a trust which Randle and Brady (1997) believe is being eroded in FE.

One of the defining characteristics of an inclusive approach is the emphasis placed on the general strategies adopted by teachers rather than providing individual or separate teaching and provision. Indeed investment in the quality of the generally available provision may reduce an individual student's need for one-to-one support. Many teachers will require support to broaden their repertoire of teaching methods and a potential source of expertise can be college-based learning support teams. Yet the status of these teams varies considerably from being integral to the management of the college to being on the margins. How they work also varies. Some are mainly concerned with offering direct support to individual students, whereas others interpret their roles more widely to include staff development for teachers and support staff. However, it is worth noting that the FEFC specifically excludes this latter aspect of learning support from qualifying for additional funding, noting that 'the costs of a learning support co-ordinator may be included where the member of staff concerned is providing direct support to an individual student' (FEFC, 1998b: 76).

Conclusion

Many of the apparent tensions and contradictions outlined in this chapter stem from philosophical differences between *Inclusive Learning* and the basis of FE provision. The ideals of the Tomlinson Report are loosely based on the principles of social justice. The 1992 FHE Act, the FE curriculum and funding methodology spring from market-individualism, emphasising consumerism, performance and efficiency.

At present what changes there are, whether nationally or at local level, appear to avoid challenging these tensions and hover on the periphery of the debates about future policy. For example, the recent Green Paper on lifelong learning, *The Learning Age* (DfEE, 1998), omitted *Inclusive Learning* from its list of key points of reference, referring to it only in the context of students with disabilities. The following issues must be addressed if the intentions of *Inclusive Learning* are to become a reality.

There is a need to continue to promote the rights of disabled people in the wider debates on social inclusion. The contention that the rights of people with disabilities and/or learning difficulties are now set firmly within the inclusion debate is not yet true within the context of the post-school sector. There is already some evidence that the debate is being dominated by concerns about larger and more potentially troublesome social groups. There is a real danger of creating separate, competing groups, which makes a mockery of the real meaning of inclusion and inclusive learning.

The aims and purposes of the FE curriculum must be reviewed and made broader than the current emphasis on academic and vocational qualifications. There remains a considerable gap between the requirements of many actual and potential students and the curriculum that is currently provided. The various reasons why adults wish to learn and the principle of equity must be reflected in the curriculum that is fundable by the FEFC.

The philosophical basis of the funding mechanism needs to change from one which is market- and outcomes-led to a learner- and curriculum-led model. The funding methodology must address the current inherent tensions between individual achievement, the curriculum offer and the quality of the learning environment. There needs to be sufficient flexibility for colleges to be able to use funding in ways that support individual students and enhance classroom practice and the professionalism of teachers.

The inclusive learning agenda must be opened up to the sector for wider debate and scrutiny. This should be supported by a sustained and rigorous research programme with academic integrity that supports classroom practice and organisational, teacher and student learning.

Finally, the professionalism of teachers and teaching in the FE sector must be recognised through the model of teacher education that is put in place and through increased job security. One of the most important aspects of the Tomlinson Report and one which was welcomed by many FE teachers was the emphasis placed on teaching and learning, so that teachers are not seen as technocrats 'delivering' the curriculum but as reflective and self-critical professionals. There can be no improvement in the quality of learning and student achievements without real investment in teachers.

Acknowledgements

I would like to thank Elizabeth Maudslay for the advice and help she gave me in the preparation of this chapter.

References

Ainscow, M., Hopkins, D., Southworth, G. and West, M. (1994), *Creating the Conditions for School Improvement*. London: Fulton.

Bassett-Jones, N. and Brewer, R. (1997), 'Strategic Management and Competitive Advantage'. In R. Levacic and R. Glatter (eds), *Managing Change in Further Education*. London: FEDA.

Bennett, N. and Hagan, L. (1997), 'Managing for Learning After Incorporation'. In R. Levacic and R. Glatter (eds), *Managing Change in Further Education*. London: FEDA.

Bradley, J., Dee, L. and Wilenius, F. (1994), *Students with Disabilities and/or Learning Difficulties in Further Education*. Slough: NFER.

Cameron, R., Owen, A., and Gee, T. (1986), 'Curriculum Management (Part 3): Assessment and Education', *Educational Psychology in Practice*, October: 3–9.

Dearing, R. (1996), *Review of Qualifications for 16–19 year olds*. Middlesex: SCAA.

Department for Education and Employment (1988), *The Learning Age: A Renaissance for a New Britain*. DfEE.

Drodge, S. and Cooper, N. (1997), 'The Management of Strategic Planning in Further Education Colleges'. In R. Levacic and R. Glatter (eds), *Managing Change in Further Education*. London: FEDA.

Dyson, A. and Millward, A. (1997), 'The Reform of Special Education or the Transformation of Mainstream Schools'. In C.J. Meijer, S.J. Pijl and S. Hegarty (eds), *Inclusive Education: A Global Agenda*. London: Routledge.

FEFC (1996), *Inclusive Learning: Report of the Learning Difficulties and/or Disabilities Committee*. London: HMSO.

FEFC (1997a), *Quality and Standards in Further Education in England 1996/97: Chief Inspector's Annual Report*. Coventry: FEFC.

FEFC (1997b), *Circular 97*, 12. Coventry: FEFC.

FEFC (1997c), *Inspectors' Statistical Handbook Version 4*. Coventry: FEFC.

FEFC (1998a), *Basic Education*. Coventry: FEFC.

FEFC (1998b), *Funding Guidance*. Coventry: FEFC.

Fielding, M. (1996), 'Why and How Learning Styles Matter: Valuing Difference in Teachers and Learners'. In S. Hart (ed.), *Differentiation and the Secondary Curriculum: Debates and Dilemmas*. London: Routledge.

Fryer, R.H. (1997), *Learning for the Twenty-First Century*. National Advisory Group for Continuing Education and Lifelong Learning.

Fullan, M. (1991), *The New Meaning of Educational Change*. New York: Teacher's College Press.

Fullan, M. (1993), *Change Forces: Probing the Depths of Educational Reform*. London: The Falmer Press.

Fullan, M. and Hargreaves, A. (1992), *What's Worth Fighting for in your School?*. Buckingham: Open University Press.

Furniss, B. and Nicholls, S. (1998), *External Quality Review – Supporting Self-Evaluation and Quality Improvement in Further Education*. PSSI Forum, June.

Institute of Employment Studies (1997), *Mapping Provision: the Provision of and Participation in Further Education by Students with Learning Difficulties and Disabilities*. Coventry: FEFC.

Iverson, A. (1996), 'Strategies for Managing an Inclusive Classroom'. In S. Stainback and W. Stainback (eds), *Inclusion: A Guide for Educators*. London: Paul H. Brookes.

Kennedy, H. (1997), *Learning Works: Widening Participation in Further Education*. Coventry: FEFC.

Kolb, D.A. (1984), *Experiential Learning*. Englewood Cliff, N.J.: Prentice-Hall.

Leney, T., Lucas, N. and Taubman, D. (1998), *Learning Funding: The Impact of FEFC Funding, Evidence from Twelve FE Colleges*. London: NATFHE.

Lipsky, D. and Gartner, A. (1996), 'Equity Requires Inclusion: The Future for all Students with Disabilities'. In C. Christenson and F. Rigri (eds), *Disability and the Dilemmas of Education and Justice*. Buckingham: Open University Press.

Macadam, M., and Sutcliffe, J. (1996), *Still a Chance to Learn: A Report on the Impact of the Further and Higher Education Act (1992) on Education for Adults with Learning Difficulties*. Leicester: NIACE.

Macbeth, A., McCreath, D. and Aitchison, J. (eds) (1995), *Collaborate or Compete? Educational Partnerships in a Market Economy*. London: Falmer Press.

Macchialora, F. (1989), 'Introduction'. In D. Lipsky and A. Gartner (eds), *Separate Education: Quality Education for All*. Baltimore: Paul H. Brookes.

Maychell, K. and Bradley, J. (1991), *Preparing for Partnership: Multi-agency Support for Special Needs*. Slough: NFER.

McCrea, S., Maguire, M. and Ball, S. (1997), 'Whose Learning Society? A Tentative Deconstruction', *Journal of Education Policy*, *12(6)*, 499–509.

Office for Standards in Education (1988), *The Annual Report of Her Majesty's Chief Inspector of Schools 1996/9*: Standards and Quality in Education. London: OFSTED.

Pijl, S.J., Meijer, C.J. and Hegarty, S. (1997), *Inclusive Education: A Global Agenda*. London: Routledge.

Randle, K. and Brady, N. (1997), 'Further Education and the New Managerialism', *Journal of Further and Higher Education, 21(2)*, 229–239.

Riesenberger, A. and Crowther, R. (1997), *Further Education: Giving Young People a New Start*. London: Further Education Development Agency.

Rouse, M. and Florian, L. (1992), 'Becoming Effective and Inclusive: Cross Cultural Perspectives'. In M. Rouse and L. Florian (eds), *School Reform and Special Educational Needs: Anglo-American Perspectives*. Cambridge: University of Cambridge Institute of Education.

Sebba, J. and Ainscow, M. (1996), 'International Developments in Inclusive Education – Mapping the Issues', *Cambridge Journal of Education, 26*, 5–19.

Sebba, J. and Sachdev, D. (1997), *What Works in Inclusive Education*. Essex: Barnados.

Stenhouse, L. (1975), *An Introduction to Curriculum Research and Development*. London: Heinemann.

West, M. (1998), 'Working With The Grain: Developing a Sustainable Model for the Self-managing School'. In M. Fullan (ed.), *International Handbook on Educational Change*. Kluwer Academic Publishers.

Young, M. and Spours, K. (1997), '14–19 Education: Legacy, Opportunities and Challenges', *Oxford Review of Education, 24(1)*, 83–97.

Young, M., Lucas, N., Sharp, G. and Cunningham, B. (1995), *Teacher Education for the Further Education Sector: Training the Lecturer of the Future*. London: University of London Institute of Education.

7 'The Business of Learning': The Student Experience

Patrick Ainley and Bill Bailey

Introduction

This chapter draws upon material collected in researching for our book *The Business of Learning, Staff and Student Experiences of Further Education in the 1990s* (1997) to describe aspects of the contemporary student experience of further education (FE). The chapter relates this material to debates and developments currently being conducted under the banner of 'lifelong learning'.

In our book we studied two colleges and showed that, despite their many differences, it was the similarities in their present situation that emerged most strongly from the interviews we conducted with managers, lecturers and students at all levels. One college, which we called 'Inner City College', was a large generalist FE institution in inner London. The other was a tertiary college, which we called 'Home Counties College' after its location. Having retailed the experiences since incorporation of the two principals and their senior management teams, middle managers and lecturers in each college, we then turned to the students. As with the managers and the teachers, we allowed students to tell their own stories to present a picture of FE today to as wide a readership as possible.

In general, FE students' intentions tend to be instrumental and transitory, often attending only part-time and always as a means to an end. In many cases, students do not stay for long – many are on courses for only a year, or two years at the most. Therefore, they tend not to identify with their college in the way that school and university students may do. Thus, colleges face the task of generating a community ethos. At most, FE students may spontaneously identify with their course, the group taking it and the lecturer who will get them through it. In many ways, part of the appeal of FE to many of its students always was that their courses were short, practical and relevant. However, there are signs this is altering, along with so much else, as periods spent in FE lengthen for many students.

Possibilities of 'progression' both within and from FE are central to the comprehensive mission espoused by the sector today and by both our colleges in relation to the communities they serve. Yet FE is not comprehensive in the same sense as comprehensive schools are; FE students do not all follow the same curriculum and their attendance is not compulsory. Even common or core (now 'key') skills are taught differently to different students. So FE's curriculum offer is broad and polytechnic, but it is not comprehensive in the same sense as the schools' National Curriculum (Ainley, 1999).

Entrants to FE from schools are guided into courses or programmes at advanced, intermediate and foundation levels on the basis of their achievement in GCSE exams and they remain largely within the courses they have chosen or that have been chosen for them. These courses supposedly enjoy 'parity of esteem', but arguably the divisions between academic, vocational and work-based study reproduce the old tripartite divisions between grammar, technical and secondary modern schools at a tertiary stage (Bailey, 1997). Indeed, characteristically different curricula (subject-based 'A' Levels and GCSEs, grouped courses leading to GNVQs, and other qualifications and job-specific NVQs), hamper efforts to combine them. Therefore, the different student groups in classrooms and laboratories, in workshops, or based in employment remain largely separate from each other at all levels except for foundation, where they are often integrated in programmes of classroom and workshop learning combined with work experience, as they were in both our colleges.

The lack of common experience by different types of student at different levels on different courses and programmes within the college, even if all share the common canteen and other facilities, occurs despite the efforts of both our colleges to organise optional 'electives' and other sporting and social activities in which students from different pathways can mix. Most interviewees, however, were unable and unwilling to discriminate directly between different types and level of course in terms of the social backgrounds of those following them. This was possibly because the nomenclature and equivalence of the qualifications to which they lead is unclear. For instance, it is unclear whether 'A' Levels for entrance to higher education (HE) and the uncertain prospect of employment thereafter were 'better' or 'worse' than GNVQ or BTEC qualifications which for some lead to immediate and possibly more secure employment. Even the Home Counties 'A' Level sociology students, despite having covered the sociology of education, asserted everyone on whatever course at the College was 'the same' and could not explain why no one in the class actually knew anyone doing hairdressing at the College. Similarly at Inner City, two 'A' Level sociologists distinguished between what they called 'A-Level people' and 'GNVQ people'. Yet from her knowledge of the membership of the Students' Union (SU) at Home Counties, the SU President there thought gender was a significant division by subject of study, but even this was 'not highly significant'. So: 'there aren't really things such as if you're this class or this type of person you therefore do this course. Everybody's treated as an equal. ... Everybody's mixed in OK.' Our summary of student experience as narrated to us in the two colleges is given under the broad headings of foundation, intermediate and advanced levels of learning.

From the foundation up

In contrast with the SU President, some of the foundation level students were very clear about how college functioned to differentiate between students while at the same time 'treating everyone as equal'. They saw this in relation to their previous experience of schooling, when most of them had statements of special educational needs. Along with the adult returners and also some of those retaking GCSEs or embarking instead upon GNVQ or BTEC courses, these foundation level students also illustrate most clearly the traditionally second-chance nature of FE provision – 'to catch up on what I missed from school'. Therefore, more than other interviewees they emphasised the differences between compulsory schooling and college.

This was explained by one student who had learning support for his statement of special educational needs throughout mainstream schooling and, therefore, had not been segregated, as he now was for most of his time in the foundation group, from other students. As he said: 'I thought it would be like that – the people on other courses would look down on you... but at college when you get there you immediately see that it's different and you try to sort of fit that environment so you would be classed as a student instead of a child.'

It was not difficult for interviewees to explain the ways in which college was so different from school. This was summed up by most as 'more freedom', 'they treat you like adults', 'like human beings' and 'you're classed as an adult'. So that, 'at college there's more respect'. This was symbolised by the first-name terms that nearly all interviewees (except the engineers at both colleges) were on with their lecturers: 'You don't have to call them "Sir" and "Miss". That shows they're treating you different.' The absence of other petty restrictions, such as school uniform, was also celebrated: 'You can sit in class with your coat on or chew gum.' 'You can go out down the town.' 'You get more breaks.' 'So it's completely different, apart from the work.'

Smaller class sizes – down to groups of about 10 in college – were particularly appreciated by students who realised, as one said: 'I just needed more time to do things that other kids could just instantly do.' He explained that because at school everyone was supposed to be doing the same thing according to the same timetable, 'They were always moaning at me for falling back on a backward level when you're supposed to go forward. Whereas here you do your best and you don't get moaned at by teachers.' In relation to peers, another added: 'It's more verbal at school because they know what they say is going to hurt you because they say you're stupid.'

Most foundation level students would have preferred to be in work than at college and hoped that the work experience component of their courses would lead to employment. As one of these students reflected, looking back on his two years at college, 'In a way college does change you. Probably because you've got your own freedom. You've got your own space as well. And you don't have to be here.' 'It's down to you,' his friend added. This belief was reinforced by teachers who repeatedly told students on all programmes that FE represented a second chance for them to make a fresh start, but typically added that, to take advantage of it, students would have to study hard, take responsibility for their own learning and success would be down to their individual effort.

Intermediate level

At this level of study the second-chance nature of FE provision extends to GCSE resits, plus at the Inner City students from abroad whose school qualifications were not recognised in this country. Students are discouraged from retaking the same GCSEs they failed at school, except for the essential English and mathematics, as results from retakes are not generally good. Many of these interviewees blamed their schools or their peers at school for their poor performance at GCSE and stated that this was why they had chosen college in preference to remaining at school. The idea of a 'fresh start' or 'second chance' in a new place was again common at both colleges.

Coming straight from mainstream schooling, or with a gap of one or two years in the cases of several of the Inner City interviewees, differences between school and college were again salient. They centred on 'freedom', as opposed to compulsory attendance with its accompanying regulations. These interviewees also accepted their individual responsibility for success or failure in this new situation, but some said they 'needed a push'. Such contradictory feelings have to be mediated by teachers seeking to motivate students to stay on course and gain their target qualifications.

At Inner City College, with traditionally low post-16 participation rates, what evidence there is suggests that there are at least as many 16–18 year olds in the locality outside the system as there are in school and college or on training schemes. Indeed, many interviewees compared themselves to those they knew who 'stayed at home doing nothing' by contrast to those in college who were 'trying to better themselves' and had 'ambition'. At Home Counties College, in an area with the highest staying-on rate anywhere in the South East, 'Unless you're an outcast, it seems like strange if you don't go on to further education.' Despite this peer pressure, which as Ainley and Green noted (1996) has 'normalised' staying-on in education in many parts of the country, many intermediate level students found it particularly hard to apply themselves consistently to their courses. This was the case, for example, with some young women interviewees who admitted they did not always return from pubs in town to Home Counties College for afternoon classes.

Both colleges had to encourage their students to balance their social lives with their study, as well as nowadays, for many of them, with part-time work. What works with one group of students has to be presented differently with another – what were openly called 'attendance checks' at Home Counties as compared with systems of 'student support' at Inner City. Similarly, tutors have to deal differently with very different individuals, including the mature students, to whose presence in classes one young student interviewee attributed the more respectful way college teachers treated their students compared with school teachers.

For intermediate level students also, smaller college classes compensated for fewer hours in class (with one-year college courses reduced to fit 16 hours) than they had been accustomed to spending on two-year GCSE courses at school: 'It's a lot more left up to you than they do at school 'cos you don't have so much time in the class for a start.' However, if classes became too small, as many did with rapid decline from the promising numbers in the first term, the remaining students and their teachers became disheartened, especially if classes were then merged.

For some, such as the two following Inner City students from girls' schools, the level of tutorial support and the smaller size of classes did not compensate for the order they missed in school: 'I think it would be better [in school sixth form than college] because there would be more people of my own age. I think they would look after you more.' So, 'in some ways I miss school. I miss sort of having the lunch times and the break times and all that stuff.' Interviewees supported the idea that FE appealed to those who were 'more mature' or 'ready for it'. 'It's hard to say if most people are ready. It depends on where they've come from – what their family situation is and the school they've been to – but most people seem ready enough. You get a few who might go back to school but the drift is more from school to college.'

The many demands that students make upon the colleges have to be balanced in the crucial 'image' that the institution projects to potential students. Creating an attractive environment and effective marketing is a major priority to which considerable resources are devoted. To help with this, at both colleges the SU (previously a fairly nominal body) was financed by senior management to organise entertainment and sporting events. As the President of Home Counties SU astutely remarked, 'We're aware of how much they need to get customers and we can use that to our advantage' when negotiating with college managers for support for SU activities and events.

Being 'new and shiny', Home Counties College had an advantage in attracting students compared with older competitor colleges. Its situation in Market Town was preferred as 'a nice place' by students from other 'rougher' towns, as they described them, where they could have gone to college. The hierarchy of competing schools and colleges locally relates to a similar rank ordering of HE institutions. The academic sixth-form college in a nearby city, together with some school sixth forms and the private schools, aimed at the 'Ivy League' of universities. Most of the Home Counties' students who intended to enter HE aimed instead for universities of the second rank, whereas at Inner City many interviewees aiming for HE had applied to local former-polytechnics.

For its part, slogans such as 'Inner City is a happening college' were not as vacuous as they might appear, but contributed towards impressing potential students. Several black interviewees stressed the attraction to them of 'a black college', as they described it, and the College built upon the positive aspects of this image with events such as a Black Awareness Week. At the same time, despite these attractions and subsidised college transport, the ending of travel grants is restricting access for many students to all but local colleges. Similarly in HE, many students are nowadays saving on costs by studying locally whilst remaining at home, as was the intention of many Inner City interviewees.

Many of the level two engineering students on their one-year course at Home Counties appeared to have confirmed their choice of going to college early in their last year at school and 'stopped worrying about it', as one said, thereafter. This foreclosed for them other possibilities such as modern apprenticeships that were being offered by some local companies. The students, however, appreciated suddenly being in demand, even from school teachers with whom they might not have been particularly popular previously: 'It was like "Come to the sixth form" and all of a sudden they were being friendly to you.'

As for college: 'Well, the College is like a business and they try to teach us as best they can, to try to provide the best service as they can, and as we enrol we're worth money to them, so they teach us and if we don't come up to scratch, or if we like start pissing around, or not have enough attendance, they would lose the money.' Consequently, even though no student understood that they represented aggregated bundles of funding units, most student interviewees confirmed the supposition of a Home Counties' Assistant Principal that 'all students have a good idea how much they are worth – between £1,500 to £3,000 a year … '. Indeed, they had often been told this by their teachers, even though in the view of some teachers this made for 'arrogant students' who were reluctant to accept guidance and who held out for courses beyond their capabilities.

All the intermediate level students interviewed at Inner City intended to remain in FE, most of them at that college. Most GCSE students hoped to progress to 'A' Levels, while for engineers their one-year BTEC Firsts prepared them for two-year Nationals, just as one-year Advanced Accountancy Technician (AAT) foundation led on to the two-year intermediate NVQ course. Aspirations were high – careers as lawyers, journalists and doctors were mentioned by GCSE sociologists. There was a challenge here for tutors and subject teachers at the same time to maintain motivation while encouraging realistic aspirations. To quote again the Home Counties' SU President, herself an 'A' Level student: 'A lot of people are in education because it's sort of the done thing and they aren't able to get a job. So... time passes them by because they're not really sure what they want to do....' This was also the case for many of the advanced level students interviewed.

Advanced level

At this level the students whose experience of FE was most similar to their previous schooling were the 'A' Level sociologists interviewed at both colleges. It would also be the most similar to the HE experience they anticipated. As one said, going to college rather than remaining in school sixth form was 'a trial run for going to university'. As a result of this continuity and as they were doing what was expected of them, they questioned their experience least. Indeed, their classroom-based mode of study had continued unchanged save that it was at a higher level. Thus, they were sixth formers whose FE built upon their previous largely successful school experience, often supported by families who, if not professionally qualified (as many of their parents were in Home Counties) were (in the Inner City) members of the churches that have been shown to play a significant part in black educational achievement (Ainley, 1998).

The newer GNVQ programmes represented an alternative route to HE for those who did not have the requisite GCSE grades for 'A' Level. For their part, GNVQ3 students and their teachers insisted that GNVQ was just as demanding as 'A' Level. In fact, the GNVQ experience was not radically different from that of 'A' Level, in that GNVQ students also relied upon textbooks, teachers' notes and class handouts, even though GNVQs are supposed to emphasise active independent learning. Indeed, 'A' Level students were constantly exhorted to 'work by themselves on their own initiative'; however students welcomed and wanted explicit direction on developing examination technique. Modular 'A' Levels, which were being introduced at both colleges, but which were not taken by any of our interviewees, rely less on final written examinations and move towards the assessment of course work if not of vocational outcomes which is the distinctive feature of GNVQs.

The BTEC phase tests, which are similar to and pre-date GNVQ assessments, were accepted by the engineering students as part of their level 3 course. They could retake them after a period, if they were unsuccessful at the first attempt. The same applied to the NVQ practical assessments for the accountancy technicians, which the classes also took together periodically – and not on individual demand or at work (which was impractical), even though this might have been originally intended by NCVQ. In the absence of opportunities for accrediting competences at work, AAT students were even more heavily reliant upon their single textbook for the course than 'A' Level, GNVQ or BTEC students at this level.

Engineering at both colleges at levels 2 and 3 (BTEC first and National) was vocationally oriented by definition. It was a full-time (16 hours a week) course, equivalent (as was the advanced GNVQ) to two 'A' Levels. This and the isolation of the engineering section within both colleges contributed to a shared vocational culture amongst the students, especially after two or three years of study. Several of the fathers of interviewees at Home Counties College worked in, or in a couple of cases owned, small engineering businesses locally. Their sons had a realistic appreciation of their job prospects (as confirmed by the college careers adviser) and did not intend to continue in education beyond level 3. In this respect, they exhibited what Smithers and Robinson (1995) called the 'discouragement effect' against progressing to HE. This was shared by other interviewees, particularly mature students if working full-time, but also by younger students who did not relish the prospect of graduating without work and in debt in three or four years' time. They felt that they would have had 'enough' of education by the time they left at 18.

These Home Counties' students were unlike most engineers interviewed in Inner City College, many of whom came from Third World countries and included several asylum-seekers. There was in any case no engineering industry locally with which they could have any contact and their notions of employment prospects were hazy at best. Therefore, they postponed the decision by hoping to enter HE. Their lecturers doubted whether these students' English and mathematics in particular would qualify them to do so, or whether if they did they would satisfactorily complete HND or degree courses at the local former-polytechnics.

Similar reservations about whether the basic English and mathematics 'key skills' of engineering students were sufficient to pass all the BTEC phase tests necessary for full qualification were registered by their lecturers at Home Counties College. Partly this reflected the school achievement of the students, which consisted of only two or three GCSEs at A–C in most cases. In contrast with this modest academic achievement, many engineering students spoke warmly of the pleasures of making things and getting their hands dirty at work and in college. Tutors at both colleges arranged additional 'key skills' support for these students, either coaching them themselves and/or arranging learning support for them. Students often did not take full advantage of these opportunities not only because there was some stigma attached to doing so but because this was an additional demand which cut into what they regarded as their free time when they might undertake part-time jobs.

Many more of these older and more qualified students had part-time jobs. In fact, there was a hierarchy of part-time employment evident amongst interviewees with 'A' Level students, especially at Inner City College, who could least afford time off from heavy timetables of study, working the longest hours – up to 18 hours a week in some cases. GCSE students, who were younger and so lacked qualifications and experience, found it harder to find part-time work. This was also because, especially at Home Counties College, more advantaged family backgrounds made many 'A' Level students more attractive to employers, not only in pubs and waitressing but in boutiques and art galleries. However, even for them, the pressures of this part-time work ate into the time that they needed to study for three 'A' Levels. Indeed, the pressures of and necessity for part-time work are widely acknowledged as contributing to lack of progression in FE (Martinez, 1997).

By aiming for HE, students deferred decision-making by another three or four years. Thus 'A' Level students who had entered college with very definite vocational intentions that they said they had held for some time during school (to be a probation officer, for example), found themselves undecided after two years of deconstructing society in sociology (Frampton, 1995).

Many students at all levels expressed an interest in their studies and said they enjoyed them. Although some of them might have changed their opinions and intentions partly due to their courses of study, it was only mature students who declared their subject of study had profoundly affected them. For example, a 39-year-old mother of four, who described herself as 'happily divorced for the past year', enjoyed her three 'A' Levels so much that she did not 'want to go home of an evening'. Typically of access students, not only had she left her husband, but 'I've dropped a lot of old friends since coming to college.... Before I was just a mother. Now I'm a mum and I'm me.' This case again exemplifies the second-chance nature of so much FE provision.

Conclusion

How does this study of students in two colleges inform the current debate about 'lifelong learning' and the role of FE colleges in 'The Learning Society'? One characteristic shared by most of our interviewees is that 30 years ago they would not have been participating in any form of post-compulsory education. Given changes in the labour market, the competition for employment and the inflation of qualifications, the participation rates for students in the 16–19 age group and among adults have greatly increased in recent decades. As one of our interviewees, retaking her GCSEs at Inner City College, said: 'You have to work harder and harder to get a worse and worse job. You have to go to university to get what 30 years ago you didn't even have to have 'A' Levels for.' Although this is something of an exaggeration, it does illustrate some of the perceptions and motivations which lie behind the considerable increases in participation rates and of student numbers in post-compulsory education in the last two decades (Ainley, 1997). Even in the case of the employed and adult, part-time accountancy students, their aim was to gain qualifications that would either advance or secure their positions. Indeed, many of our interviewees were aware of the insecurities of employment and of the almost certain necessity for them to adapt and retrain for various jobs in the changing labour market. Some even welcomed this prospect of perpetual change (Rikowski, 1999).

Our students also typified the wide age range in FE today. While Home Counties was established as a tertiary college and, therefore, has a substantial number of full-time 16–19 year-old students, it now also has over 7,000 part-time students who are mostly older. Inner City, on the other hand, has over 12,000 students of whom 63 per cent are part-time and over 90 per cent are over 19. Of course, all FE colleges vary greatly in their sizes and in the courses they offer, but our two colleges illustrate the differences between the two main types of tertiary and general FE colleges. Overall, of the 3.9 million students in the 1996–1997 session, 80 per cent were over 19. This represents a large number and a significant proportion of mature learners and shows that 'widening participation' is already a reality, a core part of the business of FE. Such adult students will form the majority of the 500,000 additional students the government aims to provide for in FE and HE by the year 2002.

The strength of the FE sector which equips it to play the leading role in this increased participation is the recent experiences of its staff, their adaptability and their ability to meet the needs of a diverse range of learners (Flint, 1999). While incorporation and the new funding methodology have encouraged colleges to increase numbers and broaden recruitment, there appears now to be a consensus, as in the *Report of the Parliamentary Select Committee on Education* (HMSO, 1998), that the emphasis on competition and efficiency savings should be tempered by a renewed focus on the quality of the curriculum, of the learning experiences of students and on the collaboration between providers of lifelong learning. It is clear that only a single framework of modular-based qualifications can facilitate the progress of adult students, many of whom will need to develop basic skills before advancing.

In recent years, colleges have improved greatly their initial guidance, monitoring and teaching of students, as is shown in the annual report of the Chief Inspector, *Quality and Standards in Further Education* (FEFC, 1996). However, the continuing drop-out rate shows that further improvements in student advice and support are necessary. This is to say that there is still too much variability in the standards of teaching and tutoring, both between colleges and sometimes within the same college. It seems to us that further improvement will have to take as its starting point the needs of the individual student. As our interviews show, these vary enormously. For example, although some younger students enjoy the freedom from school restrictions and take advantage of the fresh start in college, others would welcome closer monitoring and opportunities for social activity and mixing that is so often absent in FE.

At the level of policy, there must also be recognition of the achievement involved in the expansion of the last 10 years. Much has been made of the role of mass HE (for example, by Scott 1996), but it is in FE that there has been the real growth and it is in the colleges that the idea of a 'Learning Society' has been developed in practice to create the reality of 'lifelong learning'. It is this experience that has to be adequately financed and built upon.

References

Ainley, B. (1998), *Black Journalists, White Media*. Stoke on Trent: Trentham Press.

Ainley, P. (1999), *Learning Policy, Towards the Certified Society?* Basingstoke: Macmillan.

Ainley, P. (1997), 'Introduction', *Special Issue on 'the Student Experience' of Youth and Policy, 56*, 4–13.

Ainley, P. and Bailey, B. (1997), *The Business of Learning, Staff and Student Experiences of Further Education in the 1990s*. London: Cassell.

Ainley, P. and Green, A. (1996), 'Education Without Employment: Not Meeting the National Education and Training Targets', *Journal of Vocational Education and Training, 48(2)*, 109–126.

Bailey, B. (1997), 'The Historical Perspective, Myths and Realities behind Tripartite Divisions in FE'. In G. Stanton and W. Richardson (eds), *Qualifications for the Future: A Study of Tripartite and other Divisions in Post-16 Education and Training*. London: Further Education Development Agency.

FEFC (1996), *Quality and Standards in FE in England 1996/97*. Chief Inspector's Annual Report. Coventry: Further Education Funding Council.

Flint, C. (1999), in G. Stanton (ed.), *Speaking Up for Further Education*. London: Lewisham College and Greenwich University Press.

Frampton, D. (1995), *Towards a Nation of Shopkeepers; the Devocationalisation of the FE Curriculum*, Praxis Paper No. 2. London: Lewisham College.

HMSO (1998), *Report of the Parliamentary Select Committee on Education*.

Martinez, P. (1997), *Improving Student Retention: A Guide to Successful Strategies.* Blagdon: Further Education Development Agency.

Rikowski, G. (1999), 'Nietzsche, Marx and Mastery, The Learning Unto Death'. In P. Ainley. and H. Rainbird (eds), *Apprenticeship, Towards a New Paradigm of Learning.* London: Kogan Page.

Scott, P. (1996), *The Meanings of Mass Higher Education.* Buckingham: Open University Press, in association with the Society for Research into Higher Education.

Smithers, A. and Robinson, P. (1995), *Trends in Higher Education.* London: The Council for Industry and Higher Education.

Stanton, G. and Richardson, W. (eds) (1997), *Qualifications for the Future: A Study of Tripartite and other Divisions in Post-16 Education and Training.* London: Further Education Development Agency.

8 Reconstructing Qualifications for Further Education: Towards a System for the Twenty-first Century

Michael Young

Introduction

This book argues that despite significantly increasing student numbers both among 16–19 year olds and those over 21, the further education (FE) sector is in state of crisis. Many colleges are in acute financial difficulties and have been forced to lay off staff, and there are frequent references in the educational press to low morale amongst the staff who remain. More and more demands are being made on the sector and, although there are signs that for the first time we have a government that recognises the importance of the sector within its overall educational policy, there are few signs of any attempt to define its strategic role. A key factor determining how colleges respond to the new demands is the qualification system for post-compulsory education and training. Together with funding, qualifications are the major determinant of the curriculum that colleges can offer. Furthermore, since the mid 1980s, governments in the UK have increasingly seen the qualification system as a means of regulating the activities of the sector and the education system more generally (Raffe *et al.*, 1998). During this period, the qualification system itself has been the subject of continuing review, from the de Ville's Review of Vocational Qualifications (MSC/NEDC, 1986) to Dearing's Review of qualifications for 16–19 year olds (Dearing, 1996). This process continued with the New Labour Government's consultation based on the document *Qualifying for Success* (DfEE, 1997), which led to the proposals announced in April 1998 (DfEE, 1998).

This chapter will make two arguments about these latest proposals, and indeed the terms in which much of the debate about qualifications has been set. The first is that, in maintaining clear divisions between academic and vocational qualifications and in failing to provide incentives to encourage students to opt for the broader programmes of study, the proposals are inadequate in the face of the overall demands being made on institutions providing post-compulsory education and training in all industrial countries. Second, the proposals and the review and consultation process that proceeded them missed an opportunity to consider the kind of system that might be needed in the future. One consequence is that the proposals do little to support the broader government policies of overcoming social exclusion and promoting lifelong learning.

In seeking the basis for a more strategic approach to the reform of the qualification system, the chapter begins by locating the government's recent proposals in relation to the broader educational policy developments of the last decade and to changes in the economy and labour markets. It argues that although the government's proposals, if implemented, will offer some greater flexibility to the FE sector, they remain trapped in an out-of-date view of the role of qualifications, which takes little account of the skill and knowledge needs likely in the next century and their impact on colleges. The chapter goes on to draw on evidence of international trends to develop a conceptual framework for analysing current changes in qualification systems. A final section considers the implications of the analysis for the FE sector in England and Wales and suggests what might be involved in developing a qualification system more appropriate to the likely demands of the twenty-first century.

Qualification reform: the policy context

Qualification systems are key instruments of national policy and have traditionally been the major mechanism for selecting school and college students for employment and HE. In countries such as England and Wales, in which central government has traditionally had a largely 'hands off' role in relation to the FE sector, qualifications have come to play a unique regulatory and distributive role. They are involved not only in the maintenance of educational standards, but also in the distribution of educational opportunities. Furthermore, as successive governments have recognised, the qualification system gives them a powerful and legitimate means of influencing what the FE sector offers at a time when other policies, such as incorporation, allow colleges the freedom to 'go their own way'.

In the 1980s the government had a largely reactive approach to the reform of qualifications. It was seen primarily as a means of responding to increases in post-16 participation and new qualifications were developed for the new students staying on in colleges and schools. The New Labour Government, however, has developed a more proactive agenda around the twin themes of overcoming social exclusion and the promotion of lifelong learning (DfEE, 1998). However, despite this new policy agenda and the many qualification reforms of the last decade, the basic structure of the qualification system has changed little. As will be argued later in the chapter, the reluctance of the government to recognise that new educational policies such as lifelong learning may need a new qualification system, has been a significant barrier to the implementation of the new policies.

Despite the substantial expansion of the number of people gaining qualifications, the basic system in England and Wales is little different from that which was laid down towards the end of the nineteenth century (Young, 1993). At that time, the division of labour consisted of a relatively small managerial and professional elite, a range of distinct technical and craft occupations and a mass of semi-skilled and unskilled jobs for which no qualifications were needed. This occupational structure was reflected in the emerging tripartite system of qualifications, based on the divisions between academic, broad vocational and occupationally specific vocational qualifications, which remains with us today. Even when the most recent government proposals have been implemented, a version of this model will remain in place. It will consist of largely unchanged academic qualifications ('A' Levels), the still relatively new General National Vocational Qualifications (GNVQs), and an uneven variety of work-based vocational qualifications (mostly NVQs linked to apprenticeships and traineeships). This tripartite structure is beginning to be used by the

Qualifications and Curriculum Authority as a basis for a National Qualifications Framework, although the demand for what are often called 'other'
or 'traditional' vocational qualifications which do not fit into the framework continues and is, in some cases, growing (Ward, 1998). There is,
however, increasing evidence that the division of labour in the UK, as in
other industrialised countries, is changing in ways not reflected in the
dominant tripartite structure. For example, jobs are changing faster than
before and employees at all levels need lifelong learning capacities and
attitudes – capacities such as 'future visioning', risk taking, and 'being
responsible for one's own work' are no longer only the requirements of
managers. Occupational sectors are less insulated from each other, as
production and services demand similar combinations of specific and
generic capabilities. More jobs are becoming knowledge-intensive rather
than just skill-based and need new combinations of theoretical knowledge and practical skill that cross the tripartite divisions. New types of
job, such as those in the security services, which demand little skill, are
expanding and the traditional 'middle level' technical jobs are not being
replaced. Those in these jobs will need to have the skills and attitudes
to treat them as 'stepping stones' to careers rather than 'dead ends'. The
interpersonal skill element of all jobs is becoming an important recruitment criterion for many jobs and is no longer associated with particular
kinds of personal services.

Each of these trends point to demands which cut across the academic/
vocational divisions on which the existing qualification system is based.
The reforms of the last decade have been shaped little by such scenarios
and their predictions of the likely future learning demands and much
by incremental attempts to improve the existing system in the context
of short-term political agendas. Labour Party policy documents that
appeared before the General Election (Labour Party, 1996) recognised
that the qualifications system was in need of major reform and that
central to any reform would be the position of 'A' Levels. However,
in government, Labour's policies have echoed the fears of previous
governments that any significant change in 'A' Levels would be an
electoral disaster as the notorious 'voters of middle England' would

switch their votes to whichever party promises to leave them as they are.

Recent government proposals

Although much of the rhetoric around recent qualification reform has been in terms of economic competitiveness, the major pressure for reform has undoubtedly been demographic. In the 1980s there was something akin to a 'moral panic' about what would happen to the many 16-year-old school leavers with few, if any, qualifications, as the youth labour market was disappearing. Amongst the responses by the government were a series of attempts to provide work-based training for all school leavers (YTS, Youth Training and Youth Credits) (Unwin, 1997) and some kind of pre-vocational full-time study for those staying on at school or college (Young and Spours, 1998). Qualification reform in England and Wales since the mid 1980s can be seen as a succession of attempts to respond to these new demands while at the same time maintaining the traditional highly selective 'A' Level route for entering university at 18 plus. Inevitably this has led to contradictions and inconsistencies as some reforms, such as the modularisation of 'A' Levels, seek to widen opportunities, whereas others, such as increases in the proportion of final examinations that can count towards final assessment, seek to close them down (Hodgson and Spours, 1997).

Debates about how qualifications policy should develop have been well summarised by Hodgson and Spours (1997) in terms of three perspectives on whether academic and vocational qualifications should be brought together in a single unified system. They distinguish between unifiers, who argue for a unified system to overcome academic/vocational divisions (Finegold *et al.*, 1990); frameworkers, who accept the need to maintain the distinctiveness of the three tracks, but argue that bridges must be built between them (Dearing, 1996); and trackers, those on the political Right who argue that separate tracked qualifications are needed to take account of the different types of ability within the population (Pilkington, 1991).

The present government's proposals can be seen as a weak version of a framework approach to qualification reform. Although the broad aim of their policy 'to create opportunities for broader studies and for mixing academic and vocational learning' (DfEE, 1997) can be seen as unifying, their specific proposals appear more concerned with preserving the tracks. Few incentives are offered for students to follow programmes that involve links between the tracks. Steps that might promote links – such as an overarching certificate and the unitisation of all qualifications within a national credit framework – have been postponed at least until the next Parliament. Other elements of government policy, such as limiting opportunities for students to retake modules restricting the normal duration of an advanced level course to two years, suggest that the dominant emphasis remains firmly on maintaining the existing selective role of 'A' Levels (DfEE, 1998).

Notwithstanding the government's extremely cautious approach to qualification reform, there are grounds for supposing that a more coherent approach to qualifications may be emerging (Raffe *et al.*, 1998). The elements of such a system already in place are:

- a single regulatory body (the Qualifications and Curriculum Authority);
- a single government department responsible for all education and training (the Department for Education and Employment);
- the Unitary Awarding Bodies (EDEXCEL, AQA and OCA); and
- moves towards common funding and a National Qualifications Framework to include all qualifications.

Whether this new administrative structure will be used to introduce a qualification system that is genuinely responsive to the demands of the next century remains uncertain as a result of recent policy statements. It is unclear whether the government sees the present reforms as the first step in an ongoing reform process over several Parliaments or as an end point. Furthermore, there is little sign, as yet, of the government recognising that the role of qualifications will need to be reconceptualised if the changes in the organisation and distribution of work referred to earlier are to be taken into account. What might be involved in such a reconceptualisation is addressed in the next section through an analysis of recent international trends in qualification reform.

The international context

Although a focus on the qualification system as a major lever of educational reform has been more explicit in the UK, New Zealand and Australia than in most other industrialised counties, the need to reform qualifications is beginning to be recognised in most EU countries and elsewhere. A recent eight-country study (Lasonen, 1996; Lasonen and Young, 1998) compared reform strategies across Europe. It highlighted the extent to which the division between academic and vocational qualifications and the low esteem of vocational education are problems across Europe, although the strategies adopted to overcome the lack of parity of esteem vary widely. Four such strategies were identified in the study. First, those countries with strong work-based systems of vocational education, such as Germany, are seeking to raise the status of vocational education through internal improvements of their programmes of vocational education and specifically by strengthening the component of vocational knowledge not tied to specific occupations. Second, those countries with strong school-based systems of vocational education, such as Norway and Finland, are encouraging mutual enrichment between academic and vocational programmes. Third, those countries with divided systems and where the vocational routes are not strong, as is the case with England and France, are trying to create linkages between academic and vocational qualifications as a way of raising the prestige of the latter. Only in those countries with a strong egalitarian tradition (in the study this refers to Sweden and Scotland) are there attempts to develop unified systems that do away with tracks altogether. A number of general conclusions can be drawn from this study that are of particular relevance to the situation facing the FE sector in England and Wales. First, all the eight countries in the study are facing problems about how to include the lowest achieving 10 or 20 per cent of each cohort. Second, although work-based vocational qualification routes may in some cases offer progression to low achievers, an overall 'academic drift' is tending to isolate and weaken the status of such routes. Third, the extent to which countries use qualifications to influence educational policy varies. Those with weaker traditions of state involvement in education see qualifications as mechanisms of control and the more state-driven systems are using them to introduce greater institutional flexibility while still retaining some central control. Finally, despite their very different histories, policy makers in all countries are facing increasingly common problems. The most important of these are: the increasing proportion of the population becoming qualified and the potential for this to lead to the devaluing of qualifications in general; the increasing financial burden on the state of expanding numbers seeking qualifications; the greater diversity of learning needs among those continuing to study; the shortening of the useful life of occupationally specific skills; the persistent and increasing vulnerability of an excluded section of the population who fail to obtain any qualifications; and the continued search for curriculum principles for post-compulsory general education.

Together, these trends put contradictory pressures on governments seeking to reform qualifications. They call for more diversified systems less dominated by the traditional model of external examinations, but there are also pressures to maintain the standards with which traditional approaches are associated. This tension between the traditional selective role of qualifications and a more future-oriented role geared to promoting higher levels of participation is exemplified in a number of ways. So, qualification systems are increasingly expected to:

- offer new progression pathways through expanded electronic networks;
- combine the flexibility of modular systems with the opportunities for coherent study associated with tightly structured programmes;
- encourage progression to the highest levels of learning as well as valuing learning gains from any starting point;
- be accessible at every stage of a person's life and respond to the distinctive demands of the period up to early adulthood;

- recognise that specific skills are learned in contexts but that increasingly learners need skills to transcend contexts; and
- recognise that supporting learning in the workplace needs to be both a skill enhancement strategy and a basis for overcoming social exclusion.

Social inclusion and lifelong learning: implications for qualification reform

One of the main functions of qualification systems in the past has been to select people for higher education (HE) and jobs. The necessity of such a focus on selection is justified in terms of deeply held beliefs about the distribution of abilities in the population as a whole and the need to find 'the best people for the most important and difficult jobs'. For example, despite a tenfold increase in the proportion of each cohort obtaining two or more 'A' Levels, the view has persisted from Crowther (Ministry of Education, 1959) to Dearing (1996) that there is a finite limit to the proportion of the population capable of reaching 'A' Level standards. A second dominant emphasis of qualification systems in the past has been that they have been largely geared to the pre-employment phase of people's lives. Little attention has been given to whether adults are encouraged to continue with their learning or return to study.

It follows that if promoting lifelong learning and including as large a proportion of the population as possible in courses leading to qualifications are to be at the centre of educational policy, the whole structure and purpose of qualifications as we know them need to be rethought; even if their primary function remains selection, this can no longer, as in the past, preclude other no less important functions. Indeed, the new emphasis on promoting lifelong learning raises the question as to whether it is possible for a single qualification system to be responsive to the learning needs of the whole population and geared to both preparatory and lifelong learning. Instead of having selection as its major function, an inclusive qualification system designed to promote lifelong learning would need to give priority to increasing participation and accrediting a wide a range of types of learning taking place in a wide variety of locations. Furthermore, given that in the past standards have been maintained by selection (i.e. using assessment methods based on norm referencing), new strategies for maintaining and raising standards would be needed. Similarly, a qualification system that promotes lifelong learning will need to be accessible to people of all ages regardless of whether they are in full-time study. It will also need explicitly to stimulate ongoing learning rather than just provide evidence of adequate course completion. These requirements of a future qualification system stand in stark contrast to the recent reform proposals in England that were referred to earlier in the chapter which have focused largely on the 16–19 age group. It has been assumed that the learning needs of adults, who vary from those who are graduates to those who achieved no qualifications during their years of compulsory schooling, can be satisfied by qualifications designed for 16–19 year olds who are still in school or at college.

The argument here is not to replace a preparatory with a lifelong approach to qualifications. This would only benefit the privileged groups who already gain most advantages from the compulsory school system. What is needed is a life-cycle approach that incorporates the schooling and lifelong learning phases of people's lives. If such a system is not to be even more selective than the present one, ways will need to be found of using the experience of adults as a bridge to the systematic knowledge that they had been denied during their schooling. This is a task that is in part addressed through access courses, although it is less emphasised in mainstream approaches to adult education which have traditionally treated the accreditation of experience as an end in itself.

Giving priority to social inclusion in the reform of qualifications has a number of implications. The first, which was given much emphasis, at least in its rhetoric, by the last government in the UK, is the importance of recognising that different individuals have different learning needs and may respond to learning opportunities in different ways and at different times in their lives. Inclusion in this sense goes beyond the idea that equality involves treating everyone in the same way. It recognises that those who fail at school may succeed if alternative routes to becoming qualified are available. A second implication is that learning differences often reflect inequalities in the resources people have in approaching learning. Inclusion in this sense stresses that ladders of progression expressed formally in the qualification framework (as is the case of the NVQ levels) are necessary but not adequate for guaranteeing progression opportunities. Progression from one qualification level to another needs to be supported by teaching and by the content of learning at each level. A third and, until now, most neglected implication of an inclusive approach to qualifications is the extent to which a wide range of highly diverse learner needs can be included (or held together) in a single system. An inclusive qualification system would have to ensure that different levels and sites of learning as well as learning achieved at different stages of a person's life-cycle did not form a hierarchy in which only some learning gains are valued. Promoting inclusion in this sense would involve a significant break with current assumptions. If learners aiming for the lowest level of qualification are to feel a sense of being part of the system, they need to feel that they could, at least in principle, reach any level. If all learners are to be included, achieving low-level qualifications cannot be treated as a form of failure despite the fact that it may represent real learning and clear progression for some students. If low-level qualifications are to have a positive value, they must be linked to real outcomes and benefits and not just a placc in a hicrarchy of lcvcls which dcfincs thcm as inferior.

Towards an analytical framework

This section draws on the previous account of international trends and proposes a framework for analysing changes in qualification systems and their implications for overcoming exclusion and promoting lifelong learning. It builds on a previous analysis of systems of post-compulsory education (Raffe *et al.*, 1998) and distinguishes three dimensions or trends on which qualification systems can vary. These are:

- the extent to which a system is based on academic/vocational divisions;
- the degree of flexibility of the system; and

- the extent to which the system is based on exclusion or inclusion of some learners.

The framework has a number of purposes. It can be used to pose research questions concerning changes in the structure and functions of qualifications and the tensions this may give rise to. For example, one tension is that the traditional selective role of qualifications is likely to be in conflict with efforts to design qualifications to increase participation. It can also provide criteria for evaluating the implications of different national reform strategies – for example the unintended consequences of introducing a qualification system defined in terms of learning outcomes (Smithers, 1997).

As is the case for all educational policies, qualification reforms are shaped by the wider policy context of which they are a part (e.g. industrial and labour market policies), and by political and by other factors which may influence how they are implemented. Significant examples of such factors discussed in other chapters of this book are funding and policies on the local organisation of institutions (for example, the separation of school and college provision of post-compulsory education). The trends discussed here are not panaceas for a fairer or more efficient system. I would, however, argue, not only that there is evidence of international shifts towards more unified, inclusive and flexible systems, but that these shifts are progressive in the sense that they represent a range of attempts to modernise outdated features of qualification systems which have their roots in the nineteenth century. On the other hand, changes on all of the dimensions involve problems. They can be in conflict with each other and lead to new divisions and forms of fragmentation. They are presented here as a perspective for interpreting the narrower debates that focus on the merits and weaknesses of particular qualifications or forms of assessment and of different approaches to the design of syllabuses. The remainder of this section discusses each of these policy trends separately.

From divided to unified systems

The unification of academic and vocational qualifications has been the major axis of recent debates about qualifications in the UK, especially in England. A recent study contrasted unifying strategies in England, Scotland and Wales (Young *et al.*, 1997). It argued that the higher profile of the debate about unification in England may reflect the more powerful role that social class continues to play in distributing educational opportunities and the close connection between academic/vocational divisions in education and social class divisions in society as a whole. However, the focus of unification debates has been quite narrow, concentrating largely on the division between 'A' Levels and vocational qualifications as they affect 16–19 year olds. Furthermore, the debates have tended to polarise unified and divided systems and give less attention to possible intermediate types in which academic and vocational qualifications are 'linked', or to the process of unification itself. Nevertheless, there is evidence from international developments of an overall trend away from tracked to more unified systems (Raffe *et al.*, 1998).

Introducing the issue of social inclusion highlights the narrowness of the English debates about unification and points to the need to find a variety of ways of enabling learners to combine academic and vocational learning throughout their lives. It makes explicit that there is unlikely to be one model of a unified system and that an appropriate balance between different types of learning and how they should be related will vary for different people and at different periods of their lives.

Arguments for unifying qualifications in England, because they have concentrated on 16–19 year olds have focused on a core curriculum for all students (Finegold *et al.*, 1990; Spours and Young, 1995). However, the concept of a core curriculum requirement could become exclusive if applied to adults with limited time and diverse experiences. One possibility would be to extend the idea of a core requirement to everyone having a lifetime entitlement to both general (academic) and applied (vocational) education. In the Anglo-Scottish research project referred to above, a distinction was made between grouped and open types of unified system (Raffe *et al.*, 1998); the former gives priority to coherence and continuity of learning, whereas the latter emphasises flexibility. The problem with open types of unified systems (such as that to be introduced in Scotland from 1999), is that although they are, in principle, more inclusive of all learners, considerable discretion is left to individual institutions, thus creating the possibility of new divisions.

From closed to open systems

Openness or flexibility as a criterion for modernising qualification systems has become of increasing importance with the emphasis placed on social inclusion. Three sub-dimensions of the flexibility system can be distinguished. The first is syllabus design and is expressed in the shift from linear to modular syllabuses; the second refers to the shift from course-based to credit-based qualifications; and the third is the shift from qualifications defined in terms of inputs to those defined in terms of outcomes. Modularisation, the move to credit-based qualifications and the definition of qualifications in terms of outcomes are frequently, but not always, found together. Whether they are or not is likely to depend on whether or not the change is local or national in origin (Young, 1998). Here the three sub-dimensions are discussed separately.

From linear to modular syllabuses

Linear syllabuses define a single course of study from beginning a course to its final assessment. They are based on single entry and exit points for all students. Traditional English 'A' Levels and university degrees are linear and represent the paradigm form of syllabus in a qualification system geared to selection. Linear syllabuses are inflexible in the sense that all students who begin a course have to complete the same programme; once they have begun a course, they have no choices. With all students completing an identical programme at the same time, year-by-year comparisons are relatively easy and provide clear evidence of whether standards are being maintained. The other main strength of linear syllabuses is that they represent internally coherent learning programmes, which can be refined and updated by subject specialists over time. Modular syllabuses, in contrast, are made up of separate blocks of study, separately assessed. They allow multiple entry and exit points, opportunities for student choice at intervals throughout the course and the possibility of different routes and combinations of study. Responsibility for the coherence of learning programmes is delegated to students supported by teachers. By maximising opportunities of assessment having a formative role (at the end of each module), modular syllabuses allow more learners to remain 'included' and succeed. Evidence from modular systems on year-by-year comparisons, however, is less straightforward. It is not surprising, therefore that they are sometimes criticised for allowing standards to fall and leading to incoherent learning programmes as students 'pick and mix' modules.

If modular syllabuses are not to lead to the fragmentation of learning and the lowering of standards, they need to be accompanied by appropriate quality assurance strategies and clear systems of guidance on different module combinations. The move away from linear syllabuses places new responsibilities on colleges; at the same time, it can offer teachers opportunities for curriculum innovation and students a chance to shape the course of their own learning. As modularisation can be seen as a form of 'democratisation of educational decision making', teachers, as well as other users of qualifications, have to take more responsibility for maintaining and raising standards. If this shift of responsibility is to be effective, it will rely on groups of specialist lecturers and teachers linked to groups of users from the universities and employer organisations developing and sustaining their own standards, backed by guidelines from government and national agencies.

From course-based to credit-based qualifications

Whereas the linear/modular distinction refers to the organisation of teaching learning and assessment, that between course- and credit-based qualifications refers to the organisation of the qualifications themselves. Whereas course-based qualifications are awarded on the results of assessment at the end of a course, those based on credit are accumulated over time. Course-based qualifications were established when the pattern of occupations and university degrees changed only slowly and when most people expected to do the same job throughout their lives. As people change jobs and university or college more frequently, qualifications become increasingly important as bridges between jobs and courses. Credit-based qualifications can take account of these changes as well as the need to combine college- and work-based learning in ways that are not possible with traditional course-based qualifications. However as with modularisation, credit-based qualifications put far greater responsibility on the learner, and therefore on the support that is available from colleges and employers. Furthermore, qualifications which allow students to accumulate credits from a number of different providers and workplaces cannot fulfil the identity-supporting functions served by qualifications based on courses of study. Credit-based qualifications are potentially more accessible than qualifications that depend on completing a course in a single institution. However, they tend to individualise learning and neglect the extent to which any learning depends on participation in a 'communities of practice'. It follows that unless ways are found of linking the accumulation of credit to strategies for supporting learner participation, credit-based qualifications will not tackle the problems of the exclusion or fulfil their claims to greater accessibility and flexibility. It may be that in a credit-based system, the community-sustaining function of courses of study in particular institutions can be taken over, at least in part, by the creation of 'virtual communities' based on electronic networks.

From input-based systems to outcome-based systems
Until recently, virtually all qualifications, whether academic or vocational, were defined in terms of inputs to learners such as syllabuses, timetables and numbers of taught hours or teacher contact time. Such an emphasis on input gave certain guarantees to learners. However, it was necessarily exclusive both in terms of the forms of learning assumed to be necessary to gain qualifications and the range of people that could gain access to them. Outcomes-based models, the 'invention of the 1980s', were introduced as a major attempt to overcome this form of exclusion (Jessup,

1991), and are perhaps the most controversial of all the recent shifts in approaches to qualification design.

In theory, outcomes-based qualifications should be the basis for a more inclusive system that promotes lifelong learning. Learning aims are more transparent to learners and learning is recognised wherever it takes place and can be assessed anywhere and at any time. In practice outcomes-based approaches to qualifications have become a 'procrustean bed'. This is partly because of the association of outcomes with narrow definitions of vocational competence and their tendency to be defined in ways which exclude more conceptual forms of learning. It is also because outcomes models, such as the one on which NVQs are based, have assumed that the precise specification of outcomes can guarantee the quality of a qualification. In practice, precise specification is impossible and leads to the trivialising of learning and the devaluing of qualifications (Wolf, 1993). Outcomes-based qualifications have also been seen as a way of reducing the role of professional judgement, on the grounds that this is more likely to be based on bias and self-interest than real expertise. However, in the process of reducing the role of professional judgement, the expertise of the teacher can also be lost. If the introduction of an outcomes-based system of qualifications is to make the system of education and training more open and flexible, it has to be based on a recognition that defining outcomes can only be a guide to the design of learning programmes. On their own, outcomes cannot guarantee quality. If a national qualifications framework is defined in terms of outcomes, it will have to be complemented by the specification of possible inputs in terms of syllabuses or specific learning experiences and a stress on the importance of the professional judgement and expertise of the teacher in the development of pedagogic and assessment strategies, backed by forms of peer and user accountability.

From exclusive to inclusive systems

The concept of social inclusion has tended to refer to disadvantaged groups, such as those with disabilities or the long-term unemployed. However, if the concept is to be applied to qualifications, more general criteria, which include specific disadvantages, are needed. Here three such criteria are considered: age, site of learning and level of qualification. Age as a criterion refers to the need for inclusive qualification systems to be accessible to people at all stages of the life-cycle. Site of learning refers to the need to ensure that a qualification system recognises learning wherever it takes place and all forms that can be publicly identifiable. Level focuses on the need for an inclusive system to recognise evidence of learning gain, however small, and whatever its starting point. These three sub-dimensions of inclusion are now considered separately.

From age specific to lifelong approaches

One difference between the debates about qualifications in England and those in Scotland and Wales has been the extent to which English policies on post-16 qualifications have concentrated on 16–19 year olds. This is most in evidence when the recent Green Paper from the DfEE (1998) is contrasted with the parallel publication from the Welsh Office (WO, 1998). Similarly, the Higher Still proposals for Scotland, unlike the Dearing Review and the recommendations following it, are not restricted to the 16–19 age group. Historically, the purpose of the main post-compulsory qualifications ('A' Levels in England and Wales) has been age specific – it has been to select a proportion of those staying on at school (or college) for entry to university. This has meant not only that adults returning to study at college have had to take qualifications designed for 16 year olds still at school, but that qualifications for 16–19 year olds are treated as the benchmark for assessing all learners. A further consequence of the dominance in post-compulsory education of qualifications designed for 16–19 year olds preparing for university is that it is assumed that most students, like the majority of those in school sixth forms, will achieve the qualification in two years. Little account is taken of the many students who might achieve the same qualification over a much longer period of their life. Recent research (Fuller, 1998) on the uptake of qualifications by adults since 1970 provides interesting evidence in support of this argument. The biggest uptake of qualifications by adults is through part-time degrees, which offer the flexibility of timing not offered by post-compulsory programmes in school or college. In this and other ways, existing post-compulsory qualifications tend to exclude adults.

Qualification systems throughout the world tend to assume that qualifying is a preparatory not a lifelong process. The message of the formal system tends to be that those who are educational failures in the preparatory stage of life are, except in exceptional cases, unlikely to benefit from education later in life. Furthermore, unlike age-specific qualifications which tend to be closely linked to school-based courses, a lifelong approach to qualifications is not just a problem for those in education. If qualifying is to be a lifelong process, it will depend on changes in attitude to qualifying in the society as a whole. It will need to be based on very different relationships between people, work and the education system from those associated with a system that is largely preparatory. In a lifelong system the process of qualifying would not be something external to people's working, home and leisure lives, but would be a part of how they live as adults, citizens, employees or employers and parents. It maybe that there are lessons from the success of the University of the Third Age (U3A) about how learning can be both systematic and formal without being tied either to employment or to the prospects of higher level study. Until now, however, the U3A has consciously rejected the idea that its programmes should be linked to qualifications.

From formal learning contexts to all potential learning contexts
Another dimension of an inclusive system of qualifications is that it should recognise learning even if it does not take place in or under the guidance of a school, college or university. The growth of interest in work-based learning and the importance of all learners gaining work experience (Griffiths and Guile, 1999) are good examples of the growing recognition of the importance of informal learning contexts. This recognition has, however, not been paralleled by a similar shift in the structure and assumptions of qualifications. Such developments point to two aspects of inclusion. First, they are about raising the level of qualifications of people who have acquired skills and knowledge through their experience at work but may have been denied access to any formal qualification.

Second, they are about using people's informal learning, both at work and in other non-formal educational contexts, as a bridge to enable them to participate in and benefit from learning in formal educational contexts. Inclusion in this sense involves extending the concept of a qualification to recognise learning that does not fit traditional assessment criteria or methods but can be the basis of evidence for a person becoming qualified.

From qualification systems defined in terms of level of destination to systems based on measurement of learning gain

In many ways using the criterion of learning gain as well as that of destination in designing a qualification system is the most radical step in making a system more inclusive. Traditionally qualification systems have been hierarchical in three related senses which a qualification system for the future must overcome. First, they have, to a large extent, reflected the pyramid-like shape of the occupational structure, with the highest levels of qualification setting the standards for the rest. Second, the value and status of a qualification tends to be inversely related to its distance from those at the top; thus some (often vocational) qualifications are seen as inferior and only appropriate for those who have failed to be accepted to study for academic qualifications. Third, there are many areas of skill and knowledge which might be important for some socially useful activity or might be relevant to someone with particular learning difficulties but which are not thought deserving of a qualification at all. Two consequences of these tendencies follow. First, achievement of lower level qualifications, even if it involves considerable effort on the part of the learner, is devalued. Second, from the point of view of society as a whole the qualification system provides few incentives to learn for those who experience greatest learning difficulties. No qualification system can avoid hierarchy completely and still relate to the wider society. However, society is changing and maximising the potential of even the slowest learners is an increasing priority. It follows that qualification systems of the future will need to recognise learning gain from point of origin as well as in terms of destination reached. This is partly a question of design

– the availability and recognition of short intermediate steps between levels. It is also a question of incentives, both for individuals and for colleges to encourage learning gain wherever it originates. This issue incentive and its link to the way colleges are funded are discussed in detail in Chapter Two.

Conclusion

The history of qualifications has been, as was suggested earlier in this chapter, a history of the broadening of the process of selection. One way of expressing the longer-term changes is that systems in which few are qualified and which differentiates the qualified from the unqualified are changing into systems in which the vast majority are qualified and people are differentiated according to their level and type of qualification. As systems of HE expand and as the range of occupations that recruit on the basis of higher level qualifications has grown, this process of selection has shifted its location institutionally and in the life-cycle. Selection will always remain an exclusive, not an inclusive process. Furthermore, as more higher level jobs depend on high-level initial qualifications and are less open to those who start employment without them, those who reach early adulthood with only low-level qualifications (or none) will find progression during adulthood even harder than before. If a system of qualifications is to become more inclusive, it will need to complement its selective role in identifying talent and provide a variety of progression ladders for those in jobs that require few skills and little knowledge. An inclusive system would also have to develop new criteria and motivations for qualifying beyond those of occupational preparation and progression to HE. Selecting people both for higher paid and high-status jobs as well as for higher level study will remain a feature of any system of qualifications. Whether this tendency dominates the qualification system as a whole to the neglect of its other possible functions will depend in part on the design of the qualification system – the main theme of this chapter. However, it will also depend on the industrial and labour market strategies and government policies on expanding HE. If the range of knowledge-intensive jobs that demand higher level qualifications continues to expand, qualifications can become ladders of opportunity. If the proportion of such jobs remains static, even the most innovatively designed qualification system can only lead to credential inflation. In other words, if qualification systems are to promote social inclusion, other reforms will be needed that involve the restructuring of work in both production and service sectors. This will require new kinds of partnerships between the various stakeholders – the users of qualifications (employers and HE), the designers and regulators of qualifications (examining and regulatory bodies), the professional educational associations (those who deliver qualifications) and those seeking qualifications (students, employees and others).

Qualification reform and the role of further education colleges

The previous section discussed the development of a more unified, flexible and inclusive system of qualifications. There are, however, major implications for colleges if such a system is to realise its aims. All of the changes discussed involve the breaking up of a previously rigid qualification system. The weakness of the old system was that it was only designed for a relatively small, if expanding, section of the population to become qualified. It was based on sharp divisions between different types of qualifications and was geared largely to preparatory education and training. Economic changes and the new demands of learners have called all of these features into question. The strength of the old system was that the qualifications themselves, both academic and to a lesser extent vocational, had public credibility and provided their own forms of coherence; this was achieved provided that the student and teacher followed the course and syllabus that were laid down by the examination board. The kind of qualification system that has been suggested in this chapter has quite different implications for students, teachers and colleges. Much greater responsibility is placed on student and teachers, and therefore the colleges, for ensuring that student learning programmes are coherent and that barriers to progression are removed. Flexible types of unified systems (Raffe *et al.*, 1998) are not based on prescription, they are designed to enable learning. It will be colleges that will be responsible for ensuring that the guidance systems, the resource bases, the on-line access, the curriculum knowledge and the knowledge of progression pathways (both to employment and HE) are available to learners when they need them. Colleges will not necessarily have all these areas of expertise among their own staff. This means that they will need to develop new links with examining boards, employers, HE and other colleges with the consequent transformation of the role of many of the lecturing staff (see Chapter Nine). Government policy is undoubtedly a long way from such a reality of networked institutions in partnership with each other. It seems increasingly likely that colleges will have to lead or even pre-empt government policy if there are to be significant changes along the lines suggested in this chapter.

If social inclusion and lifelong learning are to become realities, new responsibilities will fall on three groups who are most closely linked to learners and potential learners – employers, lecturers in colleges and those working in community organisations. They, more than anyone, have the opportunity to understand the motivations and needs of those excluded from gaining qualifications in the past. It follows that an inclusive qualification system cannot be developed by government agencies, examination boards and consultants alone, as has been the case, albeit in very different ways and over very different time periods, with 'A' Levels, GNVQs and NVQs. For different reasons, these qualifications did not and could not take account of those traditionally excluded from qualifying. Therefore, we have qualifications that incorporate the needs of only a limited range of potential learners and as a result, practitioners have developed various forms of 'local' or 'quasi' qualifications such as access courses and the Awards Scheme Development and Accreditation Scheme (ASDAN) Awards. These developments have real strengths. Theoretically they come closest to recognising that learning is always a 'situated process' which takes place in particular contexts (Young and Lucas, 1999; Guile and Young, 1998). Practically they draw, more than the national qualifications, at least since the demise of Mode 3 GCEs, on teacher expertise and professional judgement. Therefore, they are able to relate more to the particular circumstances of individual learners (Young, Hayton and Leney, 1997). However, such developments remain 'local' or partial and cannot be the basis for a national system. A more inclusive qualification system would need to incorporate the experience of these developments and the way they draw on the professional knowledge of teachers and lecturers. At the same time, it would require a new approach to qualifications on the part of the professionals themselves. They would need to be more inclusive in their approach to the needs of potential learners and to be willing to recognise the importance of the expertise and experience of those not formally associated with education or training.

While teachers will need to become more inclusive towards learning that does not take place in schools or colleges, new demands will be made on those who work with learners in the community and in voluntary organisations to develop their expertise in qualifications and assessment. These are difficult tasks. They will depend upon new approaches to the funding and accountability of colleges that create incentives for them to develop outreach activities. Furthermore, new identities giving new meaning to the process of qualifying will need to be forged.

Towards a qualification system for the twenty-first century?

Present government proposals for reforming the qualification system will, if implemented, lead to 'A' Levels being broken up into six units and two three-unit parts (the first of which would be the new AS), GNVQs consisting of part (three-unit), single (six-unit) and double (12-unit) awards and a new three-unit free-standing key skills qualification. The government hopes that these changes will make a broader curriculum possible by making it easier for students to take combinations of groups of modules from both academic and vocational qualifications. It has recognised that incentives are important in a system that depends substantially on the choices of individual students. However, there is little sign that incentives will be introduced that would encourage more than a few students to move away from the traditional two or three 'A' Level programmes. There are possibilities, at the local and regional level, that a broader curriculum might be offered by colleges (and taken up by

students) even within the limited scope offered by the government proposals. Colleges could join with local employers and HE institutions in
developing local and regional progression routes based on a range of
combinations of 'A' Level and GNVQ three-unit blocks. At the least,
such developments would provide evidence of what a genuinely more
unified, flexible and inclusive system might offer. In the longer term, new
progression routes into HE and employment would need to be supported
by more radical reforms of the qualification system at a national level.

At a national level the qualifications system will need to be based on
greater unity of academic and vocational learning, more flexibility of
choice for students, inclusiveness and learner coherence. At the same
time, the government will need to trust (and hence create the space for)
regions and institutions to interpret these principles in their own way.
FE colleges have a long and respected tradition of local autonomy and
innovation to draw on based on close links with employers. It was, however, a conservative tradition not designed to respond to the speed of
modern technological innovation, nor always geared to the highest levels
of skill and knowledge. The challenge for colleges will be to interpret this
tradition in the new and demanding circumstances that they now face.
Finding the balance between guaranteeing standards across the country
and beyond and encouraging the local interpretation of those standards in
the contexts where real learning takes place will not be easy. Nowhere is
such a balance more crucial than in the design and implementation of the
system of qualifications.

Acknowledgements

I am most grateful to Alison Fuller and Norman Lucas for their helpful
comments on earlier drafts of this chapter.

References

Dearing, Sir Ron (1996), *Review of Qualifications for 16–19 Year Olds*. Hayes:
    SCAA Publications.

DfEE (Department for Education and Employment) (1997), *Qualifying for Success: A Consultative Paper on the Future of Post-16 Qualifications*. Sudbury: DfEE.

DfEE (1998), *The Learning Age*. London: The Stationery Office.

Finegold, D., Keep, E., Miliband, D., Raffe, D., Spours, K. and Young, M. (1990), *A British Baccalauréat?*. London: Institute for Public Policy Research.

Fuller, A. (1998), *Trends in Adult Participation in Qualifications, 1970–1995*, unpublished paper, Post-16 Education Centre. London: University of London Institute of Education.

Guile, D. and Young, M. (1998), 'Apprenticeship as a Conceptual Basis for a Social Theory of Learning', *Journal of Vocational Education and Training, 50(2)*, 173–193.

Griffiths, T. and Guile, D. (1999), 'Pedagogy and Learning in Work-based Contexts'. In P. Mortimore (ed.), *Pedagogy and its Impact on Learning*. London: Sage.

Hodgson, A. and Spours, K. (eds) (1997), *Dearing and Beyond*. London: Kogan Page.

Jessup, G. (1991), *Outcomes: NVQs and the Merging Model of Education and Training*. London: Falmer Press.

Labour Party (1996), *Aiming Higher*. London: Labour Party.

Lasonen, J. (ed.) (1996), *Reforming Upper Secondary Education in Europe*. Institute for Educational Research, University of Jyväskylä.

Lasonen, J. and Young, M. (eds) (1998), *Parity of Esteem in European Upper Secondary Education: Post-16 Strategies*. Institute for Educational Research, University of Jyväskylä.

MSC/NEDC (1986), *Review of Vocational Qualifications*. London: HMSO.

Ministry of Education (1959), *15–18: Report of the Advisory Council for Education – England and Wales*, Vol. 1. London: HMSO.

Pilkington, P. (1991), *End Egalitarian Illusion*. London: Centre for Policy Studies.

Raffe, D., Howieson, C., Spours, K. and Young, M. (1998), 'The Unification of Post-Compulsory Education: Towards a Conceptual Framework', *British Journal of Educational Studies, 46(2)*, 169–187.

Smithers, A. (1997), *The New Zealand Qualifications Framework*. New Zealand: Education Forum, Auckland.

Spours, K. and Young, M. (1995), *Post-compulsory Curriculum and Qualifications: Options for Change*, Learning for the Future Project Working Paper No. 6, Post-16 Education Centre. London: University of London Institute of Education and Centre for Education and Industry, University of Warwick.

Unwin, L. (1997), 'Reforming the Work-Based Route'. In A. Hodgson and K. Spours (eds), *Dearing and Beyond*. London: Kogan Page.

Ward, C. (1998), 'The Resurgence of "Other" Qualifications and their Place in the National Framework', *EDUCA, 182*, 5–7.

WO (Welsh Office) (1998), *Learning is for Everyone*. London: The Stationery Office.

Wolf, A. (1993), *Competence-based Assessment*. Buckinghamshire: Open University Press.

Young, M. (1993), 'A Curriculum for the 21st Century', *British Journal of Educational Studies, 40(3)*, 203–222.

Young, M. (1998), *The Curriculum of the Future*. London: Falmer.

Young, M., Hayton, A. and Leney, T. (1997), *Key Skills and the ASDAN Award Scheme*. London: Post-16 Education Centre, University of London Institute of Education,

Young, M., Howieson, C., Spours, K. and Raffe, D. (1997), 'Unifying Academic and Vocational Learning and the Idea of a Learning Society', *Journal of Education Policy, 12(6)*, 527–539.

Young, M. and Lucas, N. (1999), 'Pedagogy and Learning in FE'. In P. Mortimore (ed.), *Pedagogy and its Impact on Learning*. London: Sage.

Young, M. and Spours, K. (1998), '14–19 Education: Legacy, Opportunities and Challenges', *Oxford Review of Education, 24(1)*, 83–97.

9 Rethinking Initial Teacher Education and Professional Development in Further Education: Towards the Learning Professional

David Guile and Norman Lucas

Introduction

This chapter aims to develop the view expressed throughout this book that the challenge facing further education (FE) is multi-dimensional. Other chapters call for the realignment of the FE sector to be considered within the wider context of a tertiary system embracing lifelong learning and training. Our particular focus is initial teacher education (ITE) and continuing professional development (CPD) in the FE sector. We start from the premise that the quality of teaching staff and their professional development is central to a high-quality FE system. However, we argue that, despite the high expectations placed upon FE in recent years, consecutive governments have failed to develop a strategic approach to the professional education and professional development of FE teachers. Furthermore, we argue that this problem is compounded by the fact that the FE sector has to offer a much broader and more diverse set of education and training programmes to a broader range of clients than primary, secondary or higher education (HE), hence ITE and CPD are pressing concerns within the sector.

The chapter begins with a brief discussion of the history of neglect and strategic drift, which we suggest, has characterised ITE and CPD in the FE sector. We then move on to analyse the implications of recent policy developments such as incorporation, the establishment of the Staff Development Forum (SDF) and the proposal to create a National Training Organisation (NTO) for ITE and CPD in the sector. We argue that the tensions generated by these developments have been exacerbated by changes in the context of work, teaching, learning and technology. Furthermore, we argue that these economic and technological changes have generated new demands and pressures upon FE teachers for which, in many cases, they have had little preparation or support.

Finally, we argue that other factors have also hampered the development of a strategic approach to ITE and CPD in the FE sector. These include the absence of any purposeful discussion of the concepts of professionalism and professional practice within the FE sector which might have influenced national policy for ITE and CPD. We note that on the rare occasions when debates about professionalism and professional practice have occurred in FE, the concept of the 'reflective practitioner' has often been invoked as a way of defining what is distinctive about professional activity. This we suggest has resulted in a rather partial view of the process of teaching and teachers' perceptions of the wider professional dimensions of their role, and has not led to any significant analysis or engagement with the new contexts and roles in which FE teachers are expected to operate. We argue that a new concept of the FE teacher is now required which we define as a 'learning professional'.

The concept of the 'learning professional' is used to articulate a view of the 'FE teacher of the future'. It reflects a new and extended concept of professionalism that relates traditional professional concerns about teaching and learning to emerging managerial and inter-professional demands on FE teachers. We argue that this reconceptualisation of FE teachers' professional role implies a radically different agenda for ITE and CPD within the sector. We explore the implications of this position in the final section of the chapter.

The state we are in

The position of teaching staff in FE reflects the history of the whole sector. This is a history of benign neglect, the traditional marginalisation of FE colleges and the low status given to vocational education by successive governments and society as a whole during the twentieth century (McGinty and Fish, 1993). Although schemes for pre-service and in-service teacher education were established in the period following the Second World War and were given prominence in the James Report (1972), pre-service ITE was never mandatory and colleges were always able to recruit unqualified staff. Furthermore, FE never had an equivalent to the now defunct Council for the Accreditation of Teacher Education (CATE) or its replacement, the Teacher Training Agency (TTA) which has oversight of the standards and quality for ITE in relation to the schools sector.

The governance and management of the FE sector lay in the hands of local education authorities (LEAs) until 1993, when FE colleges were incorporated. Given that no clear strategic leadership was provided by government departments or their national agencies, arrangements for ITE and CPD varied enormously throughout the sector. Liaison over ITE was conducted directly between colleges and universities and was rarely subject to any systematic monitoring. Although ITE in FE was accepted as desirable by colleges and LEAs, there has, until recently, been little political or public concern about the actual nature of teacher training in the sector (Blackstone, 1998). Thus, during the 1980s and 1990s, some colleges continued with their existing arrangements for university-based ITE and their own pattern of provision for professional development, whilst others embraced the National Council for Vocational Qualifications (NCVQ) competence-based approaches. Moreover, the absence of an FE equivalent to qualified teacher status (QTS) or a national quality assurance body for FE teacher training resulted in a multiplicity of arrangements for accreditation towards the Certificate of Education and PGCE. It is not surprising that a report for the Association for Colleges raised doubts about the comparability, quality and value of many ITE courses and staff development qualifications (Young *et al.*, 1995).

Staff development, prior to the incorporation of colleges was funded through the DfEE's Grant for Educational Support and Training (GEST) budget, which, in turn, was overseen by LEAs. However, as Huddleston and Unwin (1997) have argued, staff development in the FE sector has always had a 'mixed history' and there were significant national variations in philosophy and approach. This situation was compounded by the fact that many teachers in FE (such as those in HE) perceived themselves as specialist practitioners who happened to teach rather than professional teachers (Young *et al.*, 1995). There is a strong tradition in FE that subject or vocational expertise and experience alone was adequate for teaching. This reinforced the existing low status given to vocational education and FE teachers, which played down the need to address discussions about teaching and learning. However, it has been argued that FE has a spectrum of fragmented and largely isolated traditions of pedagogy, which includes the 'school tradition' of subject-based teaching, the pre-vocational tradition currently expressed as GNVQs, the experiential tradition associated with the teaching of adults, flexible learning and the training and instruction tradition linked with apprenticeships and NVQs (Young and Lucas, 1999). There have been few serious attempts to see how these traditions might relate to one another. There is little evidence that the implications of these disparate teaching traditions were adequately addressed in ITE or CPD programmes and the main trend in the post-incorporation era has been to ensure that staff became accredited assessors for NVQ and GNVQ programmes (Guile and Lucas, 1996).

Following incorporation in 1993, the Conservative Government severed the link between colleges, LEAs and national funding for staff development and ITE. The new Further Education Funding Council (FEFC) assumed that decisions about the level of investment in CPD was the responsibility of individual colleges and not a concern of theirs (Cantor, Roberts and Prately, 1995). Those arrangements for ITE which currently exist are not surprisingly contradictory, *ad hoc* and based on the individual policies of the 460 or so incorporated colleges (Ollin, 1996). In the absence of any rational and coherent plan for the FE sector, there is considerable unevenness of value and comparability of ITE and CPD and in courses offered by HE and Evaluation and Validation Bodies (EVAs). Furthermore, opportunities for professional development are now extremely uneven across different institutions in terms of access to higher qualifications, i.e. at NVQ level 4 or 5, and progression between different academic and vocational qualifications is problematic (Guile and Young, 1996).

There is considerable diversity in the initial qualifications staff hold across the sector and in different parts of the sector. Moreover, following incorporation, there has been a fast growing tendency to employ unqualified part-time staff and assessors or instructors. NATFHE, using the FEFC's college inspection reports estimate that on average colleges are spending 30 per cent of their staff budgets on part-time staff, with some rising towards 60 per cent (Lucas and Betts, 1997). This development has meant that many staff are only equipped with competence-based qualifications such as those provided by the Training and Development Lead Body (TDLB). The TDLB's 'D' units (D32/33) were originally designed to verify NVQ assessment methods and not to serve as a qualification for teaching in FE. Therefore, it has been argued that TDLB units by themselves are quite inadequate for the complex demands of a teacher's role in FE and adult education (Elliott, 1996; Hyland, 1992), and have lead to the fear that FE teaching is becoming even less professionalised (Lucas and Betts, 1997).

Post-incorporation policy for initial teacher education and continuing professional development

The Conservative Government, however, in its last phase of office appeared to accept the need to develop a more strategic approach to ITE and CPD. Thus, the SDF was created by the DfEE in 1996 in recognition of the need to address the fragmentation and incoherence of ITE and CPD in FE.

The SDF consisted of a broad representation of stakeholders, including college principals, Trade Union representatives, the TTA and the FEFC. It had a brief to establish standards and a framework for the professional development of FE teachers, although in terms of its official remit from the DfEE its relationship to universities in the delivery of ITE is not clear. The SDF used as its starting point the functional map of the FE sector commissioned by the FEDA in 1995 (Prime Research and Development, 1995) and the Scottish Occupational Standards (SOEID, 1997). It tried initially to develop a competence-based approach to ITE and CPD. The academic and professional debate about competence-based ITE and CPD has been well rehearsed elsewhere (Hyland, 1992; Chown, 1996).

As a result of representations from a variety of bodies and extensive consultation with the FE sector, the teaching standards endorsed by the SDF moved away from the TDLB /NVQ competence model to broader standards not unlike those used by the TTA.

The Labour Government began its term of office in 1997 by accepting the need for a more strategic approach to ITE and CPD. It affirmed the importance of ITE and the professional development of FE staff and managers (Blackstone, 1998). Moreover, it recognised the need to have a framework for the recruitment, induction and professional development of FE staff which is flexible, rigorous and forward looking. The decision to waive the payment of fees for those undergoing ITE for the FE sector was a significant and encouraging step which moved FE nearer to being on a par with primary and secondary ITE.

The Labour Government, however, has not chosen to address the implications of one of the main legacies from the previous Conservative administration, namely the national framework for National Training Organisations (NTOs). NTOs were established as part of the Conservative Government's arrangements for encouraging employers to express a greater interest in and commitment to the training and development of their staff, and for de-emphasising the government's own role in promoting training and development within UK industry (Cantor, Roberts and Prately, 1995). NTOs are, therefore, principally employer-led bodies that represent employers' interests. The Secretary of State for Education and Employment has approved the SDF application for NTO status. Although the composition of the new Further Education National Training Organisation (FENTO) is not yet known, it will be employer led and is generally perceived as being too unbalanced to be the only body to represent the professional interests of teachers in the FE sector. We discuss the implications of this below.

At present it looks as if the government will treat FE differently from the other sectors of the UK's national education and training system. If, for example, the government accepts the legitimacy of the NTO for FE, this will not be extending the principle of parity of esteem between the position of teachers in FE and teachers in primary education, secondary education and HE. As Lesley Dee points out in Chapter Six, primary and secondary teachers are to be represented by a General Teaching Council (GTC), and teachers in HE will in due course be represented by an Institute, both of which stress the professional nature of teaching. FE on the other hand has only an employer-led body. In most 'professions' there is a separation between the employers' organisation, which defines terms of contract, etc., and the role of the professional body which has responsibility for defining the standards which govern a professional's 'licence to practise'. In the case of FE, this separation of power and responsibility seems not to apply. It is likely that FE will be represented by a single body, a FENTO, blurring the important distinction between professional concerns and employer concerns (Hoyle and John, 1995).

At present, the terms of reference and nature of funding for FENTO are as yet unknown. Moreover, it is not at all clear how the transition from the SDF to the FENTO will be accomplished. One worrying possibility is that the FENTO might assume sole responsibility for defining, and assessing teaching standards in FE. Such a development would go 'against the grain' of the SDF's current consultative and collaborative approach to working with universities, NATFHE and other stakeholders. The establishment of the FENTO could also conceivably limit the opportunity for further debate about future changes to the teaching standards. We are particularly concerned about this matter. As we argue later, there is not only a pressing need to review the knowledge base of the FE teacher, but there is also a need to rethink the implications of such a review for ITE and CPD. A further concern is that at present there is a proposal to create a separate NTO for Adult and Community Education alongside the FENTO, while other NTOs (such as Local Government, Science, Technology and Mathematics, Higher Education and Training) have already been established. This proliferation of NTOs could result in FE teachers working to different standards set by different NTOs. This is likely to perpetuate the fragmentation of post-16 education and training and not reinforce the need for a more strategic approach to these issues.

New demands: implications for policy and further education teachers

The sections above have described the past and recent policy context. We characterised the present position of ITE and CPD as being fragmented and voluntarist. We argued that these weaknesses have not been overcome by recent policy developments adopted by central government. In the next section we develop our argument further by illustrating how changes in the broader social, economic and technological context require a reconceptualisation of the professional role of the FE teacher. This provides us with an agenda for policy change in the future, which we discuss in the final section.

There is a growing consensus that FE will play a critical role in supporting the country's economic future, responding to companies' human resource development needs and combating social exclusion (Kennedy, 1997; DfEE, 1998). However, the implications of this new and changing context for the professional role of FE lecturers have not been addressed by policy makers.

Since the mid 1980s, a number of social, economic and technological developments – national, European as well as global – have been slowly forcing a reassessment of education and training systems and lifelong learning (IPPR, 1997; EU, 1995). Within advanced economies there have been massive changes in the nature of workplaces and a growing recognition that, in future, many employment opportunities will require higher levels of skill (Piore and Sabel, 1984; Reich, 1991). These issues have been hotly contested and extensively debated and there is considerable dispute about the extent to which such transformations are affecting all sectors of the economy and all aspects of work within sectors (Keep and Mayhew, 1997; Robinson, 1997). There is also debate concerning how far knowledge and skill are emerging characteristics of all forms of work or only apply to a minority and represent new divisions of labour in the core and peripheral labour market (Aronowitz and DiFagio, 1994).

Nonetheless, despite the contested nature of the economic and technological changes mentioned above, it has recently been argued (Ainley and Bailey, 1997) that there is now some agreement between the UK government, employer organisations and even EU policy makers, about the new economic and human resource challenges confronting developed economies. Accordingly, the key challenge is to ensure that all individuals develop the capacity for lifelong learning. It is generally accepted that the one constant in a rapidly changing economic and technological world is the need for people to be able to adapt to the faster pace of change and to new technology throughout their working lives.

It is evident that within the general context of change there are emerging new demands on colleges and FE teachers. We have separated these new demands into five broad categories. First, there are the demands that FE lecturers face in promoting the acquisition of skills and knowledge by students, trainees and employees with a very wide diversity of learning needs and attitudes (Huddleston and Unwin, 1997; Guile and Young, 1996; Young and Lucas, 1999). This requires lecturers to broaden their forms of expertise to include resource-based learning, modular curriculum design, offering advice and guidance to individual students, to maximise the potential of information and learning technology (ILT) as a resource for learning. In addition teachers need to keep up to date in their own academic/vocational specialisms as well as understanding how their specialism relates to the curriculum as a whole.

Second, a related demand upon FE teachers is the requirement to support their students/trainees in developing 'key skills'. These key skills are generic skills which are generally assumed to underpin a student's ability to transfer his or her knowledge from one context to another (CBI, 1991), and to operate effectively within different educational or workplace contexts. At present government policy for post-compulsory education and training mainly emphasises the key skills, i.e. literacy, numeracy and information technology (IT), which are mandatory for GNVQ students and those on modern apprenticeships. However, recent research (Bailey, 1991; Guile and Fonda, 1998) has argued that in future the emphasis will need to be more upon broad work roles rather than occupationally specific jobs. There is a clear implication that the challenge will be to produce students with more than functional literacy, numeracy or specific technical skills. There will be new demands impacting upon the FE sector to develop more broad-based forms of 'employability' skills and knowledge such as those associated with 'boundary crossing' and team work enabling students and trainees to take responsibility for own learning.

Third, as we have argued elsewhere (Guile and Lucas, 1996), as colleges have been incorporated, many FE organisations have moved away from 'hierarchical' models of management requiring teachers to accept greater managerial responsibilities and broader forms of professional responsibility. Therefore, teachers have had to embrace developments around more flexible approaches to learning, modularisation, setting learning targets and facilitating more independent learning. This has led to what has been described as a 'pedagogy of guidance' (Lucas, 1997). Consequently, FE teachers, in common with other professional groups (Beneviste, 1987) are increasingly having to focus more upon the 'overlaps' between their professional and managerial roles and the inter-professional dimensions of their work which are linked to that of guidance and other specialists (Guile and Young, 1996).

Fourth, the growing demand in the UK for work-based and community-based learning programmes, particularly in realising the aims of the New Deal, as well as the increasing involvement of the FE sector in the delivery of EU programmes for economic and social regeneration means that new sites for learning are emerging as well as new client groups. One consequence of these developments is that FE lecturers have been required to take on more diverse roles and act as project managers, project consultants, course tutors and course designers for the delivery of both on- and off-site courses, work which involves much higher levels of knowledge and skill than has previously been recognised (Ollin, 1996). Therefore, FE teachers are having to develop what Engestrom has referred to as 'poly-contextual skills' (Engestrom, Engestrom and Karkkainen, 1995) and learn how to move across boundaries that have traditionally divided different kinds of specialists, programme areas and sectors. Furthermore, they are also having to devise ways of helping their students/trainees to develop the ability to move confidently between different types of groups inside and outside colleges.

Finally, there are increasing pressures upon FE lectures to understand how to use the new ILT resources for enhancing pedagogy and learning. This will be crucial for two reasons. The first is the ever-extending role of IT in workplaces, as more companies expect their staff to use the latest communication technology to transfer data to other parts of the organisation and also to liaise with clients and operate more effectively across their organisation. The second reason is the potential of ILT for transforming access to the location and the overall process of education and training (Eraut, 1995; Nyhan, 1991). The New Labour Government aims to explore the value of ILT by setting up the University for Industry and the National Grid for Learning. The aim of the former is to bring access to up-to-date education and training directly into the workplace, whereas the aim of the latter is to support the professional development of teachers in primary education, secondary education and FE. In the case of the FE sector, the FEDA has offered support to colleges through the Quality in Information and Learning Technology (QUILT) programme (Cowham, 1995). Until now, however, ILT has been treated as a 'key skill' which teachers need to acquire. Although this could be a useful indicator of technical competence, the critical issue is to support staff in order to appreciate the pedagogic implications of ILT. These issues are discussed in more detail by Guile and Hayton in Chapter Five. Taken in combination, therefore, these five demands point to a very different concept of the professional role of teaching staff within FE.

Reconceptualising the professional role of the further education teacher: beyond the reflective practitioner

Certainly, some of the changes we describe above have been occurring in FE for some time. One of the first discussions about the change in FE teachers' professional roles and responsibilities was provided by Shackleton in the late 1980s (Shackleton, 1989). She conceptualised this new role as constituting a change in perspective from FE teachers adopting a curriculum-led to a learner-led perspective, and highlighted the need for the FE sector to give serious consideration to the implication of these changes.

However, there have been very few attempts to formulate a new concept of professionalism for FE teachers that would systematically reflect the developments we have described above. This is for a number of reasons. First, as Elliott (1998) has observed, little research has been undertaken on teaching in FE and there has been little discussion of the question of professionalism. Where these matters have been addressed, researchers have tended to rely upon conceptions of professionalism derived from primary or secondary education, despite their very different history and culture. Deriving a conception of professionalism from such sources, therefore, is unlikely to provide an adequate basis for understanding the diversity and complexity of the current situation on FE. Second, FE teachers have never had a professional association that could have addressed questions of professionalism. Generally speaking, the professional interests of FE teachers have been mainly represented by one Trade Union, NATFHE, which was mainly concerned with contractual duties rather than broader issues of professional practice.

In the main, when educationalists working in FE have addressed these matters, they have turned to Schon's (1978) concept of the 'reflective practitioner' to provide the basis of a model of teacher education and professionalism (Curzon, 1995; Hyland, 1992). Schon criticised the technical-rational model of professional education which viewed professionals as 'empty vessels' who need to be filled up with abstract knowledge. Such a model could not recognise the need to address the actual problems of professional practice; and failed to celebrate the professional artistry of practitioners (Eraut, 1995). This has led many FE teacher educators to use the concept of the reflective practitioner to ground ideas about professional practice in FE teachers' own understanding and experience of their working practices (Huddleston and Unwin, 1997). Moreover, it has also been used to help FE teachers to develop a critical approach to their professional practice and how they serve the needs of their clients (Elliott, 1998). There is insufficient space in this chapter to offer an extended exposition and critique of the 'reflective practitioner' model of professionalism. However, we feel it is important to explain briefly our concerns about some of the limitations of using the idea of 'reflective practice' as the basis of a model of professionalism.

From our perspective, there are three major limitations to both the concept itself and the way it has been interpreted as the basis of conceptualising the professional role of the FE teacher. First, as Eraut has pointed out, it is not at all clear whether Schon is urging professionals to discard completely the relevance of research-based knowledge or simply challenging the inflated views of its significance (Eraut, 1995). Schon emphasises the central importance of a particular form of practice-based tacit knowledge, which he defines as knowing-in-action, above other forms of professional knowledge. Yet as the burgeoning literature on student retention in FE illustrates (Spours, 1997), there are cross-sectoral problems which require the FE sector to retain a role for research-based knowledge.

Second, Schon implies that professionals will develop their knowing-in-action through the complementary processes of 'reflection-in-action' and 'reflection-on-action'. Nonetheless as Munby and Russell (1989) observe, Schon stresses the 'action' aspect of these concepts more than the 'reflection' aspect. In addition, as they further observe, in education 'action' primarily refers to the time teachers spend in the classroom with their students, rather than the extensive range of their other professional activities and responsibilities. Unfortunately, this rather narrow interpretation of 'action' can marginalise FE teachers' new broader cross-college roles, thereby implying they are a secondary concern to the real activity of teaching. Moreover, it has led some teacher educators to justify on ethical or educational grounds the continuing relevance of traditional occupational cultures and fragmented professional identities in FE (Elliott, 1996). Although we would not dispute that the classroom dimension is absolutely critical, we would argue that it has to be balanced by what we refer to as a broader, extended or 'connective' perspective on professional practice (Guile and Lucas, 1996).

Third, various writers have recently suggested the concept of the 'reflective practitioner' actually serves to separate theory from practice

(Usher, Bryant and Johnston, 1998). Although Schon celebrates the artistry of professional practice and practitioners' capacity for generating ideas and tacit knowledge, he fails to address the full implications of the self-referential nature of such 'theories-in-use' and such 'knowledge-in-action'. Usher argues that the meaning of 'theories-in-use' or 'knowledge-in-action' is highly situated. It is dependent upon interpretations made in particular contexts and in relation to specific cultural conventions and contexts. Therefore, it does not readily provide concepts or criteria that allow professionals to assess and relate different 'theories-in-use' to one another or to research-based knowledge.

Towards the 'learning professional'

Research undertaken over the last few years by the Post-16 Education Centre, provides the basis for an alternative conceptualisation of the FE teachers' professional role (Young *et al.*, 1995; Guile and Young; 1996, Young and Guile, 1997). These different research projects identified the changes in the FE teacher's knowledge base as a series of shifts away from traditional notions of professionalism. Although employing slightly different terminology, each report noted similar trends. They argued that the 'insular' knowledge base that has characterised the work of professions in the past was changing towards a more 'connective' one, and that this development reflected broader trends that were increasingly occurring in many professions as the context and nature of professional work changed. The reports suggested that the above change could be represented in terms of five shifts (Young and Lucas, 1999).

* Subject knowledge to curriculum knowledge. This highlighted the need for FE teachers' professional practice to be based on knowledge of how their specialism related to other subject and vocational specialisms and how generic (or 'key') skills can be achieved through different subjects and vocational areas and through the college curriculum as a whole.
* Teacher-centered to learner-centred pedagogic knowledge. This referred to teachers having to focus on transmission pedagogies as well as

resource-based pedagogies (i.e. having to develop expertise in assignment design, small group work, counselling and tutorial skills, and the use of ICT and other resource-based learning facilities and become 'managers of learning' (i.e. coaching students to become managers of their own learning).

- Intra-professional knowledge to inter-professional knowledge. This highlighted the blurring of roles of teachers and other educational professionals with specialist knowledge such as careers guidance or ICT.
- Classroom knowledge to organisational knowledge. This highlighted how FE teachers were increasingly having to learn to work in multi-specialist teams. Hence, they needed teamwork and collaborative skills as well as knowledge of the college as an organisation to enable them to link their college work with other local providers such employers, community groups, etc.
- Insular to connective knowledge. This emphasised the importance of teachers following the progression of their students while they are in college but also as lifelong learners who draw on their college and work experience and plan their future. It was leading FE teachers to focus on learning outside and beyond college as much as the learning that is tied to specific courses.

Taken in combination, these shifts suggest that existing ideas about the FE teacher's professional knowledge base and the conception of professional practice which underpins it will need to be rethought. It is our contention that the concept of the 'learning professional' is more appropriate than the concept of 'reflective practitioner' for making sense of these shifts and for describing the FE teacher in the twenty-first century.

The concept of the 'learning professional' serves several purposes. First, it offers a distinctive way of embracing the five shifts in the knowledge base which were described above. The concept of the FE teacher as a 'learning professional' denotes the need for an active engagement with those economic, educational and technological changes which have brought about new professional responsibilities and have profoundly altered the context of professional activity. Moreover, it suggests that colleges and FE teachers need to develop a more holistic perspective on the implication of and the relationship between these different shifts. This can be illustrated in a number of ways. As Young argues in Chapter Eight, embracing lifelong learning and the widening participation/social inclusion agenda will require a break from the rigid nature of the present qualifications system. This in turn will mean significant rethinking of current assumptions about teaching and learning, including recognising that learning occurs in many ways outside of colleges, and that FE teachers will need to find ways of relating the knowledge gained outside of colleges to more formal qualifications. These developments will require colleges to re-think how they could be supported through both ITE and CPD programmes. Young also echoes our earlier argument that teachers will need to find more varied ways of enabling learners to progress. He emphasises the challenges that will be posed as the curriculum moves from course-based learning to credit-based learning, which will embrace varied sites of learning that become accessible to people at every stage of their life-cycle. Consequently, further thought will have to be given to how CPD programmes can prepare FE teachers to address these new professional challenges.

Second, the concept of the 'learning professional' highlights the existence in FE of the growing trend seen in a number of professions which links traditional professional concerns (i.e. teaching) with more explicit managerial responsibilities (Beneviste, 1987). This trend draws attention to the need for both a more expanded definition of the forms of specialisation and expertise than are normally associated with teaching in FE, and the idea of the teacher as a learner. In the case of the former, it highlights the need for FE teachers to think about the relationship between their particular form of expertise and the process of learning. Thus, they have to develop the ability to relate their own discipline-based or vocational specialism to other specialisms, to support the development of students' more generic (or 'key') skills, and to use learning theory as a key resource to design and deliver education and training programmes and offer guidance and counselling to learners. In the case of the latter, it highlights the need for FE teachers to move beyond the practice of the classroom. This involves becoming lifelong learners themselves, supporting their students to become lifelong learners and promoting the idea of public learning within their communities. Furthermore, it requires them to develop more generic professional capabilities to respond to the demands of their evolving work contexts. We explore the implications of this position in the final section of the chapter.

Steps toward the creation of the 'learning professional'

For many in FE the idea of the FE teacher as a 'learning professional' may at this moment seem somewhat irrelevant. The financial situation and process of convergence set by the last government continues to push colleges to find 'efficiency savings' (Burchill, 1998). We accept that in these circumstances it is difficult to concentrate on issues of professional development and training. However, it is precisely because of the lack of professional standards being in place that the position of FE teachers has been so easily subordinated to financial considerations. Despite all the financial problems facing FE, the overwhelming majority of teachers are still dedicated to helping individual students learn progress and achieve (Huddleston and Unwin, 1997) and, for this reason alone, new professional knowledge and roles for the future are needed.

We would suggest that in light of our argument about the relationship between new forms of professional knowledge, new work contexts and new professional responsibilities, there is an urgent need for the government to formulate a clear strategy to professionalise the FE sector. We believe that the following steps are central to both a strategy of renewal for ITE and CPD in the FE sector.

One of the first issues that the government has to tackle is the implementation of the initiatives outlined in various policy statements for all new FE teachers to be teacher educated (DfEE, 1998). We appreciate that the question of part-time staff is complex and that it will clearly have to be discussed with the FEFC, the Association of Colleges, NATFHE and other stakeholders. We would suggest, however, that in the first instance a specific pool of targeted funding is made available through the FEFC for the training of long-standing part-time teachers. Furthermore, each college could be encouraged to establish with universities a modular ITE programme through which part-time teachers could progress towards a full teaching qualification and ensure that part-time teachers are allocated an experienced teacher to act as a mentor. For established part-time teachers, we suggest that percentage targets are set, perhaps starting with those who teach 16–19 year olds. As each year of service goes by, modules towards a full teaching certificate could be achieved. We recognise that many colleges use part-time professionals (such as solicitors) and part-time vocational specialists (such as jewellers) to enhance the delivery of various work-based and community-based programmes. We feel such staff as these fall into a slightly different category. Consequently, we think it is more appropriate to suggest that they also should be allocated an experienced teacher to act as a mentor and perhaps be subject to some form of peer review.

A second course of action that we would urge the government to take is to establish a General Teaching Council (GTC) for the FE sector. The GTC could provide a forum to help to realise the aim of developing FE teachers as 'learning professionals' by bringing about a more coordinated approach to ITE and CPD. This development could either be completely separate from the proposed GTC for the school sector or the remit of the school GTC could be extended to include FE. We would prefer the latter, as it would help to provide a more unified perspective on teaching within the education of 16–19 year olds, yet we appreciate that if a GTC were to embrace the whole compulsory and post-compulsory sectors such a unity may not be feasible, at least initially.

Despite their different remits, the GTC could try to forge common ground with the proposed FENTO with respect to certain aspects of ITE and CPD. One area for discussion might be the implications of the new knowledge base we have identified. The GTC, for example, could coordinate a review of the content of ITE programmes to identify what aspects of the FE teachers' new knowledge base should be learnt during professional practice in the college and how it relates to learning in HE.

Another area for discussion might be to take a dispassionate look at the long-term human resource development of the FE sector, bringing about a pan-sectoral approach for further professional development based upon progression routes and partnerships between colleges and universities.

Given the establishment of the FENTO and that the creation of a GTC might take some time, it will be important that the government ensures that the composition of the FENTO reflects the interests of all-important stakeholders. This development would pave the way for the eventual relationship and collaboration between the two bodies. In the period prior to establishing a GTC, the government should ensure that the FEFC gives more emphasis to ITE and CPD. This would be particularly timely as the FEFC's report (1996) has already expressed concern about the growing number of part-time staff and its effects on quality. Moreover, the FEFC could be asked to investigate how guidance could be given to colleges and other organisations on the long-term quality implications of the drift towards FE being staffed by a small core of full-time qualified staff with a large periphery of part-time, poorly trained staff as outlined above. Furthermore, new priorities need to be agreed between the DfEE and the FEFC to ensure that the FEFC identify targeted funding for staff development instead of giving just 'one line' budgets.

We would concur with other authors in this book that FE seems to be moving into a second period of incorporation characterised as a move from competition to cooperation, albeit with great uncertainty, as FE continues to grapple with the legacy of strategic drift. Accordingly, we would argue that the government needs to develop a strategy towards a more unified perspective on all strands of post-16 education and training. We believe that as part of the move towards greater cooperation an approach based upon partnership between a GTC, which would represent FE teachers professional interests, and a FENTO, which would represent employers interests, would be helpful in overcoming the present fragmentation and undervaluing of FE staff. Furthermore, the development of FE teachers as 'learning professionals' could ensure that all staff feel valued and capable of assisting students to respond to the challenges of the next century.

References

Ainley, P. and Bailey, B. (1997), *The Business of Learning: Staff and Student Experiences of Further Education in the 1990s*. London: Cassell.

Aronowitz, S. and DiFagio, P. (1994), *The Jobless Future*. Minnesota: University of Minnesota Press.

Bailey, T. (1991), 'Jobs of the Future and the Education They Will Require', *Educational Researcher*, 20(2), 11–20.

Beneviste, G. (1987), *Professionalsing the Professions*. USA: Jossey Bass.

Blackstone, T. (1998), 'Go Boldley into New Age of Learning', FE Focus, *Times Educational Supplement*, 27 March.

Burchill, F. (1998), *Five Years of Change. A Survey of Pay, Terms and Conditions in the Further Education Sector Five Years after Incorporation*. London: NATFHE.

Cantor, L., Roberts, I. and Prately, B. (1995), *A Guide to Further Education in England and Wales*. London: Cassels.

CBI (1991), *Towards a Skills Revolution*. London: CBI.

Chown, A. (1996), 'Post-16 Education, National Standards and Staff Development Forum: Time for Openness and Voice', *British Journal of In-service Education*, 22(2), 150.

Cowham, T. (1995), *Information and Learning Technology: A Development Handbook*. London: FEDA.

Curzon, R. (1995), *Teaching in Further Education* (4th edition). London: Cassell.

DfEE (1997), *National Training Organisations. 1998/99 Prospectus*. Sudbury: DfEE.

DfEE (1998), *The Learning Age a Renaissance for a New Britain*. London: The Stationery Office.

Elliott, G. (1996), 'The Assessment and Accreditation of Lecturers in Post Compulsory Education: A Critique of the Use of Competence Based Approaches', *British Journal of In-service Teacher Education*, 22(1), 19–30.

Elliott, G. (1998), 'Lecturing in Post-compulsory Education: Profession, Occupation or Reflective Practice?', *Teachers and Teaching: Theory and Practice*, 4(1), 161–174.

Engestrom, Y., Engestrom, R. and Karkkainen, M. (1995), 'Poly-contextuality and Boundary Crossing in Expert Cognition', *Learning and Instruction*, 5(1), 319–336.

Eraut, M. (1995), 'Schon Shock: A Case For Reframing Reflection-in-Action. Teachers and Teaching', *Theory and Practice*, 1(1), 9–22.

EU (1995), *Teaching and Learning – Towards the Learning Society*. Brussels: European Union.

FEFC (1996), *Quality and Standards in Further Education in England*. Chief Inspectors Annual Report 1995–1996. Coventry: The Further Education Funding Council.

Guile, D. and Fonda, N. (1998), *Performance Management through Capability*. London: Institute of Personnel and Development.

Guile, D and Lucas, N. (1996), 'Preparing for the Future. The Training and Professional Development of Staff in the FE Sector', *Journal of Teacher Development*, *5(3)*, 47–55.

Guile, D. and Young, M. (1996), *Further Professional Development and Further Education Teachers*. In I. Woodward (ed.), *Continuing Professional Development*. London: Cassell.

Hoyle, E. and John. P. (1995), *Professional Knowledge and Professional Practice*. London: Cassell.

Hudlestone, P. and Unwin, L. (1997), *Teaching and Learning in Further Education: Diversity and Change*. London: Routledge.

Hyland, T. (1992), 'Expertise and Competence in Further and Adult Education', *British Journal of In-service Education*, *18(1)*, 23–28.

IPPR (1997), *Prospects for Propserity*. London: IPPR.

James Report (1972), *Teacher Education and Training*. London: HMSO.

Keep, E. and Mayhew, K. (1997), 'Was Ratner Right?', *Economic Review*, *21(3)*, 22–28.

Kennedy, H. (1997), *Learning Works: Widening Participation in Further Education*. Coventry: FEFC.

Lucas, N. (1997), 'The "Applied Route" at Age 14 and Beyond: Implications for Initial Teacher Education'. In A. Hudson and D. Lambert (eds), *Exploring Futures in Initial Teacher Education*. London: Institute of Education, Bedford Way Papers.

Lucas, N. and Betts, D. (1997), 'The Incorporated College: Human Resource Development and Human Resource Management: Contradictions and Options', *Research in Post-compulsory Education*, *1(3)*, 329–343.

Mcginty, J. and Fish, J. (1993), *Further Education in the Market Place: Equity, Opportunity and Individual Learning*. London: Routledge.

Munby, H and Russell, T. (1989), 'Educating the Reflective Teacher: An Essay Review of Two Books by Donald Schon', *Journal of Curriculum Studies*, *21(7)*, 71–80.

Nyan, B. (1991), *Developing Peoples Ability to Learn*. Brussels: European Interuniversity Press.

Ollin, R. (1996), 'Learning from Industry: Human Resource Development and the Quality of Lecturing Staff in Further Education', *Quality Assurance in Education*, *4(4)*, 29–36.

Piore, M. and Sabel, C. (1984), *The Second Industrial Divide*. New York: Basic Books.

Prime Research and Development (1995), *Mapping the Further Education Sector. Final Report*. Harrogate: Prime Research and Development Ltd.

Riech, R. (1991), *The Work of Nations*. New York: Simon and Shuster.

Robinson, P. (1997), *Literacy, Numeracy and Economic Performance*. London: London Centre for Economic Performance, LSE.

Schon, D. (1978), *The Reflective Practioner: How Professionals Think in Action*. London: Avebury.

Shackleton, J. (1989), *The Professional Role of the Lecturer. Planning and Curriculum*. London: Further Education Unit.

SOIED (1997), *Draft National Guidelines on Provision Leading to the Teaching Qualification (Further Education) and Related Professional Development*. Edinburgh: The Scottish Office and Industry Department.

Spours, K. (1997), 'Student Retention Issues: Factors Affecting Institutional Capability'. In N. Lucas (ed.), *Policy and Management Issues for Incorporated Colleges*, Post-16 Education Centre Working Paper. London: University of London Institute of Education.

Usher, R., Bryant, I. and Johnston, R. (1998), *Adult Education and the Post Modern Challenge*. London: Routledge.

Young, M. and Guile, D. (1996), *Work-based Learning for the Teacher Trainer of the Future*, Post-16 Centre Report. London: University of London Institute of Education.

Young, M. and Guile, D. (1997), 'New Possibilities for the Professionalisation of UK VET Professionals', *Journal of European Industrial Training*, 21(6/7), 303–213.

Young, M. and Lucas, N. (1999), 'Pedagogy and Learning in Further Education: New Contexts, New Theories and New Possibilities'. In P. Mortimore (ed.), *Pedagogy and its Impact on Learning*. London: Sage.

Young, M., Lucas, N., Sharp, G. and Cunningham, B. (1995), *Teacher Education for the Further Education Sector: Training the Lecturer of the Future*, Report produced for Association of Colleges by Post-16 Centre. London: University of London Institute of Education.

10 Repositioning Further Education: A Sector for the Twenty-first Century

Andy Green and Norman Lucas

In Chapter One we argued that further education (FE) has failed to develop into a cohesive national sector, despite the post-incorporation introduction of national funding and inspection systems. The bureaucratic 'nationalisation' of the college sector has not rendered its historic diversity and 'lack of system' into a coherent whole, nor has it forestalled a continuing 'strategic drift' as regards its overall vision. The recent report by the House of Commons Select Committee on Education and Employment reflected this concern:

> The FE sector has suffered somewhat from a lack of leadership and national strategic direction. We believe there has been a significant hole in government policy in respect of further education ... various piecemeal approaches over time have lead to ambiguity and inconsistency.... Further education has reached the stage where the government now has to make choices and explain its priorities. (1998: ix)

There was a moment in the early 1990s when a strategic direction seemed to be emerging. This was during the 'salad days' of incorporation, when colleges had independence from local education authorities (LEAs) without centralised FEFC control and when the 1991 White Paper still exercised a mobilising vision. It appeared then that FE might cease to be the 'Invisible Man' of the education world, and become a leading and recognised force. The sector was to become the engine powering the drive towards the new qualification targets – a primary vehicle of the new 'learning society'. However, that early phase soon passed and was followed by a period dominated by the new funding system. This imposed high growth targets and a process of convergence, which meant lower unit costs for most colleges. Competition between institutions became intense as colleges entered the scramble for units of funding. It was within this context that the more lofty educational ideals of the new era in FE became obscured. For a further analysis of funding, see Chapter Two.

Incorporation has led to some innovation in course delivery and to a substantial expansion of student numbers amongst 16–19 year olds and adults. However, apart from its acquisition of national funding and inspection systems, FE has not been transformed into a coherent national sector. The FE sector has no clear institutional identity, including, as it does, sixth form colleges, tertiary colleges (some for the 16–19 age group and some including adults), large and small FE and specialised agricultural colleges. Institutions within the same sector often compete against one another for the same students, offering duplicate courses in the same catchment area. There is competition to recruit 16–19 year olds between schools, sixth form and FE colleges, not to mention training providers. Adult education provision is divided between LEAs and the Further Education Funding Council (FEFC), 'separating the inseparable' connection between vocational and non-vocational within a framework of lifelong learning (Crequer, 1998: 31). There are also modern apprenticeships, training for work, national traineeships and the welfare to work schemes such as the 'New Deal'. The sector now caters for a very diverse group of learners, offering a range of courses from academic 'A' Levels, national vocational qualifications (NVQs), general vocational GNVQs, access courses, HNDs, HNCs, short courses and many others. Furthermore, the post-16 system of vocational education and training is characterised by different funding levels and methodologies with a plethora of controlling agencies seeking to shape provision (Melville, 1998). The diversity and fragmented nature of post-16 provision not only makes it difficult to plan on a national level, but is also bound to cause considerable obstacles to local and regional planning.

Within this diversity there is excellence, but short-term financial considerations, forced on colleges by the FEFC, have led to longer term national or local strategic questions becoming marginalised. As Chapter Three points out, some adult teachers in FE are spending vast amounts of their time and energy trying to meet FEFC requirements, whilst maintaining the integrity of their adult provision which is often part-time, attracting relatively small amounts of funding. Furthermore, one principal has given examples of the expansion of courses, based not on local or national economic need, but on the price the FEFC will pay and the profit margin that colleges can gain from them (Perry, 1998). So-called 'unit farming' has now become quite common, including on the margins practices of dubious legitimacy.

FE is experiencing a crisis of funding and a serious soul-searching about quality, with concern being expressed about the cuts in course hours and the growing use of part-time staff to save money (see Chapter Two). As the drive for enrolments and units of funding has forced colleges into new recruitment markets, so the complexion of the college student body has changed. This, we argue, has exacerbated its longer term crisis of 'positioning' and identity. Colleges are now predominantly adult institutions, with over 76 per cent of FEFC-funded students over the age of 24, the overwhelming majority being part-time. This part-time adult provision plus the bias towards vocationalism (often sponsored by government schemes), with links to local employers, still distinguishes FE from other providers (see Chapter Three). Whilst colleges are still the major providers of 16–19 education and training, despite the late resurgence and the sustained market niche of the school sixth form, education of the 16–19 age group is a minority provision in the FE sector.

Although predominantly providers of adult education, colleges do not have a clearly demarcated constituency since the traditional boundaries between higher education (HE) (mostly new universities) and FE have become more blurred with FE delivering 13 per cent of all HE courses. During the 1990s in particular, the distinctions between training and education and between part-time, day release and full-time, grant-aided students have weakened. As more students are gaining entry to HE via access courses and GNVQs, the traditional university knowledge-based approach to teaching has been eroded by a more skills-based, employment-related one, thus bringing HE and FE closer together. David Blunkett recently told the CBI that he planned to build in more employment skills and work experience into the HE curriculum. One CBI member commented that removing the binary divide between polytechnics and universities was 'one of our great diseases' (Tysome, 1998: 3), leading to research funding being spread too thinly and new universities following inappropriate roles. Some argue that a formal merger between FE and some HE institutions is only a matter of time, whilst others predict links to provide university education locally to a wider range of students (see Chapter Four).

Formal links between FE and HE are also proliferating. Today 34 percent of FE graduates go into HE and most of the 'new students' in the 'new' universities come via FE (Melville, 1998). FE is increasingly linked to HE through franchising and access arrangements. Financial vulnerability is also undermining the autonomy of many colleges, so that some 30 of them are currently negotiating to merge with universities. Meanwhile, HE institutions, and particularly the new universities, have moved decisively into the mature student market with the expansion of foundation, access and other sub degree provision for local students. Currently, 52 HE institutions are funded by the FEFC for students on FE courses.

As we outline in Chapter One the history of the last two decades is one of the emergence of a more identifiable FE sector being blocked by competition between providers and the growing territorial battles on its borders – with renascent school sixth forms on the one side, and an increasingly expansionist HE sector on the other. The boundaries between the FE and HE sectors are becoming weaker as the vision of a seamless lifelong learning provision dominates policy discourse. So where is the distinctive market for the FE college and what will be its defining role in the future?

According to recent government statements, FE is vital for forging an inclusive society. It also has a major economic role to play: 'by reaching out to the community further education can help reduce social exclusion, increase employability and raise the nation's economic strength and morale' (Education and Employment Committee, 1998: v). Government policy has given FE a pivotal role in the 'New Deal' and in most recent initiatives on lifelong learning (DfEE, 1998). Kennedy (1997) saw FE as the major vehicle for widening participation and meeting local needs, ensuring a free, lifetime entitlement to education and training up to level 3 for all.

We agree that colleges should serve local community needs, and in doing so provide academic, vocational and general education. So much is common ground. But which sectors of the community are they primarily there to serve? Should FE provide everything, including whatever no one else is willing or able to provide?

The shape of post-compulsory education and training in England and Wales has always tended to evolve more by accident than design (Gleeson and Mardle, 1980. There was a time when it seemed that 'rational planning' and educational logic were nudging the FE sector towards becoming the comprehensive provider of education for 16–19 year olds. Tertiary colleges were increasingly popular, and seemed to have the potential to provide England with an institutional equivalent of the French *lycée polyvalent* or the Swedish Comprehensive High School (*Gymnasieskola*). They were to be large, diverse and flexible community institutions, which could provide a wide range of general and academic courses, within environments specifically catering for the needs of the 16–19 year old age group. Their popularity and success underlined the appropriateness of the vision for many young people who sought to make a transition after reaching the school leaving age.

However, the opportunity to create a structure in England and Wales comparable to that dominant in most of the developed world (i.e. having a dedicated, institutionally distinct high school sector) disappeared with school choice, grant-maintained schools, and college incorporation. The pattern that is emerging now suggests that in some ways FE colleges are drifting increasingly into the space occupied by the community college in the United States. That is to say a community institution mostly serving adults which provides a bridge between schooling and HE and training.

This can involve everything from remedial or 'second-chance' education, to vocational education and initial training, access to HE and professional training.

This scenario is in many ways an attractive one. It would make the college the key institution for developing lifelong learning and the learning society. Colleges are, despite six years of incorporation, still embedded in local communities and historically have had good links with sectors of the community which are now seen as potential sites for the dispersed learning opportunities envisioned in the 'learning society'. They have close connections with employers, professional bodies and community associations, as well as 'outreach' operations, which extend their activities into housing estates. They have always been diverse and flexible institutions, and are becoming more so. As such they are well placed to develop the new modes and forms of learning associated with the networked, flexible learning of the future. They are also, clearly, being successful in developing progression opportunities for their students to move into HE and training, not least through the opening up of the GNVQ and access routes.

Further development towards the US community college model for FE would not be difficult to imagine. US community colleges tend to be large, multi-sited institutions which dominate this type of provision in their given area – in the case of a college such as Miami Dade, for instance, being able to boast having played a formative role in the lives of majority of their city's adult citizens. Many FE colleges may approach a similar scale as financial exigencies force further rationalisations. US community colleges are notable for their commitment to open access and for the flexibility of their provision, with courses running, for instance, from 7 a.m. to 11 p.m., including Saturdays and summer vacation schools. FE colleges are also moving towards this level of flexibility, although without the resources that the community colleges enjoyed in their heyday of expansion in the 1960s and 1970s. Finally, US community colleges have long since developed a pedagogy that is explicitly geared towards student progression. They pioneered modularisation and credit accumulation and transfer, and have developed extensive systems of linkage with the university sector. The two plus two degrees (where the Community College provides the first two-year associate degree and the university the last two years of a four-year bachelors degree) has provided the route to qualification for a substantial proportion of US graduates since the 1960s. This has given a foundation for the country's claim to having the most accessible system of HE in the world. To a large extent FE colleges in England and Wales are developing similar bridges through access arrangements and franchised higher degree courses.

There is still a major difference, however, between the colleges in the two countries. Community colleges in the United States are exclusively 18 plus institutions. They are not bound to provide the pastoral environment needed by younger students and are not in competition with high schools (although they are in competition with training programmes organised by the Private Industry Councils). FE colleges, on the other hand, do still have a substantial number of younger students with distinctive needs and they are clearly in competition with schools and successful sixth form colleges or tertiary colleges which provide particular structures, support and extra curricula activities for 16–19 students. There is a lack of clear boundaries for colleges in England and Wales, which is not experienced by community colleges in the United States. Community colleges are not generally speaking in competition with the universities in the United States because their mission is clearly defined and because they are taking students who would not generally gain direct admission to the universities (i.e. whose SAT scores and school grade point averages are insufficient to get them in to universities). Colleges in England and Wales are competing not only with schools, but also with the new universities, which provide a substantial amount of sub-degree work.

FE colleges need a clearer definition of their function and clientele if they are to avoid the strategic drift described in Chapter One. This means that their boundaries, and those of their competitors, should be more clearly defined so that they are not continuously treading on each others' toes, clouding each others' missions and engaging in wasteful and destructive competition. One mid-term scenario for achieving this, which would go partly with the grain of current trends, would be that colleges should gradually become exclusively adult institutions (i.e. 18 plus), devoted to sub-degree level FE and training and incorporating all of the adult non-examination (non-Schedule 2) work which the LEAs sometimes run elsewhere. In this scenario, provision for 16–19 year olds would gradually be rationalised around sixth forms and sixth form colleges, allowing the possibility that a comprehensive tertiary 16–19 year olds sector might still emerge (if in the future LEAs regain sole control over publicly funded sixth form provision).

Although a comprehensive tertiary system would be difficult to achieve in the present context, in the long term such a rationalisation may become possible and desirable. It would rescue schools from trying to maintain non-viable sixth form provision, allowing them to concentrate on the pre-16 curriculum. FE colleges could become more focused on providing the flexible provision and support required by adult learners, leaving the particular structures and provision that the younger age group requires to other institutions.

Realigning the FE sector in this way would allow colleges to become the main site for lifelong learning with a structure and curriculum that could make progress in overcoming social exclusion. As Chapter Eight points out, the agenda set by lifelong learning policies requires a new qualifications structure, including new progression pathways and opportunities. At present FE is caught between preparatory learning (i.e. 'A' Levels and GNVQs) and lifelong learning with adult learners having to make do with qualifications that were designed for 16–19 year olds. Furthermore, the realignment that we are suggesting would allow FE colleges to address important pedagogic and professional issues (raised in Chapter Nine) and the implications for teaching and learning of information and learning technology (see Chapter Five).

Whilst colleges could focus on widening participation, social inclusion and the implications of lifelong learning for the local community, universities could become regional providers, regaining their mission of being research-led institutions providing degree and higher level education. Sub-degree provision, such as foundation and access courses, would be largely provided in colleges. Two plus two courses could be developed on a systematic nationwide basis, but with the respective roles of the FE and HE sectors clearly demarcated. Short-cycle vocational HE (including Higher National Diplomas and Certificates) might legitimately be run by universities if they could show that their facilities were required for adequate quality of provision and that they could run these courses as efficiently as colleges. However, there would be a general presumption that sub-degree work is the province of the college rather than the university. This would be good for maintaining the distinctive mission of universities, as well as for maintaining standards. It would also be good for the status of colleges if they could acquire a greater proportion of work at level 4 (i.e. HND and NVQ 4).

Recent policy statements from Baroness Blackstone, Minister for Higher and Further Education, suggest that there is government support for moves in this direction. She indicated that a large expansion of sub-degree courses such as HND/Cs should take place in FE colleges. As the number of those doing first degree courses is unlikely to expand, the Minister suggested that we should focus on 'two-year alternatives' (Thomson and Goddard, 1998: 3). The Government plans to increase the numbers in FE by 700,000 by the years 2001–2002. From 1999 there are also due to be a further 35,000 places in HE, of which 15,000 would be at sub-degree level. Colleges have been encouraged to bid for these places and it is anticipated that a significant number will go to them (Tysome, 1998).

Formal constitution of FE colleges as adult (post-18) providers would, in addition to clarifying their boundaries, help to restore their vocational mission and identity, which have become somewhat lost in recent years through their growing diversity of provision. Whilst colleges should span the academic/vocational divide, providing elements of both for most students, there is much to be said for them regaining their image as primarily technical institutions. An important part of successful vocational education is the process of socialisation into different occupational roles, and this still applies today, even when many occupations are becoming increasingly fluid and multi-skilled. One of the strengths of the German

Dual System, for instance, is that it still manages to cultivate the identity and status of the *Beruf* (vocation) (Brown, 1997). This is easier to achieve, admittedly, with apprentice-style work-based learning, or even in the monotechnic type of vocational *lycée* found in France. Nevertheless, polytechnic vocational institutions can still achieve this where they have a significant levels of provision in particular vocational areas, preferably with a substantial amount of higher level work, and where there is a robust professional culture in the vocational departments with good employer links.

Achieving close articulation with local labour markets and professional associations also requires a level of planning which has been hard to achieve under current forms of governance. We are of the view that there is an overwhelming case for FE planning and strategic funding to occur substantially at a regional level where labour market planning often makes most sense. Planning on a regional level would allow strategic thinking on education and training to take account of existing strengths and weaknesses in different areas.

Proposals for regional planning are being discussed by the Government, but are still in their early stages. However, the Lifelong Learning Minister has recently indicated that Regional Development Agencies may require schools, FE colleges and universities to work towards regional targets and respond to a new regional agenda (Tysome, 1998). Regional planning would mean new structures to bring together the regional arms of the FEFC, the TECs, the Regional Development Associations (RDAs), the regional councils of the CBI and the TUC and the Government Offices for the Regions which administer the Single Regeneration Budget. Unfortunately, the boundaries of the different regional maps do not currently coincide. Nevertheless, the New Labour Government proposals to create Regional Forums could provide an interim basis for this kind of plan until such a time as England catches up with most of mainland Europe in providing for some kind of elected regional tier of government.

References

Brown, A. (1997), *Becoming Skilled during a Time of Transition: Observations from Europe.* Guildford, Surrey: Department of Educational Studies, University of Surrey.

Crequer, N. (1998), 'Gibson Calls for More Cash', FE Focus, *Times Educational Supplement,* 27 November, 31.

DfEE (1998), *The Learning Age: A Renaissance for a New Britain.* London: The Stationery Office.

Education and Employment Committee (1998), *Sixth Report of the House of Commons Education and Employment Committee,* Vol. 1, 16 May. London: The Stationery Office.

Gleesson, D. and Mardle, G. (1980), *Further Education or Training?.* London: Routledge and Kegan Paul.

Kennedy, H. (1997), *Learning Works: Widening Participation in Further Education Colleges.* Coventry: FEFC.

Melville, D. (1998), 'Returner Learners Need Quality', *Times Educational Supplement,* 6 November, 9.

Perry, A. (1998), *Benchmarks or Trade Marks – How we are Managing FE Wrong.* London: Lambeth College.

Thomson, A. and Goddard, A. (1998), 'Message from the Ministry: Baroness Blackstone', *Times Educational Supplement,* 6 November, 3.

Tysome, T. (1998), 'Message from the Ministry: David Blunkett', *Times Educational Supplement,* 6 November, 3.

Index